THE BOX OF BEAUTIFUL LETTERS

The Box of Beautiful Letters

A WARTIME LOVE STORY REVEALED
FROM THE CORRESPONDENCE BETWEEN
LILY SMITH AND RAF PILOT MARTYN ALLIES

1939 – 1941

Compiled by Cheryl Underhill

YOUCAXTON
PUBLICATIONS

Contents

The letters written between Lily and Martyn
were found in a battered cardboard box
which had written on its side,
'BELLES LETTRES':
beautiful letters.

Introducing Lily Smith
and Martyn Allies

MARTYN'S EARLY YEARS

Martyn was born on 11th April 1920 and was a much-loved only child. His mother Margaret, known as Daisy, was the daughter of well-to-do parents Francis and Elizabeth Nickerson, who had made their money in the family leather tanning business at a time when automobiles were being upholstered in leather.

Martyn's father, Edgar James Allies, went straight from school into the Civil Service and, apart from a break when he served in Belgium in the First World War, worked his way up in the Colonial Office. In 1948 he received the OBE and in 1950 became Accountant General at the Commonwealth Relations Office.

Martyn's parents passed on to him a love of music. They both played the violin and piano and had musical soirées at home. When Edgar served with the Rifle Brigade he also played the cornet in its band and Daisy played the violin in the Epping Forest Symphony Orchestra. They enjoyed singing and Edgar would take part in amateur productions of Gilbert and Sullivan operettas. As well as going to concerts, including the Proms, Daisy and Edgar frequently attended theatre, opera and ballet performances.

Martyn was taken on various trips in this country and in Europe as his parents were inveterate travellers, and at an early age this involved travelling with his mother in the sidecar of his father's motorbike. In 1934 when Martyn was fourteen his parents took him to Germany to see the Oberammergau Passion Play in the four thousand seat open air theatre. This was the play's 30th anniversary performance which famously Hitler attended and used for propaganda purposes. They also visited Friedrichshafen to see the latest zeppelins being built there.

As a boy, attending Chigwell School, Martyn became fascinated with aeroplanes; one of his lasting school memories was of being severely reprimanded for not catching the ball during a significant cricket match because he was too busy studying an aeroplane as it flew overhead. The school had an Aeronautics Society which gave him the opportunity to meet others who shared his passion. A few close friends went on to form their own club which they initially called Skybird 132; but later, as they became more interested in model making, they renamed it the Woodford Aero Model Club. They held events, outings, debates and model-making competitions and Martyn edited and produced the club's magazine. He himself became extremely skilled at constructing model aircraft, each successive one becoming more intricate in its design and execution.

Martyn aged two with his mother

When Martyn was fifteen, he and two friends, Bob Jacobs and Peter Matthews, built themselves their own Flying Flea aeroplane. Bob's father let them use workspace at South Woodford's Mill Garage. Sadly, just as the aircraft neared completion, it became illegal to fly such planes, since there had been a number of Flying Flea crashes, including more than one that had been fatal. Perhaps it was just as well that they were never able to give their machine its maiden flight!

Along with his parents, Martyn attended South Woodford Congregational Church and while he was a young teenager his father took over the leadership of the church's Young People's Fellowship and Martyn became a member.

Aged seventeen, on leaving Chigwell School, Martyn began a degree in Aeronautical Engineering at Queen Mary College, London University and while there joined the University of London Air Squadron and gained his first experience of flying in 1938, a year before the outbreak of World War Two.

*With his father and Auntie May
at a recital in his Grandmother's house*

Aged four with his parents

LILY'S EARLY YEARS

Lily experienced a happy childhood in a loving home with her three brothers Reg, Leslie and Arthur. They lived at Chigwell Cottage, Chigwell in Essex, where she was born on 13th June 1920. Chigwell Cottage was attached to the stable block, beside the vegetable garden, in the grounds of the grand house known as Chigwell Hall, which is where her father Frank Smith worked as the butler-come-handyman and her mother Christina worked as a maid.

Lily's parents thought highly of Mr Walter Waugh, the successful chemical merchant who owned Chigwell Hall and resided there with his wife and family. The Hall was set in forty-two acres, so Lily and her brothers were accustomed to open spaces and they all developed a love of nature and the countryside, as well as outdoor games. In the grounds was a cricket pitch where the local cricket club played every Saturday. Unsurprisingly, cricket became a favoured game of her brothers – and Lily too, who became a proficient player and an accomplished bowler.

When there were special events at the Hall the children were able to watch the arrival of fashionable guests as they motored up the drive; and in the summer months when there were garden parties, they helped their parents to prepare the tea tent and serve the refreshments.

On Christmas Eve they would join the other servants and their children at the front door of the Hall and sing Christmas carols, and every Christmas Day the family would have the pleasure, for Christmas dinner, of a turkey that had been given to them by Mr Waugh. Sometimes, Lily and her brother Arthur would be taken to the Hall to entertain Mrs Waugh and her guests. They would sing and recite poetry, and at the end of the performance they would be rewarded with one penny each. The Waughs went regularly on holiday trips, mostly to Clacton-on-Sea, and while they were away Lily's father took over the running of the Hall. On these occasions the family made the most of enjoying the Hall's extensive interior and there were lots of games of hide-and-seek to be had!

When Lily was seven she was severely ill with bronchitis and Frank and Christina took their young family doctor's advice and agreed to her having a thoracotomy operation. This pioneering surgery had only an 80% success rate but fortunately, as a doctor commented in admiration when examining her aged 91, she was 'made of sturdy stuff', and fully recovered.

Lily attended the small village school in Chigwell and, while there, was awarded a scholarship place at Loughton High School for Girls. She was very proud of this fact and appreciated her time at the grammar school. From an early age she had developed a love of words, both reading and writing, and so benefitted greatly from the education she received. As well as her academic studies, she enjoyed participating in sports, singing and drama. It would seem that she was a gregarious child and teenager, and she made a number of close friendships which lasted long after her schooldays were over.

Once she had gained her School Certificate at Loughton High School she went to work as a clerk at the Prudential Assurance Company offices in Holborn, London. By this time the family had moved to Grenville Gardens in Woodford Green, East London and Lily began to attend the South Woodford Congregational Church where she, like Martyn, became a member of the church's Young People's Fellowship.

Lily with her parents and her brothers Reg, Leslie and Arthur

THE YOUNG PEOPLE'S FELLOWSHIP

Martyn's father Edgar took over the running of the South Woodford Congregational Young People's Fellowship in the early 1930s. This was a period of time when teenagers certainly wouldn't have addressed their elders by first names, so Edgar created an alternative and he was known by them as E.J. On Sunday afternoons the Fellowship would meet for discussions, or they would have guest speakers, musical recitals or poetry readings. In contrast, their weekday meetings encompassed all manner of activities from badminton and tennis to play readings and dancing.

On Saturdays they would have 'rambles'. This consisted sometimes of a walk locally but more often than not it involved catching a bus or a train to a different location where there would be a walk but also, often, a visit to somewhere of interest. From time to time they would arrange to meet up on their 'ramble' with another fellowship group. In the Easter and summer holidays the 'rambles' would be further afield to places like Paris, Holland and Switzerland and the members would need to save up a good proportion of their meagre earnings in order to participate. Edgar took immense care in planning these events and packed in as many cultural experiences as possible.

With so much time spent in each other's company and with their shared experiences away from home, the core members of the Fellowship forged strong friendships which held them in good stead in the traumatic times that were to come.

Martyn was already a member of the Fellowship when Lily joined in 1937 and they were both then seventeen. From that time onwards it was certainly a focus in their lives. They both went on a trip to Paris in 1937 and another to Holland in 1938. In the summer of 1939 Lily went with the Fellowship group to Switzerland, but without Martyn, as he was committed to going with the University of London Air Squadron to Thorney Island for their annual camp. Prior to this, in the Easter holidays of 1939 they had both been on a return trip to Paris; this was a holiday that would always remain imprinted in their memories, as it was the time when their relationship blossomed.

One of the Fellowship group, Nora, wrote a poem about the Paris 'ramble' in the style of Longfellow's *Hiawatha;* and reading it, one can certainly appreciate why these events were so enjoyed by the members and what a lasting influence Martyn's father – E.J. – had on these young lives.

Paris Ramble Easter 1939 – an extract

Gentle reader, hear my story.
Hear about our Paris ramble,
How we young ones clubbed together,
How we strove to save the money,
Scraped and saved with no regretting.
How we then set out at Easter.
Went to Paris and were seasick.
Went to Paris and enjoyed it
Under guidance of our leader
(Known to some as E.J. Allies
But to us as Nick the Elder).

He it was whose quiet humour
And his broad imagination
Kept us laughing when exhausted.
We arrived at Dieppe harbour
In the early hours of morning
Whilst the pallid moon, the Night Sun,
With her starlettes yet were shining
O'er the restless surging waters,

E.J. guides the group around Paris

O'er the harbour's salt-sea waters.
He it was who planned our ramble,
Showed us many famous places,
Showed us countless views and buildings,
While he fumbled with his guidebooks,
Dancing round or pointing skywards,
Making wild gesticulations
In the manner of dictators,
Till we crumpled up with laughter.
Such a joke was Nick the Elder.

He it was who after luncheon
Led us up to Rouen Cathedral,
Told us of Saint Joan's memorial,
Suddenly conceived a brainwave:
"Let us go inside this cake shop.
Let us feed on creamy pastries,
Squelchy, sticky, sickly fancies.
Let us go!" cried Nick the Elder.

Did we need a second bidding?
No, we rushed inside that cake shop,
Seized whatever took our fancy.
Haggled with the French assistant,
Laughing, speaking, all together.
"How much is your charge for this one?"
"I prefer the one with fruit in."
"Be a sport and have another."
"Do explain this tipping system!"
Thus we chattered in the cake shop
As we sat and talked together,
Munching, crunching, laughing loudly,
Giggling, drinking, making whoopee.

Let me introduce George Terry
Who was E.J.'s chief advisor.
He is from the tribe of Epsom,

Who are friendly to our people.
(They have often shared our rambles,
Always shown a friendly spirit.)
George had admirable patience.
Always waited for the stragglers,
Journeyed with us uncomplaining
When E.J. made the suggestion:
"Let us go inside Le Louvre.
Let us view the famous statues,
Let us criticise the pictures,
See the lovely *Mona Lisa*,
View the Watteau (what's been stolen)."
George was really quite a hero
For he "don't like picture painting!"
All the others were delighted.
And yours truly was among them ...

Outside the Louvre

On the steps of Sacré Cœur. Front row from left – Marie, Nora, Martyn, Reg and Marjorie

Lily walking with her friends. Marie on her right and Nora on her left

... Martyn is the Elder's first born.
He is also in the cake shop.
He it was who during luncheon
Made an aerodrome of spinach,
Hacked and hewed with great precision
While we criticised his manners.
He it was who by 'Le Printemps'
Flourished Lily's Coty lipstick
And incarnadined his mouthpiece.
Made himself like Greta Garbo
While poor Lily watched in anguish,
Tried to tell him it was kiss-proof,
That he'd streaked his chin with scarlet.
"It will not come off with washing,"
Warned the owner of the lipstick,
Warned infuriated Lily.
Minnehaha – laughing Lily,
Known as 'Piglet' in our circle,
Ate two snails and came up smiling,
Ate them out of sheer bravado,
Then crept to yours truly's bedroom,
Whispered faintly in the darkness,
"May I have a drink of water?
I shall taste these snails till Doomsday.
Do you think I ate unwisely?
I've got chronic indigestion,"
Wailed young Lil – no longer laughing,
Minnehaha – laughing Lily.

In Paris, E.J. far left and Lily fourth from left

Sitting on the wall with E.J.: Lily to his left, Martyn to his right

1

27th June – 7th September 1939

The Easter ramble was at the beginning of April and within days of the Fellowship group returning home from Paris, the unrest in Europe had escalated.

Back in 1937 fears had been growing that there would be another war and, if Britain was involved, the stark probability was that there would be poisonous gas attacks and high explosive bombing raids. The Air Raid Precautions (ARP) department, which had been created back in 1935, had taken overall control of preparing Britain for this eventuality and in November 1937 Parliament backed its plans to dig trenches and build air raid shelters in all towns and cities.

In the following spring Hitler claimed Austria for the Third Reich and was intent on also annexing the German speaking area of Czechoslovakia. As the crisis grew, efforts were made by political leaders to avert war and appease Hitler. Britain's Prime Minister Neville Chamberlain made three dramatic trips to Germany for negotiations.

Meanwhile Britain's ARP services were mobilised and hordes of new volunteers were enlisted. Trenches were dug by day and night, and barrage balloons appeared in the skies above London.

On Chamberlain's third visit to Germany he met with Hitler, Mussolini and Daladier of France and on 30th September 1938 the Munich Agreement was signed approving the annexing of

Sudetenland, with the understanding that Germany and Britain would never go to war again. When Chamberlain returned home and was photographed waving the white paper document in his hand it was his belief that this pact would bring 'peace for our time'. There was a euphoric feeling of relief across the country. Many of Chamberlain's fellow MPs, however, distrusted the agreement; but they felt that at least, now, the country had a breathing space in which to prepare for war.

In March 1939 Hitler reneged on his promises and German troops occupied the whole of Czechoslovakia; moreover, he announced his intention to attack Poland. Chamberlain had committed Britain to lend the Polish government all the support in its power, so finally all hopes of appeasement were dashed. Britain expanded its Air Force and Navy, increased taxes in order to boost the Defence Budget and in April 1939 announced conscription for all men aged 20 and 21.

At some time between April and June, Martyn took Lily on their first date to a performance of the ballet Swan Lake and their relationship blossomed. The threat of war, however, must have brought into sharp focus the fact that Martyn, with his love of aeroplanes and some experience already of flying, would doubtless join the RAF if war was declared, whilst Lily held strong pacifist beliefs.

As a member of the University of London Air Squadron, Martyn went with the squadron on its annual 'camp' to RAF Thorney Island where he made his first solo flight.

On 27th June 1939, Lily wrote to Martyn at Thorney Island.

89 Grenville Gardens
Woodford Green

Dear Martyn,

At last, after haunting the box office at Covent Garden for about a week, missing trains, and being late back for work <u>three</u> times, I have procured a programme ... I'm sure you'd like to see *Les Sylphides* again – wouldn't you? It looks as though you'll have to wait a little longer for *Le Lac des Cygnes*. But there's still three more weeks – and we <u>must</u> see *Petrushka*. I'm dying to see it again.

I have made a new resolution – never to be late for my engagements, and <u>never</u> to miss trains. I was punished <u>twice</u> on Saturday for the last named offence. Nora specially asked me to catch the 8:33 as she said she wanted to do some shopping. Of course, I missed it and then she told me it was to buy me a birthday present – so I had to wait until Monday!

On Saturday afternoon it was arranged that the Fellowship should go by train to Chigwell Lane and ramble from there. I allowed myself two minutes to get to the station – and missed the train! I had to stand at the gates and watch the train go out. I went down on the next train three quarters of an hour later, hoping they'd leave a message or at least the name of the place where they were having tea. (Of course anyone less 'dopey' than I wouldn't have been so mad!) When I got there, the station was bare! The porter told me they'd gone about a half hour ago but he'd no idea which way. (I knew then that you weren't home for the weekend – <u>you</u> would have waited!)

So I walked back to Loughton and got home at about 6 o'clock! I was so fed up I got out your Browning and read through the whole of 'Sordello'.

Thank you very much for the Browning and for your note inside. I read it through six times – three to make it read sense –

and three more times picking out all the unreadable words and poring over them through a magnifying glass. Your handwriting! Hell's bells! Your examiners have my heartfelt sympathy!

You missed the most gorgeous Fellowship concert on Sunday afternoon. It was a marvellous programme. They sang 'Jesu, Joy of Man's Desiring', 'He Shall Feed His Flock', 'Lift Thine Eyes', Brahms' 'Slumber Song' and lots of other lovely things. You would have liked it ...

Maisie and I are going to see *Hamlet* tomorrow. Reg [Rapkin] and his friend are going to see *Swan Lake*. I almost wish I were going there instead! ...

I'll have to stop now. My writing is getting nearly as bad as yours.

So, cheerio, all the best,

Lily

Political tensions in Europe mounted still further and war seemed inevitable and imminent. In July 1939, four Civil Defence leaflets were issued to every household in the country.

The first of these was entitled Some Things You Should Know If War Should Come. This outlined ways in which people should prepare themselves and their homes so that they would be able to react appropriately if the air raid sirens sounded. It emphasised the importance of carrying an identity label at all times and stated that more information and instructions would be issued to the public through the press and by means of broadcast announcements.

It was considered at this time that one of the greatest protections against the dangers of air attack at night would be the 'black-out'. There had already been blackout practices, when all curtains were pulled and street lighting switched off, but further instructions about how to mask windows were given in leaflet number two, as well as more advice about the use of gas masks.

The third leaflet explained the proposed evacuation scheme and the fourth described how the Government intended to control the supply and distribution of food.

When on Tuesday 21st August the announcement was made over the radio that Germany and Russia were entering into a non-aggression pact, everyone hearing the news realised that the days of peace were soon to be over.

The Prudential Assurance Society took the need to evacuate from London seriously and the following weekend moved their headquarters to Torquay. The grand Victoria and Albert Hotel became their headquarters and the staff were billeted out in guest houses and hotels round about.

On Sunday 27th August, Lily – along with two friends, Nora and Marjorie – set off by train to Torquay leaving Martyn behind at home in South Woodford awaiting his uncertain future. It now seemed more likely that he would be enlisting in the RAF rather than returning to university.

Southcourt Guest House,
Middle Lincombe Road,
Torquay
Tuesday 29th August

Dear Martyn,

I thought I would write to you while I have the chance, as we have to stay in the house this morning until the 'bigwigs' get back from their meeting. We are supposed to wait here until we receive instructions as to when we are to report for work.

I arrived here quite safely at about half past four on Sunday. Then we had to wait on the station for half an hour while we were counted out and sent in groups of about six or more to various hotels. My two friends and I were the very last – right on the end of the queue of eight hundred! We were taken to our various hotels by coach, and we've certainly managed to pick a delightful place.

Our house is right above the harbour, very high up and standing in its own grounds. We are really very comfortable here; we've got a very nice bedroom, with a large mantelpiece where I have arranged all my treasures. In the centre, in the place of honour, stands the little aeroplane you gave me. Behind it are two ballet photographs, and next to them, all the way along, are propped up my postcard reproductions. On one end is a postcard photograph of Sacré Coeur and on the other the Eiffel Tower. It's surprising to think that my dearest treasures are composed of a few tuppenny postcards, a photograph or two, a little aeroplane, a couple of poetry books and a shell you picked up for me on the beach at Pourville.

This is making me horribly homesick ...

We spent all day yesterday having a good time (instead of 'having', read 'trying to have'). In the morning we explored the town, and later went swimming. The water was beautifully warm, the beach lovely and sandy and the sun blazing hot. You would have loved it! – I can see you protesting, but you would ...

The Victoria and Albert Hotel is a large place, and in the most glorious muddle. They're trying to clear it of guests and furniture in order to move our stuff in. A good bit of our stuff is missing altogether, including fifty-four typewriters! One of the vans, packed with thousands of cards, overturned near the Oval, so all our lovely cards that we put in order (when we weren't playing 'General Knowledge'!) are now scattered far and wide and will all have to be sorted out again.

We shall be starting work tomorrow, and when we do we shall have to work hard. Some of the typists have been working up to 12 o'clock at night ...

Wherever you go, here, you run into 'Pruites' – there's roughly two thousand of us! Everyone is most friendly and practically all superiority has disappeared. The Pru are paying three guineas a week per person – it's too good to last. The present accommodation is only booked for a week. After that we shall be reshuffled and, I expect, centralised.

My absence of a gas mask caused quite the sensation I hoped it would! But it's rather a blow – the proprietor of this place is an Air Raid Warden, so I'm afraid, should anything happen, I shan't be minus one after all. It's an awful blow to my dignity – but I shall pretend I've got one!

I must really stop now, so please hurry up and write

to your lonely, homesick Lily

who sends you

all her love.

28 Glebelands Avenue
South Woodford
Thursday 31st August

Dearest Lil,

Your much longed for letter has just arrived – one of the few rays of sunshine in a very gloomy week. I was really beginning to think that you were too busy to write …

You seem to have had quite a nice little holiday, and indeed a very nice place to stay at. I hope that your luck will continue.

Yes, it is strange how much one treasures a lot of worthless souvenirs. As your mantelpiece appeared before me like a picture, I thought of my own treasures that I wouldn't lose for the world. Then as I read about the shell from Pourville the Paris ramble flashed through my mind again – peanuts at Sacré Coeur, the lipstick and Nora's hat and the snails ...

So you didn't take your gas mask, you wretched girl. For some unknown reason the Government makes every effort to protect you (heaven only knows why it should protect you to play 'General Knowledge') and you give it no thanks. In fact you scorn its help and make yourself generally aggressive. I really think the presence of an Air Raid Warden is an occurrence inspired by Nemesis ...

The only really exciting thing this week was the Prom on Tuesday. It really was a marvellous programme. I thoroughly enjoyed the two concertos and the symphony gave me a great thrill because I already knew it pretty well – I'm very tempted to get a record of it! ...

I am doing a tremendous lot of piano practice, and what's more I can play the first dozen bars of Boccherini's *Minuet*.

I played them yesterday afternoon, and when I had finished I felt so pleased with myself that I got up and bowed, first to the fireplace, then to the music cabinet, then the armchair, the door and the settee, in the true Paul Beard manner. Then I thought what a silly chap I was, and so sat down hurriedly and continued with my scales ...

Please, please write again very soon,
with ever so much love,
from Martyn

The mass evacuation of children began on Friday 1ˢᵗ September and blackout regulations were enforced. Television transmission ceased and the BBC merged its regional broadcasts so that there would be only one programme – the Home Service.

On Saturday 2ⁿᵈ September Martyn sent Lily a postcard from Waterloo Station that said, 'Have just been called up and now on my way to Southampton.'

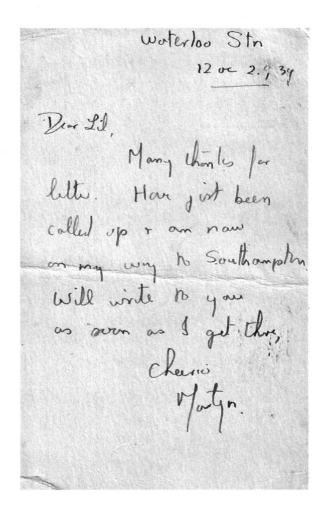

Waterloo Stn

12 oc 2.9.39

Dear Lil,

Many thanks for letter. Have just been called up & am now on my way to Southampton. Will write to you as soon as I get there.

Cheerio

Martyn.

Sunday 3rd September began as a beautiful sunny morning and many people were busy in their gardens struggling to erect their homemade or Anderson corrugated steel air raid shelters. An eleven o'clock deadline had been given to Germany to withdraw its troops from Poland and agree to cease aggressive action, and there was to be a special BBC broadcast at quarter past eleven. People gathered round their wirelesses in anticipation and finally Neville Chamberlain's sombre voice came over the airways. After a few words of explanation, he declared: 'I have to tell you now that no such undertaking has been received, and that consequently this country is at war with Germany.'

Sunday 3rd September

My dear Martyn,

... I think this is the worst Sunday I've ever known! We went to church this morning but there wasn't much solace to be had there with the front pews filled up with Territorials, and the congregation singing 'Onward Christian soldiers, marching on to war' – with all their might. There is no such thing as a <u>Christian</u> soldier – how could there be?

Martyn, darling Martyn, you won't have to go, will you? Not yet at any rate. Write quickly and reassure me, won't you. I'm so afraid for your safety. Please go down to Tiptree and make jam for as long as you can, till I come back to you again. Please God it won't be long...

We went to Babbacombe this afternoon, Nora and I, and I am now sitting on the beach. It's lovely here – great, grass-covered sandstone cliffs and the sea of ever-changing blue. With the sun shining and a blue sky overhead it seems impossible to believe that once again we are plunged into the mad insanity of war! It sounds unbelievable down here; I can't really take it in.

We went to see *Wuthering Heights* the other evening – it really was marvellous. Quite the most moving picture I've seen for a long time, but terribly sad. Lawrence Olivier is really great, you ought to see it. It's lovely to find something which engrosses you so much that you can forget ...

It's evening, just about half past six. I am picturing all the dear folks at church. I'm thinking of the vacant place next to Maisie where I should be sitting. Oh, it makes me mad that little, sniggering men should cause the precious innocent lives of their countrymen to be trampled on and broken like so many reeds ...

I am sitting in the middle of a charming picture. On either side of me on the veranda are large pots of red geraniums. Below them is the terrace with steps leading down to a velvety lawn. Beyond the lawn are shrubs and behind the shrubs is a gap in the trees through which I can see a large sheet of azure blue – the sea – and the harbour, with little boats dotted about on it.

Did you have your model aeroplane gala or fête, or whatever it's called, today? If you've had weather like ours it's been glorious! I hope all the models flew when they were supposed to and didn't let you down. Did any fly away altogether? ...

Do you have any prints of the Garden Party? Nora and I would like some. And, Martyn, it would cheer us considerably to have Nora's poem to read sometimes, so could you endeavour to get it back for me. ...

Monday 4th September

... I received your postcard this morning, Martyn, and spent the worst day so far in consequence. It came as an awful shock to me, especially after your assurances that you wouldn't be called till the last. Perhaps they weren't assurances – but I had pinned my trust to them.

I have spent today thinking and worrying and wondering about you. I couldn't eat a thing.

But when your letter came, I was so relieved. I just fell on my bed and cried, and cried, and cried – tears of joy! Now you are back in Woodford I feel you are safe.

Now I feel comparatively cheerful again. It's hard down here to believe that some hundreds of miles away men are killing one another. But Martyn, if you were called up – it doesn't – it couldn't mean you piloting a bomber plane? It is only to finish your training, isn't it? Oh, I hope so.

This won't do – I'm almost beginning to feel 'aggressive' again! ...

Monday 4th September

My dearest Lil,

... I am now home again after one of the most eventful Sundays that I have known.

I left Southampton at nine o'clock on Sunday morning by a train that was fast to Waterloo and arrived there at about half past ten. Then I caught a train at Liverpool Street for home. Quite uneventful so far. But at Leytonstone the air raid siren started. The train chugged to Snaresbrook, but there, police in tin helmets came along and told us we could either stay in the train or go to a shelter. Needless to say I stayed on the train and in due course it proceeded to

26

George Lane. At George Lane the sirens started again, and when I got home I found my people sitting in my uncle's garage which is our ARP shelter. It was a false alarm of course and soon the 'all clear' sounded.

After lunch we took my Mum, Grandma, Aunt and Bess [the dog] down to Tiptree and returned just in time for church. There were very few there though ...

After church we wandered Knighton Woods, but decided to turn back early because of the blackout.

Poor Maisie has to work overtime you know, and has no chance of being evacuated. She remarked that last week we felt sorry for you, and this week we envy you. Too true – in fact there is no point in being at home now. No Fellowship, no nothing, hardly any friends.

We went to bed rather apprehensively, and at 3 am the blessed sirens started again. Dad and self put on our coats over pyjamas and toddled over to my uncle's again. We sat there for half an hour and then the 'all clear' sounded again. Another false alarm. Still you know, all these preparations, trenches, gas masks, wardens etc., which we joked about, certainly give one some confidence now.

What is it like down your way? Do you have blackouts and sirens? – I suppose you do.

Dad probably goes to Reading tomorrow, so I'll just stay here on my own waiting and waiting, until they want me again.

I hope that I get posted to a South Coast aerodrome pretty quickly. As soon as I get a day's leave I shall dash over and see you – even if it means coming a hundred miles.

With lots of love to you,
Cheerio, Martyn

P.S. Please excuse my ghastly writing.

P.P.S. Would you please do me a favour? Write at once and tell me if one can get Bed and Breakfast at Torquay, and also try and find out if one can get to Southampton from Torquay by 11 o'clock in the morning.

Monday 4th September

Dearest Lily,

I can assure you that I had no intention of writing again today, but when I arrived home this afternoon I found two letters from you waiting for me, and so I simply had to write and say thank you very, very much. You can't imagine what a grand surprise they were, and how much I have enjoyed reading them. I have already read them three times! ...

It was ghastly to read the part of your letter that said "six months will soon go" when now it may be six years – or more – or never ...

As for what you said about the Territorials and 'Onward Christian Soldiers' – Heavens, Lil, will you speak to me when I'm in uniform? Or will you brand me as a heathen too? I'm not trying to be funny, Lil. I know how you feel about this well enough and God knows I never want to kill a German. I'm under no illusion about 'dying to preserve the right', 'fighting a war to end war' and the like. I shall die a murderer – not through will, but through weakness.

I was informed this afternoon that we were granted leave until Saturday. That is why I hastily added a postscript about trains to Southampton and Bed and Breakfast in my last letter. Don't be too optimistic about this though because I have grave fears that it won't come off.

So, dear Lil, goodbye for the present,
from Martyn, with ever so much love.

... Heaven knows, Lil, if there'll be any prints of the Garden Party. You see everything is in pandemonium here now – garden parties forgotten – photographs forgotten – everything upside down. I am now sitting in the single dark room of our house, sitting on the solitary chair that is not covered with dust sheets, trying to write by the tiniest of lights with my torch and gas mask on the floor beside me. Needless to say our Gala Day did not come off on Sunday.

You were very lucky to see *Wuthering Heights*. No chance of seeing any more films for quite a time, I'm afraid ...

Yes, Lil, I shall be training for a month or so, but then I'm afraid, a bomber plane it may be. You can be sure that I shall do all I possibly can to be put on fighters, but you can't argue with the RAF, and they just use you to suit their purpose.

Oh, Lil dear, we have had some grand times, haven't we! We've got so much out of life; we've seen the beauty of the world in all its forms; we've loved painting and poetry and music; we've had good friends and what more could we ask from the world? It would be very hard to leave you, but memories of the past give me no end of courage.

I asked Dad whether he thought that I could get a cheap ticket from Southampton to Torquay, but he assured me that I couldn't as if he thought me mad to think about it. So I'm afraid that's off, for the time being anyhow.

I enjoyed your description of the garden at Torquay. Every picture with you in it is charming, and how much I long to see that charming picture now. I pray that it will not be long before I see you again, but for the time being, I'm afraid, letters will have to be all ...

Wednesday 6th September

Martyn, dear,

... It grieves me to think that you should doubt my friendliness to you when you are in uniform. You dear, silly, boy – don't you yet know that I would forgive you if you killed a hundred Germans? I hope you never have to, of course. I know how you feel – you, who wouldn't even kill a fly! ...

Martyn, don't talk about never seeing me again. When all this wretched business is over and we can laugh once more, then we'll say how awful it would have been if – not now, not yet ...

Wednesday 6th September

Dearest Lil,

We have just had what presumably was the first raid. At quarter to seven the siren sounded, and all the police and wardens merrily blew their whistles. We could hear the planes in the distance, but soon it grew fainter and we thought that they had gone. Soon we heard them again however, and saw some of our fighters chasing about, very high up. This went on for just over an hour and then I decided to get dressed. No sooner had I started than I heard the sound of planes once more and suddenly the anti-aircraft guns decided to say a few words. I went down and watched the shells bursting, and then everything quietened down again and I finally managed to dress. The all-clear sounded at about quarter past nine. I'm afraid some towns must have caught a packet, however.

I have just received your letter, and hate to dash your hopes to the ground, but I'm afraid there is no hope of coming down. I'm sending a couple of postcards as small compensation. Think about ballet, instead of the chance of me coming down.

I also heard today that there is quite a possibility that they will send me abroad to complete my training. To Singapore or somewhere like that. That has made me horribly fed up. Needless to say, I'd much rather be in England.

So much for now,

with love from Martyn

P.S. Brighter news with regard to coming down. Could you try very hard to get Friday afternoon off?

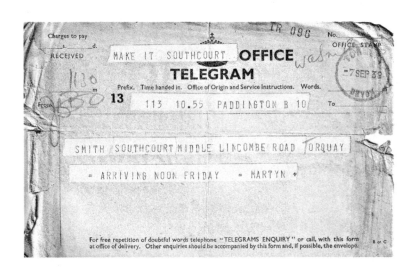

2

12th September – 23rd September 1939

After Lily and Martyn had met up and spent the rest of Friday and Saturday together in Torquay, Martyn returned to Southampton only to be told that he was not needed and could take more leave, so he made his way home to South Woodford.

Meanwhile Lily moved to her new place of residence, the Metropole Hotel, and she and her co-workers were informed that the Prudential would be remaining in Torquay for at least six months and all holidays were suspended.

Although there had been occasions when the sirens had sounded, especially in London, these had been false alarms and, so far, none of the expected German bombardments had taken place. An atmosphere of uneasiness and fear hung over the country.

28 Glebelands Avenue
South Woodford
Tuesday 12th September

My dear Lil,

It's just half past ten and I'm thinking of you working away at the V & A. It's a horribly dull, cold day. The sort of day when you must do something to keep warm. What a change from Friday! What a glorious day that was and what a glorious time we had, didn't we, Lil. Too glorious really. You know, when I was sitting on the train after saying goodbye to you, I felt more 'un-brave' than I ever have before.

Enough of miserable talk though. Fellowship and Church on Sunday were really most comforting and yesterday evening after we had blacked out the hall most of the helpers came round to our house and we had a gramophone concert. How I wished you were there too!

Do you remember the first gramophone concert that we had – and the sherry party?! We must have some more when you come home again.

I do not have to go back to Southampton but only report by phone so, if they do not want me urgently, I shall stay on here ...

Metropole Hotel
Torquay
Wednesday 13th September

My dear Martyn,

...To my extreme disgust and annoyance my mother has sent me my gas mask! You can imagine how I feel! But I've pushed it under the bed, right to the back, and left it there. So if there is a raid I shall be stuck under my bed still trying to get my gas mask!

We have started work properly now – recording, you know. Yesterday my section leader said she is considering making me a 'checker'. This means I shall have two Juniors under me! So I'm very proud of myself, as you can imagine.

I can now hear a continual stream of girls walking up the steps of the V & A to work, so I must be going too. A 'checker' mustn't be late! ...

Employees of the Prudential working at the Victoria and Albert Hotel
© *Prudential plc*

Wednesday 13th September

... This morning, Lily, I have done the shopping and all the housework. Yes, I've dusted, swept and vacuumed. I'm really quite domesticated now. My lunches are not very elaborate however. The first course invariably consists of tinned spaghetti, baked beans or corn beef and the second course of Individual Fruit Pie (apricot) or Individual Fruit Pie (blackcurrant) or Individual Fruit Pie (mincemeat)....

Thursday 14th September

My dear Martyn,

... How I should love to see you managing the domestic arrangements of 28 Glebelands! Your lunches sound great fun. I should think the local grocers are running out of Individual Fruit Pies.

It's Thursday night. How I wish the clocks could be put back to last Thursday again! It seems more than a week since I saw you. Do go to your uncle's in Weymouth and if you go, do come to Torquay. There is a little girl down here who would be oh so happy to see you.

We've had great fun tonight. We all bought cakes and biscuits and have been eating them ever since dinner. After this we had a display of 'aerobatics' and playing 'he' from bed to bed. We have since rounded off the evening's entertainment by a grand, wet-flannel fight. In this, I became most aggressive – in fact quite un-pacifistic. But I won, and have bagged all the flannels so my other room-mates are now trying to find them – but they won't, for I've hidden them all.

Just now I expect you are having a nice time with the Fellowship – lucky you! How I wish I were there. Does Don still go out to buy chips or is it ices now? Do you remember the night you tipped the packet of salt over my head? Oh, we did have fun! ...

... Thank you so much too, Lily, for the photograph. It really is a grand picture of you, Lil – and it's just how I always think of you with that 'Miss Naughty' hat, and those perky little shoes and the bag that won't stay closed! – and that sweet blue dress that blends so well with your golden hair.

We've just had lunch together you and I. You have been propped up opposite me against a marmalade jar, and we have had a full course luncheon. Yes, we started with fish (sardines to be exact) which were left over from yesterday's breakfast. Then the meat course – sausages (cold of course) left over from today's breakfast. Next the sweet – a slice of red watermelon – I hope you enjoyed it – left over from yesterday's tea. Finally biscuits and grapefruit squash – we had grapefruit partly because I remembered you don't like coffee and partly because I haven't any coffee anyway.

A grand lunch – everything one could wish for – except you. And you were just a picture ...

Friday 15th September

Dearest Lily,

… I was extremely pleased to hear that your mother has sent your gas mask. I hope she scolded you strongly for not taking it in the first place. It must be very trying for her to have to deal with such an obstinate and 'aggressive' daughter!

So, Miss Smith, you are to have two Juniors under you! I trust that now, Miss Smith, you will appreciate the responsibility of your position and will not indulge in – what do you call it – 'General Knowledge' games.

Last night we gathered in the Fellowship room again for the purpose of playing table tennis. We played a few games and then Joan brought out the Community Song Book and we sang. We sang 'Clementine', 'Coming through the Rye' and 'Loch Lomond' – but my thoughts were always elsewhere ...

Saturday 16th September

My dear Martyn,

... It has been a lovely day here – marvellously sunny and hot. This afternoon my friend and I went over Tor Abbey ruins and, even more interesting, the Art Gallery.

There is not much to be seen of the abbey itself, only ruined walls and little noticeboards saying *Site of East Column* and *Here Lieth*... These boards are planted all the way down a smooth, velvety lawn so it needed quite a little imagination. We were shown round with great solemnity, my friend and I and a little fat man who sucked acid drops very noisily all the time. He got quite annoyed with the guide because there wasn't enough of the abbey left. He kept harping on about the fact that the west side of the church, which in his opinion would have been the most beautiful, had disappeared completely.

Next time you come to Torquay, Martyn, I must definitely show you the Art Gallery. It's in a lovely old house, and contains one or two very striking pictures. There are several Turners. There's a Cox, one or two Constables, a Gainsborough and a Leonardo da Vinci. There are one or two others that I liked very much indeed by people I have never heard of, which I must show you ...

I hope you enjoyed the ramble today. I would have given anything to have been with you. Oh Martyn, I do want to come home. It seems ages since I saw you – and it's only a week ago! The thought of all the weary days to be lived through appals me. All my optimism has gone from me tonight. Tomorrow will be Sunday and I shall go to church, and I shall listen to the service, but I shall be thinking of another church – miles away from here. I shall be seeing you all sitting in the Fellowship pews, talking together afterwards – perhaps going for a walk. How I long to be there again ...

Saturday 16th September

... You know, Lily, I really didn't have much difficulty in imagining you becoming un-pacifistic during the wet flannel fight. I can just see you, you young imp, entering in with the same zest with which you seem to enter everything that's going on. But really, Miss Smith, a 'checker' playing 'he' from bed to bed and performing aerobatics! Where, oh where, Miss Smith, is your dignity? Just think of the example that you are setting your 'juniors'. Keep to eating biscuits, Miss Smith, but please – no aerobatics – tut tut!

Congratulations on bagging all the flannels, though. That really was nice work. ...

Monday 18th September

... So, Martyn, you are down at Weymouth with your uncle now? I hope you have a nice time. Oh, do come and see me. Suppose you get called up or sent away somewhere – it might be ages before we see each other again. Yes, I would be willing to come part of the way to meet you but I am afraid that an

afternoon off is out of the question. I haven't even got the nerve to ask for it. Several people were surprised at my audacity last time. Besides, I haven't properly landed my 'checker-ship' yet – I'm only officially still a 'junior'.

I am enclosing another photograph – taken in the same place as the other, and at the same time. I believe the man waits for me each Sunday morning because he knows that you would like a snap ...

Wednesday 20th September

Lil dearest,

... Another glorious day – and yet another day of war and no doubt a very terrible day for many people. Oh what a wretched business all this is. It was bad enough them taking you away at the beginning, but now it seems as if they'll keep you there for good, and apparently most of the other firms that have evacuated intend to do the same.

It looks as if the Fellowship will cease to exist as we know it. Those that are alive at the end of the war will be too far away to still be members ...

*As was often the case, Martyn included two poems with his letter.
The one written by himself he entitled Veniente Occurite Morbo,
meaning 'Meet the misfortune as it comes'.*

Veniente Occurite Morbo

'Twas as usual in the autumn that the major crisis came
When our Government was taking well-earned rest.
Some were swimming, one was fishing,
And all devoutly wishing
Hitler wouldn't try another little jest.
Yet when our worthy Premier
Recalled them, all the lot,
To a man they nobly sacrificed their leisure.
But this action it is said (though I almost had forgot),
Was only a precautionary measure.

And then came frontier incidents and tension quickly grew.
Conversation was all National Defence.
Will it happen? We were thinking
As our hopes were quickly sinking
In that sad state of continuous suspense.
Then Mr Hore-Belisha called up all the searchlight crews
For to serve His Majesty's good pleasure.
But I almost had forgot,
They announced it on the news,
'Twas merely a precautionary measure.

Then the children were evacuated from each danger zone,
And in town new piles of sandbags lay around.
Windows blackened, all lights shaded,
New white lines, where they were faded,
Appeared as if by magic on the ground.
They packed away our pictures,

All for the good I guess,
And the other things we label National Treasures.
All these, I might remind you, though you saw it in the press,
Were only precautionary measures.

On the 3rd day of September we were told we'd got to fight,
And no one yet seems quite to know just why.
Maybe a war that shall end war,
No, that excuse was weak before,
And tales of German horror make us sigh.
But that nasty fellow Hitler
Is a really wicked lad.
Next he'll try to take our land from us by seizure.
And so we've got to stop him
Although this war is mad.
It's simply a precautionary measure.

Thursday 21st September

... It seems almost pointless to write, Martyn, as I am hoping by the time you get my letter that you will be on your way to see me. Oh, Martyn, come quickly – I am trying not to hope very much, but it is hard.

I love the poem, the one about the precautionary measure. It's really very good – but who is it by? Did I ought to know? I can't think, unless it's you. If it is, I think it's very good indeed.

Yes, Rossetti's poem is lovely – but it's too sad for us, isn't it? If you were here with me I should feel reassured. I'm tired of letters. I want to see you, Martyn, hear your voice. Do come if you can.

Gosh! That's the gong! Breakfast!

You need to not worry if the Pru decide to stay down here for ever; I shall give in my resignation 'toute suite'. But I don't think they will, it's too expensive. At the end of October they are going to allow each person a guinea a week towards their board and lodging. So this means at least £1500 per week. Even the Pru can't keep that up for long ...

Friday 22nd September

... I was overjoyed, Martyn, to read the first part of your letter, but the second half wasn't so promising. Pray heaven that the train ticket arrives in time. This suspense is dreadful! But it will be lovely if you do come ...There's really nothing more to say except that I send you all my love, and hope that we shall be together this time tomorrow.

So, till then, my darling,
all my love, Lily

3

25th September – 25th October 1939

Presuming that the trains from Weymouth to Torquay ran as scheduled, Lily and Martyn would have spent the rest of Saturday and all of Sunday together. Lily was desperate though, not only to have more of Martyn's company, but also time at home in Woodford Green with her family and friends.

Metropole Hotel
Torquay
Monday 25th September

My darling Martyn,

I believe you have been wishing the most wonderful thing for me – and wishing it very hard. For – what do you think? The most marvellous, gorgeous, wonderful thing that I've been longing and hoping for – I'm coming home!

When you went away this morning, I think you took part of me with you – my heart – there was only an aching void where it ought to have been. All the morning I tried to work but it was hopeless – I could only think of you, each moment being taken farther and farther away from me. It seemed that I had said goodbye to part of myself. And for how long? Somehow my 'infernal optimism' couldn't face up to it.

Then, after lunch, my senior came into our room and said, "Holidays are to be resumed. I will get out a list and you must tell me when you want them." This brightened things up considerably.

It was not till an hour later that I had the marvellous idea of coming home this Saturday. You see, it's my Saturday off so I can probably get my week's holiday quite easily. The girls that went last weekend were allowed to travel up by the 2:15 pm train from here, so I expect I shall be able to.

Don't you think it's a lovely idea? If I wait longer there may be a raid or something. Or, worse still you may be called up and have to go to some aerodrome miles away. Isn't it better to try and have my week now? Or is there too great a risk of you being called up suddenly and thus spoiling our plans?

Do write ever so quickly and let me know, Martyn, won't you? We may be able to have that long awaited week together after all. Won't it be heavenly! You must work out another itinerary. Though if we only sit on Woodford Green, I shall be happy! 'Happy' – a little word like that is impossible to describe my feelings. I want to dance, and sing, and laugh and shout! I shall have to compose my feelings sufficiently to go out and post this letter and if I don't go now, I shall miss the post. ...

So, goodbye for now my dearest.

All my love to you,

Lily

28 Glebelands Avenue
South Woodford
Tuesday 26th September

My dearest Lily,

Your letter arrived about five minutes ago, but I have only just got over the shock!

What a glorious shock though! It really is too, too grand for words – I just simply can't find words to express how happy I am. And you know, when I left you last, as the train went along by the edge of the sea near Teignmouth and I saw the cliffs where we had wandered on Sunday gradually merge into the sea, I thought to myself "Goodbye for a month – perhaps more. Oh, if only it were Saturday again." For I could see no future prospect of my coming down for some time, and although I've hoped and hoped that you would get your holiday, I couldn't believe there was really any chance. And now you're coming! Oh Lil, it really is marvellous. – I shall start planning the week right away.

I had wished that the week would come in November or at the end of October, but as you say, Lil, it's too great a risk to leave it and hope that I shall still have leave then. No, Lil, please do try and have next week ...

The Croft,
Maldon Road,
Tiptree
Wednesday 27th September

... Yes, Lil, you simply must come, for I heard yesterday that they've finished training the Regular RAF now and so will start on us very soon. It'll be awful if they recall me before the end of next week, but I don't somehow think they will.

So, Lil, darling, you've simply got to come!

We had a great time last evening in the Fellowship. It was quite a "gambling hell"! We had darts, cards, Lexicon and Wibbly-wob, and George and self gave one of our piano duets! In spite of all the attractions, half the girls simply sat around and knitted!

They are blacking out the big hall this week, so there will probably be badminton again next week. I do so much hope you're home. Won't it be fun playing badminton again! ...

Wednesday 27th September

My very dear Martyn,

... I am so glad you want me to come home this Saturday because now that the opportunity has come, I don't think I could wait another day.

I asked my senior this morning whether I could have my week's holiday and she said "Certainly." So, I shall definitely be coming home this Friday. I shall be catching the 2:15 pm train from here and that should arrive at about eight o'clock but it may be late. If you come and meet me – I should love you to

– we must arrange a definite place or it will be difficult in the blackout.

Please ask your Pop to arrange a ramble this Saturday. I am sure he will. See what you can do to persuade him anyway …

This afternoon we are going to have a 'sewing bee' to make curtains for the office during the blackout. It will be a nice change from recordings.

It's time to go back to work, so I'll have to stop now.

Till I see you, all my love, Lily

Thursday 28th September

My dear Martyn,

Much to my annoyance I am not being allowed to catch the 2:15 pm train on Friday. So I have just been to the station to enquire about later trains. The only one that is any good goes at 8:58 pm from here and arrives at Paddington at 4:05 am – not so good. I shall spend the rest of the night in the waiting room and then catch the first train from Liverpool Street station to George Lane.

This isn't going to be very pleasant but it will be better than waiting until Saturday morning, and not arriving home till 4:30 pm. You won't of course be able to meet me – but you are quite at liberty to come round after breakfast. I shall be so happy to see you.

Oh Martyn, I am so thrilled – I don't know how I'm going to live through the next two days! And if I don't go now, I shall be late for work.

So, till I see you, all my love,
Lily

After her week's holiday in Woodford, Lily returned to Torquay.

Sunday 8th October

... It is just half past eight, Lily, and I am thinking of you nearing Torquay – further and further away from me every minute. As your train steamed out this afternoon and your hand disappeared from sight, I felt horribly hot and my throat all dry, but I cheered myself up with the thought that it wouldn't be for long ...

Tuesday 10th October

Dearest Lily,

... I've been reading the first part of *The Forsyte Saga* and somehow it's shattering my faith and ideals. Love of art that degenerates to mere hypocrisy or desire for possessions; love of persons that seems eternal and yet fades away in marriage! I wonder if it's better to die when one's ideals are still bright and before one has tasted personally of the cruelties and cruelness of the world. And yet I don't want to die now, because I'm sure that we would always get on well together. Remember our dream of a bungalow, Lil? And yet I'm obsessed with doubts about us, and life – and everything. Oh, Lil, darling, I expect you're fed up with my wailing ...

Clifford's got to register for service next week and he's trying to reconcile it with his pacifist views. He said that he had weighed up everything, and as it would mean losing his job to be a Conchie [conscientious objector], and as he had a debt to his people, he had decided to register, but would try to get in a section of the Army that doesn't actually fight. He tried to convince me that he had a clear conscience on the matter, but from the vigour of his assurances it was obvious that he still had lurking doubts.

You've got to be a revolutionary or an angel to make a good pacifist! I don't know whether you're really a good pacifist when I think of wet flannels! But you're an angel all the same ...

Wednesday 11th October

My dearest Lily,

... The message came through that I had to attend a pay parade in London tomorrow morning. So back I go again! I had a good mind to ring up the RAF and say, "No. To hell with my Personal Allowance! You can keep it. I'm not coming to fetch it." But then I remembered our bungalow, darling, and repented ...

I never expected to love anyone – I never wanted to, and now that I do I'm not so sure that I like it. You see it's made me alter my whole plan for life. I wanted to be a wanderer – to tramp the world picking up jobs here and there – living now like a beggar and now like a baronet. All very romantic, I suppose, but not so impossible as wanting to be an engine driver.

And now in the space of a few weeks everything is changed. Is it a passing, mutual infatuation, Lil? Time will show, but, God, I pray that it is not.

Oh, Lil, dearest, it can't be, it mustn't be – forgive me please for ever thinking of it ...

Thursday 12th October

Dear Miss Dopey Piglet Smith,

… Your recent letter arrived by first post this morning and so bucked me up that I rather regretted writing the dismal letter of last night …Really, Lil, it's marvellous to know you are coming back again. So far, the war has been one succession of anti-climaxes – or should I omit the 'anti'. I keep on saying goodbye to you, and feeling like hell for days afterwards because I think I should not see you for months – and then you write and say you're coming home or else I find that I can come and see you!

Oh Lil, it is grand. I feel like rushing about and dancing for joy!

There's probably going to be a fellowship ramble to Sadlers Wells, and even if it doesn't come off, we could go together. The snag is that it's *Madame Butterfly*, but still, Puccini is better than nothing. What do you think about it?

Your optimism is a real tonic, Lily, and I feel thoroughly ashamed of my doubts. I think I sometimes have fears about things as a sort of insurance against them happening. I mean that if you are prepared for a thing, it doesn't usually happen, and so if I'm prepared for the worst, I imagine it will probably never occur.

Doubt you, Lil? Good heavens, no! I feel that you are simply unchangeable – if you did change, it would give me a terrible shock …

Sunday 15th October

… When I read through your letters, Lil, I feel that it's horribly mean of me to moan every time I write. Heaven knows, I love you madly now and the possibility of it being infatuation seems absurd. Only time will show whether it is or not.

But enough of all this, darling, let's talk about next weekend. I've discovered that there is a concert, though I don't think it's a terribly good one. Haydn is good and Corelli's music is rather like Handel's I believe, so that should be enjoyable too. The Brahms is a bit heavy ... but quite jolly though. Which would you prefer, the concert or Sadlers Wells? Please let me know. If we are going to Sadlers, we might get up a party ...

Tuesday 17ᵗʰ October

Lily dearest,

... I have got the tickets for the concert on Saturday. I hope that suits you. You see there is to be no fellowship ramble to Sadlers Wells and at present there is no ramble arranged at all, not even a walk! But there is badminton in the evening and you will be able to see the others then.

The Forsyte Saga is marvellous and I find it terribly hard to put down the book now! I shall be eternally grateful to you for inspiring me to read it.

I heard from my pal John French today. He is at a Flying Training School at Chippenham. The worst part of it is that he is flying 'twins' – twin-engined aeroplanes – already, and so it looks as if he will be put on bombers! Not a very rosy prospect, but unhappily one can't pick and choose one's machines and duties. He says that he doesn't expect to be "beating up Adolf" before the beginning of next year, so he will have had four months training at least and he had already done many more hours than me ...

Wednesday 18th October

... You might think, Lily, that I deprecate pacifism – but far from it. You know I admire you tremendously for being a pacifist, but I just cannot believe that peace will come by just refusing to fight. If pacifism is to be a paying proposition, the world must be educated up to it. It must be educated to a love of beauty, to a love of those things which are all men's common property.

War has come again, but don't let it quench your efforts for peace – I know it won't ...

Tuesday 24th October

Darling,

Your letter has just come, but oh Lil, all your optimism seems to have gone – quite vanished!

You know I'm not really pessimistic altogether. I'm pessimistic about the future and optimistic about the present, while you seem pessimistic about the present and optimistic about the future!

Things really aren't at all bad. I know I'm having a much better time than you – at home with the crowd and all that – but then look how much worse it might have been for all of us, or rather for both of us. I might have been in the Army, and been whisked across to France like poor Sticky. You might have been evacuated to Scotland, billeted in little houses and granted no free passes home! It could have been much worse, it may be much worse yet, but I pray that it will not.

No Lil, it's only eighteen days now, sweet one, so cheer up and count your blessings!

Yesterday I heard on the radio a short anthology of poems, and among them was one called 'Do you remember an inn, Miranda?' I think by Belloc. Do you know it? Another of the poems that was read was Masefield's 'Cargoes'. I had never realised how much I liked it, and how much the rhythm fitted the different boats ...

So dearest, goodbye till tomorrow,
with all my love to you, Martyn

Wednesday 25th October

My dear Miss Smith,

I have to acknowledge your letter of the 24th inst. and note with pleasure your promotion to the rank of 'Checker'. As you are no doubt aware, I have a very great respect for Checkers, mainly owing to their scarcity in this quarter, and so naturally I have a great, indeed an increased, respect for you as a Checker. Your title shall be in future 'Miss Piglet', or would you prefer 'Miss Dopey', or would you prefer just 'Lil darling'? I like the last myself.

I'm jolly glad to see that you've bucked up a bit – I expect it's your promotion that's done it!

You really are a scream with all your plans for when I should be posted and where. Anyone would think that I owned the blessed RAF – instead of being a diminutive specimen about which they have completely forgotten! ...

I'm afraid there is no more to say, except that I love you an awful lot, and spend most of my time just looking forward to November 10th.

So goodbye till tomorrow, dearest one,
love, Martyn

4

30th October – 27th November 1939

Britain had expected that following the declaration of war there would immediately be extensive bombing so there had been a flurry of activity to ensure that everyone was prepared for the onslaught. People's lives changed in many ways but there was a determination to keep going come what may. A real hardship in everyday life was the strict enforcement of the nightly blackout and there were many accidents caused by this.

However, in the first few months of the war there was very little offensive activity from Germany. After all the build-up, this lull made the public uneasy, resentful of what they considered to be unnecessary restrictions, and distrustful of the Government's leadership. This period became known as The Phoney War.

Two months had passed since Martyn had been called up but he was still no nearer to receiving his pilot training. There were other matters, however, that greatly concerned him.

28 Glebelands Avenue
South Woodford
Monday morning – 30th October

My dearest Lil,

You may have sensed by my periods of pessimism lately that something was worrying me. Something in fact was definitely wrong. Well, at last things have come to a head and yet I'm afraid the real crisis is still to come.

You may or may not have noticed that for some months past the policy and activities of the Fellowship have been more or less decided by a little clique consisting of E.J., Alice, Joan and Joe, but mainly Alice and Dad. In fact everything that Alice wants goes. Alice has been so full of ideas, and Dad is so keen to carry them out, that it hasn't been found necessary to hold a council meeting for almost four months! ...

On Sunday evening I got Jack chatting on the subject and found that not only did his ideas on the subject completely agree with mine, but he told me that there were many other people who felt the same way, and many who had more grievances against the present state of things than I could have imagined. He complained bitterly that if he suggested a thing, he had to suggest it at least ten times before anything was done, while if Alice suggested it, it was done at once ...

We are so busy arranging rambles, visits, games, badminton etc., in fact making the Fellowship a sort of Mutual Enjoyment Society, that we've completely lost sight of its real aims. Surely, we really have three aims: –

Understanding Christianity – Putting it into practice – Cultivating ourselves. We dabble a bit in each of them, but for the most part our main aim seems to be self-centred enjoyment. You see I have a pretty poor opinion of what we're doing at present – I feel we've got into a lazy rut. And I found Jack agrees with me, so we're going to try to improve things with a bit of action. Dad's got enough push and imagination to make anything go ...

Monday evening

... Heaven only knows what will happen for I've now told Dad that I'm not the only one that's dissatisfied with the 'Alice clique' and he says that he thinks he'll have to resign. That would be the most ghastly thing imaginable, for Dad's whole life is the Fellowship and though perhaps I shouldn't say it, I doubt whether we could have a much better leader. It's only a small thing really and to resign would, I feel, look as if he condoned the influence of cliques and favourites. And I'm sure he doesn't – in fact I don't think he really realises that he's been encouraging a clique.

I'm sorry I've written all this, but I had to tell you the whole story so that you could bless or condemn. Oh, Lil, it makes me feel so rotten. If only you were here now – I could do with some of your comfort ...

Tuesday 31st October

My darling Lily,

Your letter has just arrived, and I am thinking that by now you have got my last disturbing epistle. I'm terribly anxious to know how you feel about the matter and shall be greatly relieved when I receive your next letter.

With regard to the 'favouritism', I suddenly made up my mind to take the bull by the horns and took a step which now gives me a cold sweat when I think of it, but I feel it's the best way through ...

Jack and myself, assisted by Reg Rapkin, and I hope some others, are going ahead with an ambitious plan of campaign and I'm going to try and present it at a council meeting on Sunday. I shall be jolly glad when all this trouble is over, but at the same time this miniature 'crusade' is making my blood tingle. This plan of action is a great idea and I'm going to put my heart and soul into getting it carried through. I do hope that you are 'for' it – I do wish that you were at home to help us carry it through ...

Wednesday 1st November

Dearest Lily,

I've made the most terrible mistake, which I'm afraid will wreck everything. Dad has been brooding over the trouble since Sunday and this morning he told me that he realised my 'confederate' was Jack and couldn't understand why Jack should have been so grossly unfair as to suggest there is a clique and to libel Alice of all people.

Then I blindly did the most mad thing I could possibly have done. I showed him your letter.

It completely struck him down and he said, "Well, now there's nothing I can do but resign."

Oh, God, I've pitched the whole Fellowship into the fire now and I shall repent it to the end of my days. And I've wrecked our life too. I shall have to leave the Fellowship and all my friends in it too.

The war is a blessing really. I shall go pretty soon. – I'll see I do. Till then I shall live a life that will be just hell, but so will quite a few other people's thanks to me.

I have abused your confidence, Lil, and I'm sorry – as sorry as I could possibly be. But what's the use of that now. Forgive me if you can, Lil, but there's no reason why you should. I just don't deserve it.

I expect this is the last letter I shall write to you. I expect I've already seen you for the last time, but please believe me now, in spite of what I've done, I do love you with all my heart and ever shall.

So goodbye,

Martyn

Friday 3rd November

My very, very dearest Lily,

I really don't know how to begin this letter, whether to say how sorry I am I wrote that last letter, or whether to tell you how infinitely grand and sweet I think you are.

I just had to tell you what I had done, and it seemed to me I had knocked the bottom out of everything and lost everything worth living for.

I waited in suspense for your letter and when I got it I realised how wretched of me it was to have feared your reply – to have forgotten how dear and perfect you were in everything.

On Wednesday morning I honestly felt that Dad's decision was completely final. I lived the rottenest day in my life and felt there was no hope for the future. But thank heaven, maybe thanks to Alice, the clouds have lifted. Dad has decided to mention the dissatisfaction on Sunday and arrange a secret ballot to establish whether the Fellowship still has confidence in him. I told him that I felt the result would be a foregone conclusion, but if it would ease his mind, it would be a good thing. I'm afraid we've trod too near the edge of the precipice to bring in our plan at the moment. Those reforms will have to come in gradually and very tactfully.

I don't know whether you've written to Dad, and if not, whether it could still be to advantage in the new circumstances. But just as you like ...

There is a gap in the collection of Lily's letters through October and November, doubtless due to the reaction that some of them had fuelled by their content. The next letter that Martyn wrote was more of a hasty, short note.

Sunday 5th November

Lil dearest,

I am writing in haste to catch the post. There's been a ghastly bust up and at present it looks pretty fatal. I'm afraid your letter did no good – rather the opposite in fact.

Say nothing to Maisie or Prissie. Have a feeling they are taking the other side.

Love,
Martyn

Monday 6th November

Dearest Lily,

I am afraid that things are turning out far worse than I ever anticipated.

Your letter to Dad, has I'm afraid, done far more harm than good. He says that your defiant attitude of 'not withdrawing anything' proves that we have all raised the trouble because of personal grudges ...Dad raised hell yesterday afternoon. He related the whole story, with every lurid detail and even quoted chunks from your letter, although he didn't say who it was from. Alice knows, though, and if she tells Joe, the whole Fellowship will know in no time.

There was a terrific argument after Dad's little speech. Joe and Joan both took Alice's side naturally and so more or less admitted that they were in the clique.

Hilda said that she was aware of an undercurrent of the trouble but was sufficiently confident in E.J. to let things go on as they were. Audrey spoke a lot about bringing it before the council, but admitted to me afterwards that she felt that Alice had been behaving rather foolishly for some time.

I spoke to quite a few people after church and most of them appreciated the trouble, but accused me of tackling the subject without any tact. Dad will not admit to a single charge, in whole or part, but insists that if there is any blame, it rests entirely with him and not with Alice. He says now that he will definitely resign the leadership at the AGM.

Alice has already resigned and I have decided finally, now, that I will do the same. I shan't be re-elected at Christmas anyhow ...

Patching things up is going to be jolly difficult, if not impossible, and it will take a few weeks at least for things to blow over.

I'm wondering whether it wouldn't be better for you to postpone your visit for a few weeks, for I can assure you that it won't be at all pleasant next Sunday. I know you have been looking forward to coming home an awful lot, and I hate the idea of having to wait another three weeks, but I'm afraid the atmosphere next Sunday won't be at all exciting.

Please think this idea over carefully, for in a month's time things won't be so bitter and the majority of the Fellowship will have decided whether we are the criminals or not ...

Wednesday 8th November

Dearest Lily,

You have no doubt received my telegram by now, and are probably pretty amazed. I do hope it didn't come too late.

I am still a bit dazed about last night. Either things have blown over, and amazingly quickly, or else it's a big hoax.

I went round there expecting fireworks, but instead of that I chatted to Joe, played badminton with Alice, shared chips with Joan and joked with Maisie. Personally I feel considerably freer now that the whole thing has come out.

After my effort on Sunday of running down Alice, denouncing the clique, telling the council that it was incompetent and telling the whole Fellowship that it was using the organisation as something on which to pin pleasures – surely this was an amazing reception.

I don't think now that you need fear coming back – or should I say 'that I need fear you coming back', for probably only Alice and Dad know that those writings were yours. Anyhow if anyone has reserved their cold shoulder for you they'll soon wish they hadn't, for any cold shoulders in this affair belong to me and I'll jolly well see that it hurts you as little as possible.

So darling, come home if you possibly can.

Oh Lil, I do want to see you now – you must come home – when shall I meet you on Friday?

All my love to you, dearest, bye,

Martyn

Lily did return home for the weekend and the Fellowship's problems must have diminished for just a week later they held an 'American Tea' which Martyn describes with enthusiasm in his next letter.

... I do wish that you had been here, Lil, for the 'American Tea' yesterday. We really had a great time. Reg and self, assisted by George and Tony, arranged the grammy recital which I think went off quite well on the whole. Everybody seemed quite pleased with it and we have got to do another at a Church Social on Thursday week.

After the recital we had the cinema show. Following the film of rambles, we had the Garden Party film – it really is excellent. There is a charming picture of you dashing across the lawn, skipping over chairs and other debris that was lying around. Following the films we had quite a jolly concert by the choirs and then we packed up the American Tea and concluded the evening with badminton. There have been no further developments regarding 'the trouble'. I simply can't imagine how things will eventually pan out. You can be sure that I won't let Maisie know who wrote the letter. I've already made enough trouble for you without making any more and the last thing I want to do is to be the cause of your breaking your friendship with Maisie. Maisie and myself have always been good pals up to now and I wish I could tell her the whole story.

I don't want to be in the bad books of anybody, but Maisie is one of the last people I want to be at loggerheads with – for more reasons than one – you will appreciate that fact.

Oh well, such is life as I always say – we must just wait and see.

Well my darling Lil, bye till tomorrow.
I love you with all my heart and soul,
Martyn

Thursday 23rd November

My darling Lily,

I went up to town to report today and after doing the aforesaid duty I wandered down Charing Cross Road, eventually arriving at the Ballet Shop – do you know it? It has in it a marvellous stock of books and pictures of ballet and needless to say has the periodical entitled *Ballet*. I bought a copy of both of the two numbers that have been published up to date – there will be no more till the war is over. And I'm sending you one of them now. I'm keeping the other till I've read it – I hope you don't mind – and will send it to you next week ...

I'm jolly glad to hear that you are having a good spot of leave at Christmas time. Even if you came home before then I am afraid that I shouldn't be at home! I have to report at Southampton on Tuesday and they will then give me details for reporting at RAF Saint Leonards, near Hastings, on Wednesday. Yes, I am to be posted at last!! ...

5

27th November – 31st December 1939

As luck would have it, Lily was able to sneak an extra weekend home by using another girl's free pass, so she was able to spend some time with Martyn before he left for St Leonards. Returning to her Torquay hotel late at night, in total blackout, was more problematical.

Hotel Metropole
Torquay
Monday 27th November

My dearest Martyn,

Well although I can't post it, here is a letter from tonight as I promised.

I arrived here quite safely after a very comfortable journey which I spent mostly in deep slumber … I changed trains at Newton Abbott and arrived at Torquay at quarter to five in the morning. But then my troubles began. The crowd of about fifty gradually split up leaving the station in groups of twos and threes and made off down the road for their respective hotels. I followed on by myself expecting to recognise somebody from the Metropole. Soon everyone had disappeared leaving me trudging along in the teeth of a violent gale! Apparently no *Metropolers* had caught the train.

I walked on in complete solitude in the pouring rain and howling wind! When I got to the top of our road, which I found without too much difficulty, I suddenly had a horrible thought – I hadn't bothered to get a hotel key! What if the door was locked? Every other time there have been so many people going in that it hasn't been necessary to produce the key which one is supposed to use when it's later than quarter past eleven. I hurried on, ran up the steps, tried the door and to my horror I found it was locked. I rang the bell – nothing happened. I rang again – and again and again! There wasn't a sound – only the wind howling and the rain pouring down. I alternately rang and listened for about ten minutes, but at length, getting desperate, I walked round to the side. I looked up at the windows of our room and perceived one to be wide open, so, waiting until there was a lull in the tempest, I shouted up at the top of my voice. I called again and again, and at length when I was just about to give up altogether I saw a torch flickering and two of my friends appeared at the window. Never have I felt so relieved! I went back to the front door and a minute later the door opened and my friend and the hotel porter appeared and let me in. I was escorted upstairs and after sundry explanations we all tumbled into our beds.

Today hasn't been too bad. I didn't really feel the least bit tired – only I wished for the weekend all over again. But really I feel a deep happiness and a heartfelt gratefulness that once again I should've been allowed the exquisite joy of seeing you, of feeling your arms around me. My darling, we are lucky indeed – aren't we? We weren't meant to be away from one another for long. Please God the war will soon be over and we shall be back in the old, happy days once more...

... I regretted very much, Lil, that I couldn't come to Paddington with you. I was very much tempted to skip the Council meeting but I'm glad I went.

When we got home from the meeting, Dad said that he felt that I should have been quite justified in skipping the meeting in order to see you off, but that he thought it was very creditable for us to have forgone that pleasure for the sake of the Fellowship.

I felt considerably bucked that he said that, for I felt very sick that I couldn't go up with you. But we have got a debt to the Fellowship, Lil. Had it not been for the Fellowship, we should probably never have met and for that reason alone I feel that it is our duty to do all we can to make it successful. I know you feel this way really, my darling, and that is one of the reasons why I love you so much.

At the meeting Douglas made a speech on Alice's behalf and Hilda gave her a few pats on the back. Joe, to his credit, said very little but at the end said quietly that he hoped that if such trouble occurred again, there would be more tact and less mud-slinging. The only other happening was that it was decided to start a devotional meeting on Wednesday nights and it was left in Reg's hands to arrange it.

I have now written to Alice to smooth things out.

This weekend, more than ever before, I have realised how much, and how deeply, and how passionately I do love you, my dearest ... Be strong, my dear one, and I will be strong too, and then our love will not fade or wane. I prize it so very, very highly – I prize you so very, very highly and I want to love you for always ...

Tuesday 28th November

My darling Martyn,

... I am wondering how you are liking your new surroundings? I hope you have found some congenial friends. Are you enjoying yourself, marching round Saint Leonards? Do you feel homesick? You'll be home before I shall – lucky, lucky you.

I trust you have made satisfactory arrangements with the Flight Lieutenant as to when he will wash your hair? Doubtless he has also promised to buy the shampoo! I do so hope that he doesn't let the soap go in your eyes! I am shaking with laughter at my own funniness! You always said I was funny, didn't you? ...

In your letter you said, 'supposing our love should fade and wane.' Do not be afraid, Martyn, as long as 'you' are 'you' and 'I' am 'I' we shall always love one another. I am only afraid of a cruel fate that may take you from me, but it won't – it can't. When once this war is over I shall feel safe, secure in your love.

A friend of mine has got the Sadlers Wells programme and a season of ballet is starting from Boxing Day ... Martyn, I would love to go, wouldn't you? ...

Alexandra Hotel, Hastings
Wednesday 29th November

My dearest Lily,

I have just finished supper and have to pass a couple of hours before roll call and lights out. Naturally I decided that one of the best ways to spend the time would be to write to you and so you will have to put up with a long description of my experiences, which may or may not be boring.

I reported at Victoria at 8:45 this morning and the train finally left at 9:45. We had a coach reserved for us and in general travelled down in comfort.

When we arrived at Saint Leonards they piled us, complete with kit, on to lorries and carted us around to this hotel. When we heard that we were going to the Hotel Alexandra I think we rather imagined a palatial residence, simply dripping with luxury. The Hotel Alexandra is no longer like that though!

It has apparently only just been taken over by the Air Ministry and we are the first people to inhabit it. Arrangements for receiving us were not by any means ready. There are still crowds of workmen knocking it into shape but at present it looks as if it has been decidedly knocked out of shape.

I am sitting in the lounge or anteroom as it will be. It is about as big as the Fellowship and Primary rooms put together and it contains just about a dozen antique chairs. But there are two hundred and forty fellows at the hotel! All the lampshades have been removed and all the lamps except three. There is no carpet, but only the felt that was once beneath the carpet. In fact the whole hotel is a scene of desolation.

I am in a room with four others, though the room is smaller than the choir vestry. We have beds, of a style, but we have to sleep on straw palliasses and rest our heads on straw-filled bolsters. We are provided with four blankets each, though, so we should be fairly warm.

When we arrived we were given a meal almost immediately and on the whole it was pretty good. Steak and kidney pie, spuds and cabbage, followed by prunes and custard.

We spent the whole afternoon in our rooms waiting for something to happen. Finally what did happen was that at four o'clock we were told that there was some tea for us. This consisted of sausage and mash, bread, butter, jam and tea.

After tea we had an ARP drill. That sounds a lot, but in fact it meant that we all marched down to the cellars and were packed together like sardines for about ten minutes. At last at about half past six we were allowed to leave the building and it was then that I scribbled your postcard and groped my way along the seafront until I discovered a pillar box. Our hotel, by the way, is right on the front and we do our parades actually on the prom.

At seven o'clock we had supper – seems all meals, doesn't it – and this consisted of cold beef, bread and butter, and cocoa. Even if the food is not hotel food, one does at least get plenty of it!

At present there are three washbasins between about a hundred fellows, so things are going to be rather difficult. Even the blackout is not effective and although they have darkened the windows we have had to cover our windows with blankets before being allowed to use the light. They seem to anticipate that things will be straight by next week and on the whole I think that things will be quite pleasant.

There is a strong and fairly official rumour that we shall have a full week at Christmas. If we don't have leave at Christmas, I shall go absolutely mad, for that is the one thing I'm looking forward to with all my heart now.

When I first arrived at this place I sensed a peculiar smell, or rather a peculiar atmosphere. I knew somehow that it was familiar, but could not recall it for a time. Then I suddenly I realised what it was like – the hostel at Amsterdam! The general whiteness and bareness and the peculiar odour produced by the mixed smells of wet paint and cooked meals took me back to Amsterdam. Grand times that seem so far away!

I'm afraid that we shall always be feasting on pleasant memories, for some years – for a good few months at any rate; memories of Amsterdam, Paris, Sawbridgeworth. And for us too, some very special memories – the boat coming home, Wanstead Park on the night before you went, Kew, and all the times that we have been to Connaught Water and Knighton Woods.

Oh my sweet darling, those times were just heaven. The whole time's heaven when you're near. Fancy, in less than a month we shall have five days of heaven. Darling, how I am longing for that time.

Excuse me being so sentimental. I love you so madly now, and it is the only thing that I can think of.

I must close, so until tomorrow, goodbye, darlingest.

All my love, Martyn

Wednesday 29th November

My dear Martyn,

... Thank you for the ballet magazine. I am looking forward to reading it – I keep on looking through it and gloating over the pictures.

We've just been having a grand time in the room. We've got three beds all in a row along one wall and we've also all bought new wire hairbrushes. So we've had a grand fight! We jumped from bed to bed until the clothes fell off and we fell off onto the floor! As a great favour I then performed my *dance specialité*, the Dying Swan – choreography by that great artiste of mimicry *Mademoiselle Lilianova*.

Thank you ever so much for the 'Arc de Carousel' picture too. It's lovely and will go beautifully with the 'Sacré Coeur'. It has taken my thoughts right back to that lovely sunny morning when we sauntered through the Tuileries and under the arch to the Louvre ...

My darling girl,

Your letter has come – and what a letter! It really is perfectly grand of you to write such a lot. I hope it is sufficient reward to know that I thoroughly enjoyed reading every one of the thirty-eight pages. Thirty-eight pages! Surely that is a record!...

I can't say that I've made any friends down here. I am not one that makes friends quickly. But at the same time I'm enjoying myself as much as it is possible. I am one of those people who enjoy themselves, what shall we say, passively and not actively. I don't want amusements made for me and I don't delight in toddling around with a crowd of other fellows.

Give me a fair amount of spare time and let me do as I like and I am perfectly happy. I don't mean that I always like being by myself, for when I'm with my real friends I'm ten times happier, but I'm not prepared to sacrifice my taste in films and amusements in general, in order to be with some acquaintances.

Sorry to inflict that bit of self-psychology on you, but I think you understand me in many ways better than I know myself ...

Monday 4ᵗʰ December

My darling Thinglet,

I have perused only two sides of one sheet of your letter and I found to my horror another reference to my 'tender feet'.

Now really, Lil, this is too, too much. As I have pointed out before, your feet bear no comparison to mine; for a start, they are miles too small to work efficiently and are most extraordinary devices anyway. But my feet, I should also like to point out, are big and tough. That verdict is final. The matter of tender feet – ugh – is now closed and further reference to it will be coldly disregarded!!!

And now the business about 'Sergeant'. Please, Lil, say not a word about it. I have already been teased by almost every person I know, and really the joke is growing rather stale.

Yes, I am a Sergeant – I just couldn't help it. All those who join RAF Volunteer Reserve as pilots automatically become Sergeants. At least, they did before war broke out. Now you have to rise through the ranks. If I do get my commission, I become a Pilot-Officer (not a Flight Lieutenant yet!).

I am at present feeling very elated, for another letter from you has just come. Two letters in one day, it's really grand! But it only compensates for the absence of letters that I had to endure last week. And it did have to be endured – for your letters are so much a part of my life now, and as soon as I have received one, I start looking forward to the next ...

Today we had our first taste of our daily programme. At quarter to nine we commenced with an hour's drill – yes, we march up and down, and salute, and about turn, and slow march and do various other antics.

Next we had a lecture on signals (not railway!) for an hour. Then another hour's drill before lunch. After lunch we had an hour and a half's Maths and then another half hour's Drill. By the way, I don't know what you mean by 'brain softening'! Are you insinuating that my work is less intellectual than 'checking'!

I had a very lengthy epistle from Dad this morning. Marjorie has apparently suggested a Fellowship party at Christmas and Dad asks me what I think of the idea. I'm just writing back to say 'dashed good idea' ...

Oh my darling, my love for you seems to grow stronger and deeper every day, and my whole soul just aches for the time when I shall be with you again. Thank heavens it won't be long ...

Only eight days more, Lil – what a grand thought ...

Thursday 14th December

Lil darling,

... What is all this about a mysterious woman who hisses at you and glares with black evil eyes? It all sounds very curious to me – do you think she is a spy?

If I was you I should abstain from making declarations of your opinion on the International Situation – she might hear the 'Careless Talk' and so give 'Assistance to the Enemy'.

Be careful that she doesn't try and poison you with deadly nightshade soup or with stew of cursed frog legs. (Probably cursed snails would be more potent!!)

So it's cold at Torquay now! Well, I regret to say that it's not exactly warm here. In fact while we were doing P.T. this morning on the prom, with nothing on but shirt, shorts and socks, it started snowing! How would you like that?

One week, Lil!

No words can express how I'm looking forward to it. I just feel like dancing around on the chairs and yelling my head off.

You know I'm not so sure that not seeing each other always is so bad after all. It makes me, at all events, prize your company so much more, and the short times we have together are so precious and sweet ...

My darling girl,

I have just had one of the most shocking bits of news that you could possibly imagine. We are most probably not going to have any Christmas leave!

The fact is that a lot of fellows from another squadron pinched all the silverware from some café and then got drunk and goodness knows what else. The result is that they have put Hastings out of bounds and unless the fellows own up by this evening, there will be no leave.

We are all naturally mad about it and everyone is going around with long faces and taking a generally pessimistic view.

I'm just hoping for the best and hoping very, very hard, for Christmas leave has been the one object in view since I came here.

Oh darling, I've simply got to see you. If I can't get away, please come down and spend a day with me.

Why must some people be so dashed selfish and stupid? Oh Lil, I hope to heavens they don't cancel it. I've been looking forward to seeing you for so long.

There's really nothing else to say now. I pray that my next letter will contain better news.

All my love to you, dearest,

Martyn

Fortunately Martyn's leave wasn't cancelled and they were able to spend time together and enjoy some of the Christmas festivities with their families and friends.

Thursday & Friday 28th & 29th December

My very dearest Lil,

A whole day has now passed since I saw you, and at the moment I cannot somehow realise that thirty days have got to pass before I see you again. I feel so terribly lovesick now. I hardly seem to be able to think about anything but you, trying to imagine that you're near me, remembering the softness of your funny little hands, the cool smoothness of your cheeks, the sparkle in your eyes when you smile and the exquisite tenderness when you say 'darling' ...

I had been looking forward to Christmas so eagerly that I feel completely lost now.

All the thrill of giving and receiving presents, Christmas cards, Christmas pudding and carol singing gone for a whole year and heaven knows what may happen before then.

The only bright spot on the horizon is January 27th. I'm longing for that day. Fancy, it's exactly four weeks today! Not a very long time really but how each of those twenty-eight days will drag! ...

Sunday 31st December

Lily my darling,

I am living in comfort now. We have got a fire, a superb roaring coal fire, and so, with the radio as well, it is almost like home. But only almost!

I saw Nora on Friday before I left and we had a long chat about the troublesome times of six weeks ago. We talked for quite a while about the Fellowship and I found her ideas quite helpful and invigorating. We both bemoaned our fate at being so far from the 'home front'. As I'm writing this Nora is in the train travelling away from it again. I do wish that I was home now so that I could do something about the devotional evening and the Tuesday night talks and all the other plans I had. ...

Well, tonight ends the year 1939; a year that has been perhaps the most eventful in my life. Apart from little things like wars etc. there's been one very big event – I needn't tell you what it was.

I don't really know when it started but I think it must've been at Easter, on the boat coming home. How marvellous it would be to have all that holiday over again. To have all the time since Easter over again would be grand. But we must just look forward to 1940, that's all.

Well, dearest, I must close now, so goodbye till tomorrow,

All my love to you,

Martyn

6

8th January – 21st May 1940

After the festivities of Christmas, when thoughts of the war had temporarily been put to one side, people in Britain experienced a truly dismal time. Efforts to increase the country's military resources and defence systems increased and fear grew of imminent German attacks.

The winter weather was the coldest it had been in forty-five years and even the sea along parts of the south coast froze, as did seven miles of the River Thames.

In January the Government introduced food rationing, so queueing at grocers, butchers, bakers and greengrocers became commonplace.

Sadly, none of Lily's letters have survived from this period; so the following letters were all written by Martyn from St Leonards and South Woodford.

RAF Initial Training Wing
Alexandra Hotel
St Leonards-on-Sea
Monday 8th January

My darling Lil,

Thank you very much for the twelve page letter and the little packet of photographs. They really are grand, dear, and I should like enlargements of all of them; but I must be content with one and should like the one you suggested, if you please. I don't know what plans you have for the miniatures but could I have one or two to keep in my wallet? Just one of you looking serious, one of you beaming upwards and one of you beaming at me – to help me imagine that you are near me in the times when you are so far away. ...

When this war is over, I do believe that it will be the duty of those who survive to do their very utmost to see that it will not be their fault if such a calamity happens again.

I can't say I have a great deal of faith in pacifist leagues or leagues of nations accomplishing the job, but I thoroughly agree with Prissie that the machinery that should be used is the church. It's a bit of machinery that's got to be cleaned and oiled, though; cleaned of all its hampering tradition and fear of progress, and oiled so that it strides forward and makes itself a part of the life of the man in the street ...

I feel that there are two ways for the church. One is for it to champion the cause of the oppressed and suffering with every ounce of energy that it has got and the other is to establish itself as the centre and patron of the arts and learning, and even sport, much as it did in the Middle Ages ...

I am more and more convinced that Christ is the one thing that matters in the Bible and Christ simply as a pattern for life.

All the talk of Christ rescuing us from Hell Fire does not interest me much. The one thing that I feel we should appreciate is that Christ's life was all beauty, self-sacrifice and consideration for others.

Christ should be the pattern for life from the common-sense point of view alone, for if all lives were led like His we should have the heaven on earth that everybody really wants. This is the desire of communists, conservatives, Congregationalists and even fascists – even though they are all fighting amongst themselves because they all think they have the right way.

Maybe Christianity isn't the right way but it has a far more absolute standard than communism or the other 'isms' can boast of ...

If you and I and Prissie and the Fellowship and Dad are all still here when the war ends, we've got to put our backs into making our Fellowship and our church influence the whole neighbourhood and not only that but we've got to make the Christian church influence the whole world. Yes, I know it sounds absurd and fantastic, but I'm sure it could be done ...Now for some bad news. They are indeed tightening up on things here. We are having more P.T. and extra Maths and Signals – going on till half past six! Also, if you are late in or don't clean your buttons you are on the mat at once ...

... You will be amused to hear that I have started making models again. I have started one of an Airspeed Oxford and one of a sailing ship, the *Flying Cloud*. Heaven knows when I shall finish them! ...

And no, I do not have to wear RAF pyjamas with red, white and blue stripes or anything like that ...

Tuesday 16th January

My dearest girl,

I have just started reading *The Case for Federal Union* by W.B. Curry. As you probably know it is a Penguin Special and if you have a chance to read it, do take the opportunity – you really mustn't miss it.

I have read only fifty pages of the book but what I have read has convinced me that there is a very strong case for federal union and I think that as a piece of political machinery it appeals to me much more than communism or pacifism or any other method for righting the world. I think that it will thoroughly appeal to you, for it is essentially pacifistic in aim. It concentrates not so much on the evil of war as on its sheer stupidity, wastage and detrimental effect on human progress and comfort.

But where, as far as I can see, it differs from the pacifist ideas, is in its method for attempting to obviate war. "The policy of non-resistance," says the author, "is too contrary to human nature to have universal effect, and anyhow what really should be done is to remove all likelihood of occasions for the display of non-resistance".

Furthermore, pacifism is a negative quality. Simply renouncing war is going to get us nowhere and what is needed is a government that is capable of removing the root causes of wars and solving all small dissatisfactions. You must read the book – it really is an inspiration to me and seems to be a really practical proposition. Furthermore it has the advantage that it has already been tried out in America, Switzerland, and South Africa and has worked!

Do read it as soon as you can for I am sure that if there is to be any international unity at the end of the war we've got to start now and decide how it may be done and prepare for it as well ...

Monday 5th February

My very dearest Lily,

I have now the far from onerous task of replying to five letters from you!

Yes, there were three waiting for me when I arrived home last night, and I have had one by each post today.

Let's start from the beginning. I'm glad to hear that you are getting on well with *Federal Union*. Is it the book by Curry that you've got, or the pamphlet I gave you? The canvassing I did at home last Sunday seems to have worked wonders. I put three copies of the Curry book in the library and about six pamphlets – and they were all taken out! ...

My darling girl, as I've read through your letters I've realised so clearly how infinitely fortunate I am to have someone who is so sweet and so lovable and so loving.

You say, 'Don't let's wait till the war is over to get married'. How that echoes in my own heart, Lil, and what a temptation it is to consider it. If we could live together for a few months – but we would only be together for a few days at a time – a few hours at a time – hardly different from things now. And for me to make you a widow, just think what that means, for just a few weeks of bliss would be an unforgivable crime. But I love you so very deeply and passionately, Lil, and long for the time when we shall be married.

My dearest one,
Martyn

Thursday 8th February

Lil darling,

I'm very pleased to hear you've got your bonus, and of course the resulting blouse, shoes and costume! But what about a hat? – Surely you were not able to resist one of those weird creations with which you delight in adorning your golden locks? Nevertheless, we certainly shall be 'posh' shan't we – I'm afraid we shall have to forsake Corner Houses for Frascati's in the future! ...

As the month of February neared its end, so came round another weekend's leave for both Lily and Martyn, which they spent at their respective homes in Woodford. After a couple of happy days Lily returned to Torquay and Martyn to St Leonards.

Lil, my dearest one,

... It has been a simply marvellous day here – and it has filled me with a glorious 'all is well with the world' feeling, although heaven knows that it isn't! But then as far as I can see all is well with my world and as far as I know all is going to be.

My darling, each time you come home you make me love and admire you more and more. Each time I realise how much you mean to me and how much I want to keep you.

When I first got to know you I expected that I should love you in a sort of platonic way – that I should love you because you had ideals and interests that coincided with mine. I love you all the more now that I have found how far your ideals surpass my own ...If the things that I cared most about a year ago were aeroplanes, the things I cared least about were girls, and if there was one thing I intended never to do, it was to fall in love! And now it's happened and that love has developed into an adoration and passion that frightens and bewilders me.

Oh my sweetheart, a year seems such a very long time, but I'm afraid it certainly can't be less. Dad would probably collapse from shock if I told him and would say that I was too young. But why too young?

I know the outlook's not too rosy, but I am in just the same boat as crowds of fellows who are already married. And if we wait till the war's over we might have to put it off for years and years.

What do you think your people would say? – I expect they would feel that we were both too young. That is, of course, if they are willing at all to trust their daughter to the mercy of one who is so lazy, aimless and brainless?

But then you have to decide too. It sounds pretty conceited for me to say that I'm sure you love me, but you're so perfect that I know you wouldn't say you wanted to marry me if you didn't mean it. But you would be taking a terribly big risk, Lil, and might have to make a very big sacrifice – all on account of one who isn't worth it and who has far more vices and far fewer virtues than crowds of other fellows you will meet in your life.

Think carefully, Lil – I say that not to put you off, but because I love you with so much more than a passing whim and it is a terrible thought that you might be unhappy as a result of making me happy.

My darling, I love you with all my heart,

Martyn

Wednesday 6th March

My darling girl,

I am sorry to have been so long replying to your letter, but I have been on guard duty since teatime yesterday and just simply hadn't a chance to write. I was Guard Commander again and since the wheels have started running more smoothly, the Guard Commander has been inflicted with many more duties and I have hardly had a moment's rest, certainly not enough moments to write to you, and certainly not ones that were sufficiently restful for me to perform that most difficult task of saying to you what I really want to say.

When I dream of marrying you, as I confess I often do, my thoughts seem to form a mirror in which I see all the beastliness of myself. – All my dullness, and selfishness and laziness, all my bad temper, and sarcasm and stupidity and childishness. And then these thoughts seem to say to me: you have no right to force anyone else to endure such a character and if you really love her you should forget all your desires.

And then I feel that I want to cry with despair and bury my head in the ground. Sometimes I wish that this war would prevent me from ever having you, for you deserve someone far, far better than me.

Then I realise that I simply can't do what my thoughts tell me I ought to do. Something, probably my selfishness, tells me that I don't really want to bury my head in the ground, but rather to lay it on your breast and feel your sweet hands caressing my hair. Whatever my conscience or logic or common sense may tell me to do, I know somehow that the only thing that I shall be able to do is to hang on to you with all that's in me.

You're so essential to my happiness – such a magician at dispelling all my cares and doubts and forebodings, that I dread the idea of letting you go. ...

Saturday 9th March

My dearest girl,

I have just received your two letters and they have made me so happy, so gloriously happy, that I feel I want to sing and shout for joy.

Oh my darling angel, it's grand to know that you love me so, and as I read through your letters my whole being seemed to tingle with a marvellous delightful thrill. But you have a serious fault, Lil; you flatter me quite unjustly. Remember that you have known me for only a year, while I have known myself for almost twenty years, and if you don't believe that what I said about myself was true, you will find it out in due course. I have learnt it by bitter experience.

But when I read that you're prepared to put up with me, though you don't put it that way, it makes me terribly happy and I marvel at my luck in finding such a wonderful girl! If it was luck!

I have never known such perfect bliss as during the last few months. If only we could know whether it was going to last, Lil. You are so optimistic and I am inclined to be too – but yet, it all seems such a perfect fairy tale. A perfect romance with a happy ending – I suppose there are such things? I simply must believe that everything is going to be fine – it is so marvellously fine at the moment. My heart is overflowing with love for you ...

Sunday 10th March

... If only this was 1944; if only we were both twenty-three and the war was over and I could marry you without people talking about 'being too young', 'neglecting careers' and things like that.

You know, Lil, in some ways the war is a blessing. If there had been no war, I should have had to stay at college for another two years and there would have been no possibility of us marrying for three or four. Now at least there is a possibility of it being only one or two years, even if the possibility is rather slender!

I have been gazing into the fire and dreaming whilst listening to Max Bruch's concerto coming over the air from somewhere ...

… I was most pleased to hear that the hair looks 'awfully nice' now. What you must have endured, you silly, funny girl. I can't imagine myself going through agonies in order that my hair might look smashing. Washing it – sorry, I mean having it washed – is quite painful enough! I'm longing to see it though …

Thursday 14th March

Lil dearest,

The weather is steadily growing worse and at the present moment I am sitting by the window watching the snow hurtling down in a miniature blizzard! Yes, it started snowing again this morning and already there is about an inch on the ground. But in spite of the weather I am feeling considerably joyful – and why? – to my great relief and happiness I have got Easter leave!! I told you in my last letter that only a quarter of the squadron were to be given leave and this morning they had a ballot to decide who should go. To my amazement my name was the last one to be drawn! Isn't that remarkable luck!

So I shall get off after duty on Thursday – exactly a week today! …

... I'm afraid Easter, in common with most of our times at home, is going to be a dreadful rush! I'm beginning to wonder whether we shall eventually have any time alone!

You see I suggested to Dad, when I was last at home, that there should be a local Fellowship ramble as well as the Easter ramble at Bournemouth. After all, it's rather tough luck on the people who can't go on the big trip if everything closes down. The result is that George has just written to me and told me that he and Dad discussed this idea and decided to ask me to run a ramble on Good Friday morning. So I agreed to run it, providing George maps out the route. He had already suggested that we spent part of the time getting seasick on Connaught Water!

Then in the afternoon there is a performance of the *Messiah* at Loughton and as my Ma is playing in the orchestra, I feel I (or we!) ought to go along. Personally I always enjoy hearing the *Messiah*.

So you see, Friday is pretty full already and although we shall probably be able to have the evening together, I think it would be a rather jolly idea if we went out before breakfast.

What do you think to that – do you think it's quite impossible?! ...

Martyn, like his father, was an inveterate organiser and between the two of them they managed to create an interesting Easter trip to Bournemouth for the Fellowship, and an action-packed four days for Lily and Martyn themselves. Then it was back to St Leonards for a couple of weeks or so for Martyn, and a return to Torquay for Lily.

Lily my darling,

It's the most awful day, cold and horribly wet, all of which has made me most dull and homesick. At least, not exactly homesick, but rather Easterholidaysick, Fellowshipramblesick, and more than anything – far more than anything, very Lilysick!

We had Navigation from half past eight till half past ten and were set to work through a question paper. I doubt whether anyone did though, for we all had that Monday morning feeling – at least a Tuesday after Easter Monday feeling – which is considerably worse.

I just sat and gazed at the paper but saw nothing that was written on it. Instead I saw the last few days as vividly as in a film.

I remembered the play, and the ramble, and the *Messiah* and the concert at the Pavilion.

Then I remembered the train journey down to Bournemouth that was so like a honeymoon and our walk on Sunday night when one kiss lasted the whole length of the chine! Oh my sweetheart, those times thrilled me with the most perfect happiness ...

... Can you bear a shock? I have written to four different places for particulars of correspondence courses! Yes, you have now caused me to wake up to the fact that I've got to prepare for when this war ends. So I'm going to go right ahead. Then, if and when the war ends, I shan't be left high and dry with nothing that I can do. I still favour either architecture or advertising. ...

Thursday 28th March

Lily darling,

I was very pleased to receive your letter today and to learn that you had survived the ordeal of returning to Torquay.

Please don't thank me for little things like meals and bus fares. I only hope that very soon I shall be able to give you things that are really worthwhile giving, and anyhow, the happiness that little things like those can give you is very small compared with the tremendous amount of happiness you give me. Had I spent a million pounds on you to date, you would have already repaid me a thousandfold.

I have just been to the pictures to see the Marx Bros' *At the Circus*. It was quite amusing, but not so uproariously funny as I expected. Last night I went to see a performance of *Lilac Time* and with that too I was disappointed – most disappointed really! It was about ten years ago when I last saw it ("ahem" says he, shaking his beard!) and I remember that on that occasion I was most thrilled. But really the dialogue is terribly sentimental and wishy-washy and some of the humorous episodes are like pantomime turns.

But next week there is something definitely worth going to at the White Rock Theatre. Can you guess? It is the Arts Theatre Ballet! Yes, for a whole week, straight from its run in London. You can bet that I shall be there almost every night!

Tomorrow Hastings is to be greatly honoured. We are to have a visit from the worthy Secretary of State for Air, Sir Kingsley Wood! He's going to inspect both the Wings here, so we've got to do a march past and also a display of P.T. It will at least be a change from the usual routine.

Must close now, so good night and goodbye till tomorrow, sweetest one,

I love you so much, Martyn

... There has been considerable excitement here today, for ninety-eight men have been posted to aerodromes. They are all those whose names commence with the letters A to H, though of course I am not included because of my commission. All the A's and B's are going to Prestwick, so, as you can imagine, I'm not at all sorry I'm not going! The F's, G's and H's, lucky beggars, are going to Fairoaks, near Chobham, in Surrey, which is comparatively close to London and to home. I wish I was going there! ...

The C.O. came up to me as I was leaving the hotel last night and told me that he had heard that my discharge papers had just come through to the Wing, so it is very possible that I shall only be here for a short time now ...

28 Glebelands Avenue,
South Woodford
Sunday 7th April

... Well, I am home again on indefinite leave and it may be three days or it may be three months before I am posted again.

I'm so glad you liked the photo of me. As a matter of fact I discovered it on Friday, in the shop of a local photographer, a whole series of photos taken on the occasion of Sir Kingsley's visit and amongst them was a real close-up of myself ...

Martyn goes on parade on Hastings seafront

92

My dearest Lily,

... I must tell you about the concert on Saturday. There were twenty of us – a remarkable number for a symphony concert, as you will agree. All the usual ones were there – Maisie, Joe, Joan, Alice, Prissie etc. The program included the *Pastoral Symphony* and *Emperor* piano concerto and also the introduction to Act Three of *Lohengrin*. Leslie England was the soloist and the whole programme was most enjoyable ...

Last night Reg came round after church and he and Dad and myself had a most profitable discussion on Fellowship matters. We had a go at the devotional evening question and have evolved some new ideas which may be useful. We are trying to suit all tastes by having four different kinds of meeting for each Wednesday in the month ...

Thursday 11th April

My darling girl,

I'm glad to hear you enjoyed your Peace Pledge Union meeting. You know, Lil, you mustn't become too unpatriotic, or I, as a member of His Majesty's Air Force, shall have to put my foot down!

The meeting about the devotional evening last night was most successful. Eighteen were present and we had quite a lively discussion. My four week scheme was finally accepted with slight modifications and Reg, Prissie and self were elected as a committee to get on with the job of drafting a final plan. ...

Martyn celebrated his 20th birthday on 11th April and during his following weekend's leave he took Lily to see a ballet which was probably Sadlers Wells' performance of Coppélia, since that had been recommended to them.

Monday 22nd April

Lily my dearest,

I have just finished breakfast and so that I shan't be tempted to put it off, I decided to write straightaway. It is a warm and glorious sunny morning – a marvellous morning just like yesterday. I almost said a perfect morning, but it's very, very far from perfect, because it's so different from yesterday.

Yesterday I felt perfectly happy, but today I feel just thoroughly dull and fed up. When I waved goodbye to you last night and saw your carriage vanish into the darkness, I really couldn't tell whether I was most happy or most unhappy. I felt numbed by the realisation that for three weeks I shouldn't feel your light hands caressing my hair or the softness of your cheek against mine, but then I said to myself this weekend wasn't a glorious dream – she wasn't a glorious dream, but she's real and soon there will be another weekend that will be just as real and just as glorious! As long as there is Lily, what have you to be unhappy about!!

I arrived at Liverpool Street station just in time to see the 10:30 train steaming out so I had to resign myself to a three quarters of an hour wait. I felt too tired and too lost in my dreams to care much, so I went on the platform and sat on a trolley until the train came in.

I don't know whether it was the huge openness of the station and the cool moonlight, but something seemed to

94

have a most soothing effect on me and I felt strangely happy as I sat on the trolley and lived the weekend all over again.

I remembered all that we had done, and all that I had said to you and you had said to me. Sometimes we didn't seem to understand each other – perhaps you are still wondering what I meant by saying you had 'funny' eyes. 'Funny' was quite the wrong word. You have the most delightful, sparkling, expressive eyes that I have ever seen, and that is not flattery – it is simple fact – and I ought to know for I have gazed into them often enough ...

Tuesday 23rd April

Lily my darling,

... You will no doubt be interested to hear that I wore my birthday present dressing gown this morning. Mum wanted to make my bed and Dad wanted to have a bath so there was no alternative but to install myself in the drawing room and read. On such occasions I usually put on my overcoat, but I thought to myself, "No, Martyn, now is the time to baptise the dressing gown," and so the dressing gown had its official debut. It also has its own special home now, for yesterday I purchased a chromium wall hook from Messrs. Woolworths Ltd. and this is now fixed to my bedroom door; and from the hook the gown now hangs.

I have just been round to your house and collected the book of knitting patterns. I have carefully studied the four examples at the back of the book but in spite of the mediaeval appearance of helmet A, and the Arctic atmosphere of helmet B, I really think I prefer the one that is illustrated on the cover – the one in fact which is

described as 'Aero Cap'. I think it looks most slinky and I'm thinking that after the war I shall be able to use it as a summer flying helmet when I cruise around Britain in my Air Ministry 'surplus stock' aeroplane ...Sunday 5th May
Lily dearest,

I must say that your last letter gave me an awful shock. I really didn't think that you would to take the plunge to leave Torquay. I expect though, that you've quite made up your mind and it's no good trying to persuade you to reconsider your decision now. I don't know that I really want to dissuade you, for although I can't say I think it's a very wise step, I know how much happier you would be to be home again and I know how much I want you to be home!

This morning I have been to your church at Chigwell Row. When I went round to fetch Les and Florence's wedding present list I saw your Dad and he was most keen that I should go along to the Anniversary Service. It is a charming little church, isn't it? Today it is really summer-ish and the coolness and the smooth light from those stained glass windows helped to make the service most delightful. We must walk there some Sunday morning when you are home again.

From the sublime to the ridiculous – yesterday afternoon we all went on the Fellowship ramble to the zoo! Once again it was just like summer and there were crowds of people there – almost like a bank holiday, but not quite so bad. We did have a very jolly time though and I wished so much that you had been there ...

Lily dearest,

... I was pleased to hear that your section leader described you as "absolutely radiating excitement and happiness" – never was a truer word said, or a more descriptive sentence used – you always do just that: "radiate excitement and happiness". And you do it so well that it has an effect on all those round about you – we all seem to absorb your radiation and it does us such a lot of good!

Oh Lil darling, how I wish she had been right in thinking that you were leaving to be married – how marvellous it would be if you were! ...

Tuesday 21ˢᵗ May

My dear Lil,

You can guess how delighted I was to receive your letter and learn the great news of your final homecoming! Really you do have the most amazing luck – I just can't understand it. Would it be very unkind of me to say that the Pru seems to want to get rid of you!?! No, that is a wicked thing to say, isn't it – I'm sure it's as a token of their esteem and gratitude that they're excusing you the last two weeks.

Oh my darling, it's grand to think you'll be home again so soon – I can hardly believe that I shall see you again in three days' time ...

... And by the way, I think I should remind you – don't forget you only want a single ticket to Paddington! ...

7

Lily's return to Woodford coincided with a disturbing period of the war. Hitler's advance on France had led to the British forces being trapped in Northern France and an enormous operation was set up to rescue them, which we now know as the evacuation of Dunkirk. This event, although a defeat in war terms, was such an incredible achievement that it gave a great boost to the country's morale.

Churchill, as the newly appointed Prime Minister, hailed the rescue in his 'We shall fight them on the beaches' speech, but warned that the country should not 'assign to this deliverance the attributes of victory. Wars are not won by evacuations.'

At the end of May the Emergency Powers Act was passed which effectively gave the Government control over all persons and property and regulated almost every aspect of everyday life.

Britain prepared itself for an invasion by land. All signposts were taken down and destination boards were removed from buses and trains. Barricades and tank traps appeared on coastal roads; and large sections of the east and south coast, which normally at this time would have been entertaining holidaymakers, were designated as Defence Areas which could only be entered with a permit. Seafront hotels were requisitioned, swimming in the sea was banned and machine guns were positioned on seaside piers. Men were encouraged to join the recently formed Local Defence Volunteers which later became known as the Home Guard.

On 14th June German troops entered and occupied Paris and four days later Churchill told the House of Commons, 'The Battle of France is over. The Battle of Britain is about to begin.' Within days, fifteen million copies of a leaflet entitled If the Invader Comes were distributed giving fundamental rules that needed to be obeyed. In the event of an attack, the order was to stay put until given permission to evacuate. Other instructions included: keep watch for anything suspicious; do not give a German anything; do not believe rumours or spread them; and be ready to help the military. Remember always, the leaflet said, that the best defence of Great Britain is the courage of her men and women. Think before you act. But think always of your country before you think of yourself.

Against this backdrop, Lily and Martyn had the delight of six weeks in each other's company, since they were living in their respective family homes in Woodford.

On 13th June 1940 Lily celebrated her 20th birthday and Martyn's present to her was accompanied by a specially created, handwritten document.

I, the undersigned,
do hereby deem that the enclosed shall be regarded as a token
of my persistent faith in one, LILY MAUD SMITH, whom,
in spite of her many evil and wicked ways, namely the habits of :
pretending she is no longer a littul gel
uttering the words 'jus never minit'
using the expression 'jus cos'
and 'yew woodunt rilly woodjew'
and numerous others,
I still believe to have a soul that is capable of being saved,
and I hereby pledge myself

to do all in my power to effect this solution.
Signed, this thirteenth day of June
in the Year of our Lord, Nineteen Hundred and Forty.

E.M.Allies

I, the undersigned
do hereby deem that the enclosed shall be
regarded as a token of my persistent faith in
one, LILY MAUD SMITH, whom, in spite of her
many evil and wicked ways. namely the habits
of   pretending she is no longer a littul gel ;
uttering the words ' Jus never minit ';
using the expressions ' Jus cos' and 'Yew
woodunt rilly woodjew';
                    and numerous others.
I still believe to have a saul that is
capable of being saved, and I hereby pledge
myself to do all in my power to effect
this salvation.

              Signed, this Thirteenth day of
June, in the Year of Our Lord, Nineteen Hundred
and Forty.

Lily's experience and confidence were increasing in her job as clerk at E & A Shadrack the coal merchants, whose office was right by South Woodford underground station, and Martyn was waiting patiently – or probably impatiently – to be called up for his flying training.

Finally he was posted to the Initial Flying Training School at Meir on the outskirts of Stoke-on-Trent and billeted with a family whose daughters both worked in the potteries. This was at a time when the potteries were belching dense smoke out into the atmosphere so it was necessary for planes to take off and land by flare path, even when, above the smoke, the sky was cloudless.

219 Weston Road, Meir
Stoke-on-Trent
Tuesday 6th August

Lily darling,

Well, here I am, all settled down for a six weeks' course! The aerodrome is less than five minutes from Meir Station and also on the bus route to Stoke, which is a distinct advantage. When I reported to the adjutant, he sent me to Flight Lieutenant Gibbons who is the Commander of the Flight and my instructor, and he sent me to get my flying clothes, which I did, and then to Pilot Officer Plunkett who was to fix up my digs. Plunkett is a very decent fellow, about twenty-four, and only got his 'Wings' last January. He fixed for me to stay at the same place as he was staying with a Mrs Ambrose and it is most satisfactory.

We have to work quite hard flying from 8:15 till 12:00 and lectures from 1:15 till 5:30 and vice-versa on alternate days. They do not recognise weekends here and we work every day, with one day off every week which is usually Saturday or Sunday. If I have a Saturday off, I shall apparently be able to catch the 7:30 train on Friday night arriving at Euston at 10:45, and all will be well as long as I am back by 8:15 on Sunday morning. This, I'm afraid, knocks out Proms, Sadlers Wells and everything else but at least I should be able to get home for a few hours to see you, and that really is all that matters.

Well, my dearest, I'm afraid I must close for today, as I've got to write to Mum and I want to get to bed early.

So goodbye, and all my love to you, sweetest,

Martyn

Tuesday 6th August

… Well, darling, here comes my second epistle from the Black Country. Is this the Black Country? Anyhow, if it isn't, it ought to be, for really the general dirtiness of everything is incredible. The district seems to be shrouded by a perpetual fog – a kind of grey haze which one can actually taste! Most of the roads and pavements seem to be constructed by the simple method of stamping the dust down and it is impossible to keep one's shoes clean. After a half hour's walk down the street, one acquires a coating of dust which it would take a week to obtain in London E18. One's clothes become filthy in an amazing short space of time, and Plunkett tells me that one really needs a collar a day, and three shirts a week!

The whole atmosphere is most depressing – dirty, drab, redbrick houses, all quite plain and bare, and mostly very dilapidated, with crowds of little children in patched and tattered clothes – my goodness – give me the East End any day!

Of course, everywhere are potteries and in Longton, which is only a few miles from here, one can count those funny brick bottles as easily as the London barrage balloons – there seem to be countless hundreds of them.

I seem to be giving you a very dismal picture of my temporary home town. I may be piling it on just a wee bit, but it really is pretty grim. Nevertheless I think I shall enjoy my stay here. You see, it is a very good aerodrome, the instructors, lecturers and officers all seem very decent and my days here are splendid. The food is first class, I have a cosy bedroom with a comfy bed, and I can use the lounge, garden etc. just as I like. Living like a lord, in fact!! This in some measure compensates for what I am afraid will be a scarcity of homecomings. As I told you yesterday, we only have the one day off per week, and it would mean leaving here at 6:30 on Saturday evening, home at 10:45 and having to leave at 5:10 on the Sunday night; eight hours travelling and twenty-one shillings and nine pence for an effective eight hours at home. So, I'm afraid, rather too much to be indulged in weekly. But I think it will be worth it every fortnight. In fact I guess it will be necessary every fortnight! …

I am longing to receive a letter from you, but don't expect one before Friday morning. I must close now, Lil dear, until tomorrow.

So goodbye and heaps of love to you,

Martyn

My darling Martyn,

Thank you for your letter – it has seemed ages in coming …I was very glad to hear that conditions are so favourable for you. You are fortunate to have such comfortable digs.

But I was very disappointed to hear about leave – or rather the absence of it! One day is going to be so terribly short! … Can't you save a day from one week and tack it on to another? What I want to know more than anything else is, are you coming home this weekend? I do so hope you are. Please write back ever so quickly and let me know.

I should love to hear everyone 'sir-ing' you – it's must be awfully funny! (I should laugh ever so!) That's because you look so smart in your uniform!

Yes, it seems as though you'll have to work hard. So, you'll only be flying half the time – have you got much more to learn? …

After Fellowship Circle last night Margery walked along with me to the top of our road or I should have been very lonely. I certainly shan't attempt any outings in town (Proms, Sadlers etc.) if I've got to walk home alone. So you won't be the only one to miss things! …

I am thinking about you all the time, wondering how you are, frightened sometimes for your safety – please keep yourself alive and well for me darling because I need you.

All my love to you my dearest,

Lily

Wednesday 8th August

Lil dear,

Just a note to tell you that I may pop home for Saturday. If so I shall arrive at 10:45 at Euston on Friday night. I should be delighted to see you if you could be by the big stone pillars at the entrance. I will telegram you if I do decide to come, and should be pleased if you would let Mum know. Please don't be too hopeful, for it is only fifty-fifty.

Love in haste,

Martyn

While Martyn and Lily were enjoying precious hours together in London, in Germany final preparations were being made for Operation Eagle Attack which was to be an all-out assault on the Royal Air Force.

Sunday 11th August

... I arrived back at half past nine last night – not bad really – had supper and went to bed.

This morning we had a church parade. We had to march up to the church and I had to march with the officer in charge at the head of the parade. After the church service we marched back again and spent an hour being lectured on Armaments – Vickers guns to be precise. We should be having a lecture on Administration this afternoon, but the weather, which was frightful this morning, has improved, so we may have some flying ...

My dearest Martyn,

It's only twenty-four hours since we were with each other and in just a week's time we shall be together again! It was that thought which cheered me up all the way home yesterday. I kept thinking that in exactly a week's time I should be setting out to meet you again. I'm longing for Saturday to come!

On my way home I stopped at Leytonstone and was successful in matching up a handbag and a pair of gloves to go with my shoes. They are awfully nice – I shall probably wear them today.

I've started embroidering one of the chair backs now. I've only done some of the green parts but I think it's going to look very nice. I'm awfully glad we got them before you went away for it fills in all the odd moments. And somehow, doing that brings you nearer to me.

It has been very hot and sunny here this morning and I have been wondering whether you are having the same weather, and if so, whether you are flying. I suppose I ought to hope so for your sake, but when I think of you 'up there' – I'm afraid! Be careful, won't you.

I must get ready for Fellowship soon – or I'll be late.

Oh! And don't forget the photo you promised me! Please smile!

Shinawamatalonmerdonslamonacerfla ~~~~~~ (that means I love you ever so much and long for you to be with me).

If you were here I'd kiss you, but as you're not, I send you heaps of love,

from your adoring little drunkard!

Monday 12th August

... I was much amused to hear about the Church Parade – I wish I could have seen you at the head!

We had a most interesting discussion in Tony's garden re 'Should restrictions be put on Jews?' We voted; and the side for no restrictions won. (My side!)

After church Mr Lemon [the church minister] shook hands with me. "How are you? Not quite so happy this week, are you?" Fancy him knowing! I didn't tell him that I'd only just said goodbye to you ...

Tuesday 13th August

Lily darling,

I haven't had a letter from you today, but I expect that you have been unlucky and missed the seven o'clock post. I'm hoping that one will appear in the morning.

My expectations of a fine day today were not realised, although it was not actually wet, it was very dull and extremely misty and definitely too bad for flying. So of course, we have had the inevitable lectures – today on Armaments and Administration.

This evening I have been into Hanley to have my identity card photographs taken – and I have also had one taken for more private use! You will be pleased to hear that I grinned from ear to ear! And I take no responsibility for the cartoon that will doubtless result!

We have amassed heaps of notes during the last few days and I must sort some out this evening.

So, here's goodbye till tomorrow and heaps and heaps of love to you, my dearest one.

Bye, sweetheart,

Martyn

Wednesday 14th August

... When Mr Chapman went out of the office yesterday afternoon, I thought, once I'd finished the work he'd given me, I should be free to start my letter, but instead I had to attend to my office duties and had quite a busy time! Lots of people came in to pay bills and order coal and then one of the coalmen came to say that three people were out so would I give him three other people to deliver to. I was quite rushed for about two hours and really enjoyed myself! ...

Have you had any raids at your place? When I heard about the ones on aerodromes in the south east, I was worried – but you're more east, aren't you? ...

Brother Les has been given the sack, in view of his conscientious objection to war work, so is now looking for farm work ...

Thursday 15th August

Lily darling,

Thank you for yesterday's letter – it did reach me by first post this morning. I was most intrigued to hear that you were rushed off your feet with office duties on Tuesday afternoon – I guess you felt like a managing director as you answered the phone calls and interviewed the clients!

But this brings me to some tragic news. What I had feared all the week has happened. There is to be no weekend leave and we shall be flying all day Saturday and Sunday! As you can imagine, I feel thoroughly fed up, and I expect you will feel the same when you read this letter.

No, ducky, we haven't had our aerodromes bombed yet, although they're quite expecting it. Quite a lot of towns about twenty miles from here have been bombed and although the bombs have made nasty messes of some roads, houses and tennis courts, there don't seem to have been many casualties.

Incidentally we are certainly not South East, if anything we're North West, not so very far from North Wales you know, but really we are right in the Midlands.

Well darling, I must close now and do some work before going to bed. Oh, I do so wish I could see you at the weekend – it is going to seem so long waiting another whole week.

Bye for now, sweet one, I love you so,

Martyn

Friday 16th August

My dearest Martyn

... Surely this is a record – I had three letters from you by first post this morning – such nice letters they were too, thank you darling! I felt very remorseful, for in my last letter I accused you of not writing for two days – sorry! I apologise most humbly.

Those letters made such a difference to me, Martyn – they sent me to work humming a tune; they made my smile real and less mechanical. The past events had left me tired and harassed, and when that big ray of sunshine – your homecoming –

disappeared I felt so unhappy. But today is different. Those few words telling of your love and longing have made things seem worthwhile again ...

It's 9.30 pm and the guns are going. This is our sixth air raid today but yesterday we had seven! ...

In your letter you say that you wish you were in air-raid-stricken Woodford. How terribly thankful I am that you are escaping these awful restless nights of incessant gun-fire and the sickening drone of enemy planes! ... I would give anything to get away, to have a single night or day without a warning. How I wish that I could be with you in some quiet place with no whistles blowing every hour.

If you were here, darling, and saw the havoc and destruction, the homeless evacuees wandering about, you'd get an awful fit of the blues and all my love and kisses would be of no avail to cheer you. So I think I'd rather wait and have a cheerful, carefree, teasing Martyn come back to me!

Don't forget to tell me immediately you know anything about coming home. And darling please come quickly because every day I get more impatient to be with you, in your arms.

Goodbye my love,

Lily

... p.s. I can think of nothing more breathtakingly wonderful than being yours 'for keeps '!

p.p.s. An incendiary bomb has just fallen opposite in Wanstead Rd, but by a miracle in between two houses, and now the fire is out.

Friday 16th August

Lil darling,

In your letter you talk about meeting me on Saturday. By now you will know that there is no chance of me being able to get home. Although I am still feeling pretty fed up, I am slowly resigning myself to another week here. I don't think they could possibly stop weekends twice running, so I guess I should be definitely home next Saturday or Sunday.

I have done almost three and a half hours' flying now and I have just started circuits and landings. I did one landing today, but it was pretty poor as I straightened out too high, but I managed a couple of take-offs quite well.

Must close now, dear, and swot up some navigation, so cheerio till tomorrow.

All my love to you, Martyn

Saturday 17th August

My darling girl,

It's just about ten past nine. I expected that at this time I should be on the way home to see you and instead I am writing you a letter! Still never mind, as you say, 'It's no good crying over spilt milk.' We must just hope like hell that they don't try this trick again next week.

It has been a glorious day here – quite hot and blazing sunshine. The clouds were very high indeed so on one flight we climbed to four thousand feet and practised spins. The Magister spins pretty steeply, so they are quite exciting. I also did about forty-five minutes of circuits and landings, but wasn't at all hot on them this afternoon. My circuits were too short and take-offs too bumpy, so I didn't feel too pleased with myself.

I am wondering whether you have had any more air raid warnings during the night, or during the day for that matter? They had two 'purples' (machines very near) at the aerodrome last night and quite a few people heard bombs dropping. Needless to say, I was fast asleep! ...

On Sunday 18th August 1940, the Luftwaffe, in an all-out effort to destroy RAF Fighter Command, flew 850 sorties involving 2200 aircrew. The RAF resisted with equal vigour, flying 927 sorties involving 600 aircrew. Three of the air fields targeted were North Weald, just to the north of Woodford, Hornchurch to the east, and Thorney Island, where Martyn first learnt to fly. This air battle became known as 'The Hardest Day'.

Meanwhile, since Martyn was denied any leave in order to have more flying practice, Lily went on the Fellowship ramble.

My dearest Martyn,

I had so looked forward to seeing you – to say I was disappointed when I received your letter is putting it very mildly!

I had decided to have my hair washed and set rather than go on the ramble, but when I got your letter, I cancelled my appointment at the hairdresser's, for it seems rather pointless to have nice, newly washed hair if there are no gentle fingers to touch it. I made myself go on the ramble instead. I thought it would do me good, and I was glad I went for I felt much better while I was out. We took much the same route as the Bedfords walk. Do you remember? We went through the forest at Lambourne End and on to Crabtree Hill – a delightful spot that! We sat down there for a little while, just as we did last time, and admired the view with Havering in the distance and that long avenue, down which we walked before, and the long, long cornfield and the two farms that look as though they're cut out of a French landscape.

We had been hearing the sound of distant planes and after some searching we were able to locate them, flying terrifically high. As we watched, there was the sound of a gun and a puff of white smoke appeared. We all went under a tree – it was quite exciting! The very least we expected was falling bombs! But nothing further happened – only another bang, so we proceeded on our way.

We reached Havering, had tea and walked back home along the same route that we took on our return from the Bedfords. George and I sang a lot of Community Songs, with Maisie and Tony joining in occasionally. We got behind the others and when we reached the road at Lambourne they were nowhere to be seen. We walked along the road towards the Maypole and ran the last part of the way as a bus was coming. When it drew up, we saw that the others were on it. We arrived at the Bald Hind and as we alighted we saw against the sky a huge red glow with flames occasionally showing.

We then walked to the Crooked Billet and got on a stationary bus. Your Pop suggested some ices, so rushed off the bus to get some. He'd only just gone when the bus started! We thought he'd run down the hill and get on at the bottom, but when we reached there, he couldn't be seen!

I made out a ticket for your mother's coal yesterday, so I phoned her to say it was coming and had a little chat. She too was very disappointed that you weren't coming home.

Have you had any more warnings? We had another on Friday evening making three in twenty-four hours! One was at quarter past five. We finished work at half past so once again I made my way home through silent, deserted streets and passed wardens who looked at me suspiciously.

Well, I think I've nearly written enough – and the dinner is requiring attention. Mum's in bed so I'm in charge of culinary preparations.

I wish it was Saturday tomorrow – I do want it to come so much …

Sunday 18th August

My darling Martyn,

… I wanted to write again so that you would be sure of getting a letter on Tuesday.

We were just finishing lunch today (by the way my cooking was quite successful and pronounced fit for human consumption!) when the siren went. The raid lasted about an hour and left off just in time for me to go to Fellowship.

We had quite a pleasant time. Your Pop read a good poem – obviously chosen because he has a son in the RAF! I chose the first chapter of *The Beloved Vagabond* by William J. Locke. You really ought to read that book, you know. Would you like me to send it to you?

After tea we had another air-raid warning! Consequently, church didn't start until twenty to seven and there were very few in the congregation ...

Sunday 18th August

Lil darling,

I am feeling extremely mad! They stopped my day off so that we could do more flying, and can you guess what it has done? – Yes, you're quite right, it's rained almost all day! This morning we were bundled into a lecture room with no lecturer, and just told to do some work. This afternoon we simply waited around for the weather to clear and it's slowly got worse. They just had to give flying up as a bad job.

I heard on the six o'clock news tonight that a battle was raging over London, and I'm sincerely hoping that Woodford hasn't received any stray bombs or pieces of falling aeroplanes.

Last night I woke up and heard raiders overhead and ascertained that a considerable number of bombs were dropped at Newcastle-under-Lyme about ten miles away. Also, two bombs were dropped only about two miles from here ...

Tuesday 20th August

Lily my darling,

... You seem to be having quite a merry time with air-raid warnings. I wonder that you haven't heard any gunfire or bomb explosions, for the real excitement couldn't have been so very far away. How typical of Hitler to have chosen the very day on which you cook the dinner to send his aeroplanes over. Still, the main thing was that your cookery was so successful. I really must sample it someday soon ...I had a letter from Dad this morning, and he told me that you went on the ramble and he thought you'd enjoyed it. I should have loved to have been with you when you indulged in community singing! Did you give a performance of 'I'm Knitting a Singlet for Cecil'? I shall never, to my dying day, forget when you sang it in the train homeward bound from Paris!! What a grand time that was, wasn't it!! Dad mentions that the bus went without him as he was getting ices, but he doesn't say whether he was forced to consume ten ices himself! ...

I'm Knitting a Singlet for Cecil

I'm courting a lad such a nice sort of lad,
    but he's so sentimental you'll say.
He's asked for a keepsake to wear next his heart
    to treasure when I am away.
So I'm knitting a singlet for Cecil,
    a nice woolly singlet for Cecil,
It'll keep him as snug as a bug in a rug
    as in its embrace he will nestle.

It's fancy where it should be plain
    but I can't pull it all out again,
It's low at the back and the front it's a 'v'
And the armholes are not where I meant them to be,
But it's soft so it's sure to remind him of me,
    That singlet I knitted for Cecil.

I couldn't afford so much wool so
   he'll have to keep giving a pull,
He'll have to use flakes when he washes the thing,
But just like the ivy I know it will cling,
And lots of fond memories it's certain to bring,
   That singlet I knitted for Cecil.

My keepsake he'll never forget,
   it'll tickle his fancy you'll bet,
It's such a nice colour he's sure to look swell,
It's the woolliest wool that the wool sellers sell,
It'll tickle him where he can't scratch as well,
   That singlet I knitted for Cecil.

So I'm knitting a singlet for Cecil,
   a nice woolly singlet for Cecil,
It'll keep him as snug as a bug in a rug,
   as in its embrace he will nestle.
It's the first time that I've knit one of these
   and it's shorter than fashion decrees,
He might get a chill both behind and afore.
   I think I will add just a few inches more
And then he can tuck it in his bottom drawer,
   That singlet I knitted for Cecil.

Freddie Robins

8

20th August – 31st August 1940

Fierce aerial battles had raged over southern England as Hitler tried to gain air superiority before embarking on a land invasion, but the Air Force had gained the upper hand.

On 20th August Churchill made his famous speech in praise of the pivotal efforts of the RAF crews against the German Luftwaffe.

'Never in the field of human conflict was so much owed by so many to so few.'

89 Grenville Gardens
Woodford Green
Wednesday 21st August

My dearest,

We at Woodford are all alive and well – no bombs yet! There have been no air-raid warnings since Sunday evening ...It seems that you had a very narrow escape when the bombs dropped only two miles away. Thank heaven that you are safe!

I was bitterly disappointed when I received your letter this morning and learned that I may not see you for another week! Surely, Martyn, they will let you come here before that? It seems incredible to me! I have been looking forward to Saturday so much! I can't really believe you, that I shan't be waiting for you at Euston and that there won't be that glorious moment when you kiss me again, but I suppose I must just be patient and wait until you do come. I'm hoping as hard as I can that it will be sooner than we think.

By the way, when I'm writing to you, Mum and Dad invariably ask to be remembered to you! I always forget to put it in.

Thank you for the photo. I think it's a very pleasant snap, but, I'm sorry darling – I don't think it's very like you. Everyone else (the family) says it's awfully good! I definitely like the smile, but it looks more like Laurence Olivier than you! However in spite of these remarks I must confess that I can't resist taking it out and looking at it many, many times! Sometimes I put it to my lips and wish it were real!

Do you know how you ended your last letter? 'Must close now deer'! Now, Martyn, I really must object to that – 'dopey', 'smithy', 'sneezewit' and 'piglet' are allowed – on occasions – but 'deer' definitely 'no'. (It was your bad handwriting I suppose!)

Oh darling, please come home to me soon because I do miss you so terribly.

I love you sweetheart,

Lily

219 Weston Road, Meir

Thursday 22nd August

… Yes, Lil, it is going to seem a very long time if we have to wait a month or so before seeing each other again, but as you say, it may be sooner than we think, and we must just hope for the best.

You remember how I told you that Ken had invited me to go up to his home in Manchester? Well I've now found that there is a train I can catch. Hence I've decided to dash up to Manchester one evening, probably Monday, stay the night, and then dash home early the next morning. I am quite looking forward to this excursion, for I haven't seen Ken's people for about two years.

It has been very windy again today and I have only done about forty minutes' flying. We went up and did a series of spins and then ended up with a spot of low-flying. We flashed over the ground at about a hundred feet and waved to all the farmers and milkmaids etc. in the fields below. Quite a jolly time!

Now Lil darling, you really mustn't accuse me of calling you a 'deer'! You surely do not think that I would be so unseemly as to address, in such fashion, one by the name of Lilian Maud Smith. No, Maudie, it was 'dear' I called you, not 'deer' and in case my bad writing should confuse you again I will say – must close now 'dearest' till tomorrow, so goodbye and sweet dreams.

All my love to you,
Martyn

Friday 23rd August

My darling Martyn,

Once again Mr Chapman has gone home in order to lunch with his relatives. It's now three forty-five and he's not yet back, so I'm manageress! I really do like it here very much now, for, even when he is present, I often attend to customers or answer the phone. Today I felt very flattered when he said (after several phone messages from Mrs Ashwood –unnecessary according to him!), "Why, you are worth a dozen of her!" I can only hope that I don't look like a dozen of her – she being on the rather large size.

Last night I was peacefully sleeping when at about four o'clock, I woke up at the sound of a gun! A second later there were five heavy crashes as bombs fell! Gosh, I was scared – it sounded as though they had dropped in our garden – the plane was certainly just overhead. About two minutes later (too late to be any good) the warning went! As guns were still firing, Arthur and I decided to get up. We went downstairs, made some tea and took it up to Mum and Dad who were still in bed – then, as all was quiet again, we went to bed ourselves. The all-clear went after about half an hour.

This morning I learnt that five bombs were dropped in Edmonton High Street demolishing shops and a cinema. We could scarcely credit that it was so far away (though near enough!), the noise was so terrific! ...

Friday 23rd August

... I was interested, Lily, in your account of the devotional evening and especially intrigued that you thought your readings were "rather good". Oh, my dear little lump of pure conceit, it's no good; your little nose is sticking up far too high in the air! We shall definitely have to put a ring through it and pull it down again! (On further consideration I think that might make you look too much like a piglet, so we will keep the ring for somewhere else, if you have no objection!) ...

It rained again all day today, so they gave us a Signals exam this morning and we had our Navigation and Airmanship exams this afternoon. The Signals wasn't too bad except for receiving Morse from the signalling lamp. For that part of it I got more mistakes than correct letters. Airmanship was pretty simple and Navigation would have been ok had I not made a stupid error in a geometric problem so putting me right out and landing me with a lot of wrong answers. I'm not exactly itching to see the results!

I'm afraid you must have had a pretty thrilling night last night, if what the newspapers say about attacks on London is correct. I do hope you don't have any more for a while ...

Saturday 24th August

Lil dearest,

... I can imagine that you were slightly windy when the planes planted bombs on Highams Park and Edmonton the other night. When I read that north-east London had been attacked, I guessed that you would have heard something of it this time.

My goodness, you are a lucky girl to be able to go out on the razzle three nights in one week! An opera, a Prom and a ballet – and all in the space of four days. You certainly have made me very envious!

I have done two and a quarter hours' flying today – the most for a single day so far.

The results of our Navigation and Airmanship exams are not up yet, but the Signals I regret to say, is! I passed the buzzer test, having no mistakes on sending, and only one in receiving, but in the case of the lamp I got a hell of a lot wrong and failed by about ten marks! I'm not particularly worried, for I expected to be hopeless at the lamp. After all, I had never seen a lamp till I came here, and up-to-date I have done one hour's receiving on it and no sending whatsoever. In fact I had never tried sending on it until the test itself! ...

Sunday 25th August

My dearest Martyn,

.... We've been having quite exciting times here. On Friday night there was gun-firing and the sound of bombs dropping some way away. On Saturday morning there was a warning – another one in the afternoon and a third at half past eleven at night. Nothing much happened in the morning; I was just going to put my coat on ready for work when the siren went and so I started out an hour later than usual. In the meantime I entertained our baker and his helper who were sheltering in our house.

In the afternoon Maisie and I were going to Leytonstone to buy some shoes. The train came in just as the siren went, but we decided that probably nothing would happen so we continued. However, the train was only going to Snaresbrook so we got out there and were advised to take shelter. We went over the bridge with one or two other people while the raiders could be heard overhead. When we reached the barrier there was suddenly a terrific burst of gunfire. A warden who stood outside shouted, "Quick, you'll have to run for it!" and we all ran like mad for the shelter which was in the railway yard. The planes and guns sounded just on top of us – it was pretty awful. We reached the shelter and stayed there until the all-clear. When it went we decided to go home to tea.

But I was not to be deprived of my shoes! So in the evening I set off once more, alone... I've got some lovely ones, real Dutch sabots (at least real Lilly & Skinner Dutch sabots).

Last night I went to bed early as I felt dead tired (no sleep the night before because of the air activity). I was in a deep sleep when the siren woke me – guns and planes again for about two hours! I didn't get up – I felt much too sleepy. The all-clear woke me up again but I soon fell asleep. You've probably heard the result of that raid – we could see the sudden glow of fire which the incendiary bomb in the city caused.

But now all is peaceful again – though I find myself always listening, always on the alert.

I was afraid for you when I heard about the Midlands raid – I hope you are alright.

The bombs that we heard so clearly the other night dropped just behind the Kingfisher. There was one bomb dropped at Chigwell Lane and others at North Weald. It had stopped train services so presumably they were somewhere near the line.

I'm afraid this letter is very war-ish but it's my only important news and the main topic of conversation here. There is something else that's very important to me – but I haven't discussed it for three weeks. You see, there is a boy who is tall and dark, with a tender mouth whose kisses thrill me to happiness and whose caresses fill me with contentment – and I do so wish he could come home to me.

Bye, precious one,

Lily

Sunday 25th August

... This is my second letter to you today, so that you won't be without one on Tuesday – you'll probably get three!

We had an awfully nice time with Fellowship at Mr Tonkin's the beekeeper. He had, as usual, an unfailing store of things to tell us. Your Pop acted as 'choir' and read the hymns. Mr Tonkin read two stories, both very interesting ones, and together with the hymns and a prayer they made up the afternoon's service.

Afterwards came as usual the refreshments – plums, apples and pears, all of which we found very acceptable.

Mr Tonkin then entertained us with a dress rehearsal of what happens when he approaches a hive. He did look funny, complete with helmet, net and smoke bellows! It was very amusing.

By that time it had gone five so we went home to tea.

This evening I went to church, of course – a rather more inspiring sermon than usual. Mr Lemon's remarks will probably amuse you.

They are as follows: –

"Well" – shaking hands – "how are you?"

Me: "Very well, thank you."

"Not very happy, eh?"

Me: "Not very."

"And the author of your joys and sorrows – where is he?"

Me: "Stoke-on-Trent."

A few more questions about your position, then to the company at large:

"Oh well, Lily can still smile, I see!"

Evidently I do still smile – sometimes I don't feel like it! Rather quaint wasn't it – 'the author of my joys and sorrows'. Joys, yes, he's right there – but don't give me any sorrows, will you?

I'm trying to stop wondering now when you will come home. I only think how very wonderful it will be when you do come – it will be, won't it? Do you feel this longing too, Martyn? – A longing for kisses, for someone to put their arms around you – for someone you can say things to, silly things, private things. Or am I being awfully sentimental?

You see it's in my heart all the time – you!

Lily

Sunday 25th August

Lil darling,

It's just about nine o'clock now, and I'm wondering whether you have been for a walk with Maisie to Knighton, or whether you have gone straight home after church.

I'm wishing very much that I was at home just walking back with you. I'm wishing I could put my arm round your waist, and squeeze you close to me, and then feel your head resting on my shoulder. But it's no good wishing, for the fact remains that I'm just sitting down in an armchair at Meir, writing you a letter and feeling most homesick and lovesick …

I haven't been to church this evening, for we didn't finish flying till six o'clock so I've been listening to a recorded performance of the Grieg A Minor Concerto. My little radiogram is working quite satisfactorily now.

This afternoon I had my solo test – a flying test by one of the instructors to see if you're fit to go solo. As far as I can make out, I didn't do at all badly. My two main faults were that I didn't land quite into the wind and when I had taken off I tended to drift to the right. I did a couple of nice spins though, and in my opinion, my landings weren't at all bad (conceited?!). The fellow who examined me said in effect, "You're alright but mind those faults," so I'm hoping that I should be off solo tomorrow.

Do you remember me telling you about a fellow named Amhill who was posted here on the same day as myself? Well, he is one of the unlucky ones who have been suspended. He has only done nine hours' flying and they suspended him because he was not progressing, and was not 'of the right temperament', whatever that means!

It really is beastly luck and I'm hoping that such a thing doesn't happen to me.

I expect that you have had some more excitement with air raids. We had a warning last night at half past ten and the all-clear went at eleven o'clock. We had no bombs or gunfire though.

All my love to you as ever, my dearest,

Martyn

Monday 26th August

My darling Martyn,

.... I had just got into bed last night when the warning went, so I got up, went downstairs and did my embroidery. It lasted about three quarters of an hour and then I went up to bed and slept very soundly until morning. I was amazed to learn in the morning that I had slept right through another air-raid!

We had another warning this afternoon and as planes were overhead Mr Chapman escorted me to the stationmaster's sandbagged office. It was soon over though and no damage done in our vicinity. But thank heavens you didn't go to North Weald or Hornchurch – they've had it very badly. One of our coalmen who lives at Canning's Town didn't come to work until eleven o'clock this morning. Poor fellow, he was in no state for work and Mr Chapman sent him home to sleep. He'd been living in his shelter for about two days with bombs dropping all round, some of them delayed action ones. It was pitiful to see his face blanch when there was a sound like a siren. ...

.... I think I know, Martyn, what the authorities mean when they say Amhill is not 'of the right temperament' – they mean that he does not have that devil-may-care bravery, that cynicism which says, 'We've got to die some day. Let's have some adventure, some excitement first, and die dangerously.' I suppose we women, who must just stay at home and worry and hope, will never understand that trait in you – for us the broken hearts when you don't come back ...

Wednesday 28th August

My dearest Martyn,

We had quite a hectic time last night! I went up to badminton and played until about quarter to nine when Maisie came and said that in view of the likelihood of air-raids she wasn't going to *Tosca*. I then began to wonder who I could get to go with me instead. – George declined with thanks! So I thought next of Reg and without more ado Maisie and I went up to his house and I asked him – and of course he immediately said he'd like to come. He had to use a good bit of persuasion on his mother – but in the end we won! So I'm going with Reg tonight – I hope you don't mind! I promise I won't flirt with him – much!

We left Reg's and were walking home when as we reached the top of Maisie's road the siren went and so I went to Maisie's house and spent two and a half hours, fairly comfortably, in their kitchenette. We began to feel sleepy, after sitting there for such a long while, so had just installed ourselves in the drawing room on the settee (Maisie and I) when the all-clear went. It was about ten to twelve when I walked home (by myself!) beneath a beautiful starry sky. They were relieved to see me at home!

I had just snuggled into bed when the wretched siren went again! However, I soon went off to sleep and even the all-clear didn't wake me ...

On Monday, the night we had the six-hour raid, Maisie and Joan were at Loughton and had to stay in a public shelter till the all-clear at quarter to four! I think I'll take my embroidery tonight in case we have to shelter for long.

Last night there were some bombs dropped in Sydney Road – that road near the police station on the High Road.

Is there any more news about your leave? I should be so terribly happy if you could come home on Sunday! If you do, by any wonderful chance, we must make an arrangement in case there is an air-raid – a waiting room or something.

I think of you all the time and long for you to be with me. I want to whisper something in your ear – I believe I told you before – "I love you".

Bye, precious one,
Lily

Thursday 29th August

Lily darling,

I have just arrived home to tea, and have found your letter waiting for me.

I do hope you enjoyed *Tosca*, for if you are really enthusiastic about it, you might succeed in converting me to become a Puccini fan, though at the moment I doubt it! Of course, I am frightfully jealous! – but just as much as I would be if you went with Maisie or Laura or anyone else! I am jealous of everyone who has a chance to be near you (even Mr Chapman!!) now that I am so rarely able to be with you myself. Apart from that I am most pleased that you were able to get Reg to go, for I do want you to go to shows as much as you can. Was Maisie still ok for the Prom? Or did she decide to forgo that too? I hope you haven't had to wash that out, for it really was a topping concert.

The raids certainly are becoming a veritable curse now, aren't they! The bombs were too horribly close to Grenville Gardens for my liking – if the bomb toggle had been pulled twenty seconds earlier or later, there might have been a nasty hole in front of your house! If they give Woodford Green a miss for three or four months, I'll be ready for them with my Spitfire! (I hope!!)

We had another warning last night at ten o'clock but after staying with the others for half an hour, I got fed up and went to bed. I then managed to sleep through planes flying overhead, bombs dropping, and the all-clear – for all the others in the house heard them and I didn't. I expect we shall have another warning this evening at about ten o'clock – it is quite a regular occurrence now and they nearly always come about the same time.

I was told that some bombs were dropped near Trentham, about 5 miles from here, on Tuesday night. I flew over that way today, so decided to investigate. I practised steep turns all round the district, at the same time searching the ground below, but I saw nothing. I have done quite a spot of flying today – two hours' solo and an hour's dual, so I'm feeling quite pleased with myself! It has been very windy and bumpy, but on the whole the weather today has been pretty good. If I keep up the effort of doing three hours a day, I'll be able to complete my fifty hours by next Sunday week.

You will not be the only one to listen to a concert tonight, for just as you start listening to the Prom, I shall start listening to a performance of the Mendelssohn's Fourth – on the Home Service programme! When they broadcast things like that I am certainly most pleased that I have got my little radio.

Now, you ask me about coming home on Sunday. Well, ducky, the possibility of a day off is apparently not as faint as I imagined, so if you receive a telegram sometime on Saturday, please don't be surprised! I trust you will be able to meet me by the platform as before. If an air-raid occurs I expect they will divert you to a shelter, and when I arrive, I will enquire where the shelters are, and so find you. If I can't find you half an hour after the train comes in, I shall phone home, tell them where I am, and then wait for another half hour. So if you haven't found me half an hour after my train arrives, please phone home and find where I am. Don't count on the telegram too much though!

Heaps of love to you,
Martyn

Thursday 29th August

My darling Martyn,

I was very relieved to get your long letter this morning. It had taken a long while to get here; I suppose the raids have hindered things.

Thank you for the photos. I think your identity one is simply topping! It's really awfully like you. I thought you were going to look awfully grim for your identity photograph! I'm jolly glad you didn't! You see I've proved my point about how much nicer you look smiling than serious, haven't I?

Oh-oh ... there's the siren!

Up to now – twenty past seven – we've had three warnings today! At quarter past twelve, ten past three and quarter to five. I stayed in our office with Mr Chapman until the planes and guns were heard and then he insisted that I go to the sandbagged room on the station. They didn't last long. The last one was the nearest – quite a battle too! But by about half past five things had quietened a little, so I came home. By the way we had no warning last night! We were amazed. Apparently planes were over several times but there was no siren. It seemed quite strange. Of course I was furious to have missed the Prom for nothing but it wouldn't have been very pleasant coming home, expecting a raid to start every minute.

You really are exasperating, Martyn! I ask you heaps of things that you never answer! I asked you when you would be leaving Stoke for good. Is it in a fortnight's time or am I being too optimistic?

It doesn't comfort me much to hear about your sheer stupidity saying 'we will fight like devils to have the privilege of dying in an aeroplane'. It was cruel to say that, Martyn – to me whose entire future happiness depends on your living. Don't say these things to me – Martyn, please – if you knew how they hurt! Can you not be comforting, reassuring! ...

Friday 30th August

Darling Lily,

This is just a note to tell you that, unless anything unforeseen happens, I shall be arriving at Euston at 10:45 as arranged. Hope my arrangements regarding procedure in event of an air-raid are ok. Hope we shan't have to use them though!

Well, ducky, must close now, so goodbye till Saturday night.
All my love to you, Martyn

Martyn's identity photograph

9

1st September – 13th September 1940

Lily successfully met up with Martyn in London late on Saturday
1st September despite this being a dangerous time.
    After the initial bombing of London, Churchill authorised the first
bombing attacks on Berlin. Hitler was incensed by this and announced
that Germany would retaliate with one hundred times more.

219 Weston Road, Meir
Monday 2nd September

Lily darling,
    … I shall only write a short note tonight, Lil, as I need to
go to bed early. The reason is that I didn't arrive home till five
o'clock this morning and so have had only six hours' sleep in
two days! The train was an hour and a half late, arriving at
Stoke at three o'clock. There was no means of transport from
Stoke to Meir so I had to stay in the waiting room from three
till four thirty, at which time I was able to catch the first bus.
    I simply couldn't do anything right today – my flying was
awful, and I got really desperate! Still, I'm going up to bed
now and hope I shall feel more normal in the morning. I do
hope you got home safely and weren't caught in a raid …

My dearest Martyn,

I hope you arrived at Meir safely and that you didn't have to walk. As it happens, we didn't have an air-raid last night after all! So I could've come to Euston with you, but the walk home wasn't very pleasant even at that early hour! It was very dark. But I had the memory of you all the way, and the feel of your arms around me, and the touch of your last kiss!

It was as wonderful as I thought it would be, seeing you again! I do so hope you can have next weekend as well, but I mustn't think about that. I'll just hope they send you home when you finish in two weeks' time.

Martyn – you remember our conversation on Sunday morning about getting engaged at Christmas, and how you remarked that I've always said I didn't want a long engagement? Well, I've changed my mind. I always used to think that it would be the height of boredom to be engaged to a man for perhaps a year, to see him every day, to always be dependent on his wishes. I thought one would get tired, disinterested. But we're different! I know that engaged to you, married to you, even parted from you – I should still go on loving you all the time – and could never be happier than being with you every day, every minute, every second. That is why I said that on Sunday. I wanted you to know. Are you sure like that, darling, certain sure?

The siren has just gone. It's half past four and Mr Chapman is still at Wanstead, but I'm not going to the stationmaster's room – I'd much rather stay and write to you and if I don't post this tonight you won't get it till Wednesday.

There is a dogfight starting! So I thought I'd better get under shelter. Then Mr Chapman came back just as I was preparing to shut up. I've been watching and I could see our fighters diving about and there're great puffs of smoke!! It looks over Hornchurch way – probably the aerodrome again! ...

Tuesday 3rd September

Darling Lil,

... I am feeling considerably better now than I did this time last night. Honestly, I haven't felt so down for a long time as I did then. Firstly I was dead tired, secondly I was sick with the realisation that the longed for weekend with you was over and thirdly my flying was so terrible that I was in a state of complete despair! I'm not so tired now though and although I'm still tingling with the happiness of Sunday, I am no longer wishfully looking back, but I'm expectantly looking forward to another such delightful day in a week or a fortnight.

Furthermore my flying was back to normal today, and although at lunchtime I was really dreading the thought of going up, when I got up I flew quite well and had a most enjoyable afternoon. I did a couple of cross country flights – one with my instructor to Matlock and then one by myself of about a hundred miles to Elsmere, Oswestry and the fringe of the Welsh hills. The hills were a really grand sight as they stretched like a huge forbidding wall across my path. Altogether I've done about four and a half hours' today.

I was awfully pleased to hear that you had changed your views about getting engaged. I'm sure you wouldn't regret it. If we did find that we got tired and disinterested then the engagement would have served its purpose by indicating that we weren't suited to each other. For surely, if we get tired of being engaged, it would be quite fatal to get married! I should like to become engaged to you soon, even though we may not be able to marry for a year or so.

I am more and more sure that our love is no passing craze, but that it's really going to last. I had been half expecting the thrill of seeing you to die off, but after last weekend I just don't believe it can! I was just as excited as ever to see you, just as breathlessly happy whilst I was with you, and just as sad when I had left you ...I love you,

Martyn

Wednesday 4th September

My darling girl,

I haven't had a letter today but I'm not disturbed about it in view of the post being so erratic these days.

It has been a glorious day again and this afternoon I went on a cross country to Northampton. Unluckily I temporarily lost myself on the way down and took an hour and quarter for the journey instead of three quarters of an hour! I had passed Burton-on-Trent and was going along very nicely, picking out my landmarks, when suddenly I saw the outskirts of a town on my left. I knew that this shouldn't be and imagined that I had drifted to the east and struck Leicester, so I altered course to the west. Actually, I had drifted to the west and arrived on the wrong side of Nuneaton, so should have altered course east!

Anyhow, after about three minutes I suddenly saw an aerodrome, then another aerodrome and then a third, all in a line. I was very tempted to land at one of them and find out where I was, but then, lo and behold, ahead of me I saw a balloon barrage and below it a very large town.

Needless to say, I was soon facing in the opposite direction, having guessed that this was Birmingham! After a few more minutes I caught sight of the wireless masts at Rugby, and so I knew for sure where I was. A quarter of an hour later I was on the ground at Northampton, having made a detour of about fifty miles! Coming home I kept a straight course and did the eighty miles in less than fifty minutes.

Well, ducky, goodbye for tonight.

All my love to you, sweetheart,

Martyn

Thursday 5th September

My darling Martyn,

... We had a very exciting time last night! I went to Fellowship Circle – there were six there – and we had just got down to discussing the plan for Befriending the Forces (I expect you know more about it than I do) when the siren went. So we all went home. I had only just got indoors when the guns came into action. They were terrific! Our house really shook with the vibration. Arthur and I watched events from the kitchenette window; we could see the plane clearly for some time in the searchlights but though the guns kept up a heavy barrage I don't think they got it ...

Thursday 5th September

Lil darling,

I was pleased to receive your letter of Tuesday this morning, and to learn that no bombs were dropped near you on Monday night.

We have had raids each night this week, though I slept through those on Monday night and Tuesday night. Last night however they dropped quite a packet near Trentham and our house received its first vibrations.

This morning I went to Trentham to try and find them but did not succeed. It hasn't been a very good day for flying so we have been doing other things like crosswind take-offs, and landings, and precautionary landings. I'm afraid that we are not having a day off this weekend as we shall be flying all day Saturday and Sunday and exams start on Monday. I can't say I'm looking forward to them at all.

I must close now but will write a longer letter tomorrow,

all my love to you,

Martyn

Friday 6th September

… I spent a very enjoyable forty-five minutes this afternoon doing aerobatics with my instructor! We did loops, stalled loops, slow rolls, flick rolls, half rolls, rolls off the top of loops and goodness knows what else. Really a most amusing pastime – I must give you a taste of stunting in my private plane when the war is over!! …

Friday 6th September

… I was just getting ready for work when the siren went, so I thought I'd write to you Martyn, whilst I'm waiting for the all-clear. There is an enemy machine diving about and making smoke trails across the sky – I've been trying to spot him but he's right in the sun. Gosh! – There's just been a burst of machine guns firing quite close!

It must have been very thrilling to fly all by yourself to Wales! It seems wonderful – and frightening to me! I'm very glad I only hear about it afterwards – after you're back safe and sound. Be careful, darling, won't you.

Your letter made me very happy, Martyn dear. I keep thinking about the lovely things you said. Yes, we must be honest with each other, and if our engagement doesn't work – we won't get married. But I feel as sure as you do that our love is deep, and real, and sincere. I think it always will be. Surely those six weeks when we saw each other all day were quite a good test. True we had one or two disagreements but when we made up I'm sure that we loved each other more and understood one another better. And if our quarrels are never more serious than those we ought to be happy, Martyn!

The all-clear went at ten o'clock this morning – since then we've had two more, lunchtime and teatime respectively.

There was no letter from you this morning, but one came by this afternoon's post. It was very disappointing though! You had ignored the subject of weekend leave completely! I eagerly scanned each sentence – but in vain! Martyn, you might have just mentioned it – I felt horribly disappointed! I presume you're not coming.

Your little escapade over Birmingham sounds rather dangerous to me – don't lose your way anymore! Although accounts of your exploits in the air are interesting, they frighten me. I like your love letters best of all. It is those that bring me happiness and contentment.

Write some more, Martyn.

Good night, darling love,

Lily

On Saturday 7th September the Luftwaffe shifted its focus from bombing British airfields and aircraft factories to conducting air raids on London. The Blitz, as it became known, began at about four o'clock in the afternoon. Masses of German planes appeared over London and for two hours dropped high explosives and incendiary devices. Later that night there was a further onslaught and by the morning 430 people had been killed and 1,600 were badly injured. The raids had primarily targeted London's hub of industry and trade but this dockland area was densely populated and housed many of the poorest working-class citizens of London. The day became known as Black Saturday. The bombing of London continued without respite for another 57 nights and many of London's landmark buildings were hit, including Buckingham Palace.

Sunday 8th September

Lil darling,

... From this morning's paper it seems as if you had a pretty awful time yesterday, and I'm praying that you're quite safe and sound in Woodford. I also understand that troops have been dropped somewhere, and they certainly seem to be expecting the invasion to start here, for all the Home Guard has been called out, and six coach loads of troops have arrived at the aerodrome to deal with any troop-carrying planes that might land.

Yesterday morning I had my Fifty Hour Examining Officer test and didn't put up a very good performance. Early in the morning I had really been flying well, but about twelve o'clock, when he took me up, it had become quite bumpy, and this put me off on my climbing and gliding turns. Most of all it put me off on my instrument flying, which is always pretty bad, but yesterday was frightful. I thought I'd made an awful mess of things (I probably had!) but the only remark that he made when we came down was, "Your instrument flying wasn't so hot; you're too heavy with the rudder." So in view of the absence of curses, I presume that I have not yet been chucked out!

I am thinking of you now, just having your lunch, before getting ready for Fellowship. I do so wish that it was last Sunday, and that I was able to come down after lunch and meet you, instead of having to walk back to the aerodrome and continue flying. Still, maybe I shall next weekend, so I mustn't moan! ...

Lily my darling,

Your letter of Friday which arrived this morning tells me of more and nearer raids, and I'm terribly afraid that your next letter will bring news of unhappy events on Saturday. I'm hoping hard that no bombs fell near you. We haven't had any excitement for two nights now, so we're expecting something to happen tonight.

We had our Armaments exam this afternoon and I think I passed alright. I also completed my quota of fifty hours' flying today and shall probably only do two or three more this week.

You have probably heard that, owing to the invasion, all leave has been cancelled, so I'm afraid the chances of me being able to come home next weekend are more slender than ever.

Yes, my dearest, I now feel that, in spite of our half-hearted quarrels, that six weeks was a good test of our love, and I'm sure that our love came out of the test with flying colours! As you say, if we're engaged and never quarrel more than we did then, I'm sure there's no excuse at all for not getting married!

I'm sure our love is as firm as a rock, for I am sure I love you now as much as I ever have.

Lil my dearest one, and darling, I do want you so much for keeps.

I love you, dear,
Martyn

Lily darling,

I was rather afraid that the post would be in a turmoil as a result of the recent raids, so I was not terribly surprised when no letter from you arrived today. This Blitzkrieg is a real curse, for as you probably know, all leave has been cancelled and I'm afraid there is little or no chance of coming home this weekend now. We have been told that we shall most probably go to our new station on Saturday night and won't even have a day in town. Too bad, isn't it, but I have not given up all hope yet!

It is almost like the end of term now for we've finished flying and are just wandering around the aerodrome. Tonight we are having a celebration with the instructors at a posh pub in Hanley.

I heard from a fellow who took the reports from the Flight Commander to the Chief Flying Instructor that on my report it said 'shows common sense and should make a good service pilot' – so I'm feeling quite pleased with myself (conceited!). I believe that I'm recommended for 'twins', though I wanted to go on to fighters; but I'm not quite sure yet.

Well, ducky, I must close now and have a bath (as I haven't had one for a fortnight!).

So goodbye, darling.
All my love to you as ever,
Martyn

Lily darling,

I was most pleased to receive your long letter this morning, but was not nearly so pleased to hear about what happened on Saturday night. I admit that I expected that Woodford would not have missed things altogether, but it certainly shook me to read that incendiaries had struck the shops and the Plaza, and that your road was littered with shrapnel. I do wish that you were up here with me in this comparatively safe and peaceful area!

We had our Signals exam this morning, and I was pretty sure I would fail, as I am so bad at receiving Morse on the lamp. Luckily I only got fifteen mistakes after all, plus one on the buzzer, so I had a total of sixty-eight marks, and hence a pass. Admittedly it wasn't a very brilliant effort, but I'm feeling quite pleased with myself all the same!

We have nothing to do at all tomorrow except swat for the Airmanship and Navigation exams on Friday.

I expect the postings notice will go up tomorrow, so I should be able to tell you in my next letter how far I shall be from home. I asked my instructor today what planes he had recommended me for, and he said 'twins'. So it doesn't look as if I shall be throwing a Hurricane about after all, but I'll ramble about instead in a flying boat or a heavy old bomber.

Lil darling, I do so want a day off this weekend so that I can see you again. Already it seems an age since we were together – and being with you is such a marvellous time! I'm still hoping that Sunday morning will see us in our haunt on the golf course, or perhaps even in Knighton, for I have such a longing to feel you close to me and hold you tightly and kiss your lips.

I do love you so much, my sweetheart,

Martyn

Lil darling,

Your letter this morning really shook me to the core – gosh, you must be having a frightful time now. I do so wish that I was at home to share the danger with you, instead of being stuck up here on a blessed rest cure. I expect that you, almost driven mad by bombs, would give anything to be away from them, but though it's stupid and strange, I, having only heard bombs in the distance, am just itching to be in the thick of it! Silly, isn't it!

How terribly tragic the evacuation from Silvertown is. It seems ghastly that those poor dockland folk, who have a pretty awful time anyway, are the first to be really affected by the results of war. Here is an opportunity for the church, the Fellowship and the Fellowship Circle to practise what they preach. It seems to me to be a golden opportunity to do a magnificent piece of work, and once again I am mortified that I am out of it all. I do hope that the Church and Fellowship has snatched up the opportunity without hesitation.

I was delighted to hear how you had distributed ices to the children and managed to take such a lot of clothes up to them. Would you suggest to my Mum, if you see her, that I have two sports coats, two macs, a pair of grey bags and maybe an overcoat that might be useful. I don't see why I shouldn't part with a dozen handkerchiefs or so, and I'm sure there are some ties and a cricket shirt that could go too. And my winter undies could go, for I can get some more when it gets cold.

If I get a day off this weekend I'll sort them out myself!

And that reminds me that I am still hoping for a day off, though the posting list has still not gone up, so I don't know where or when I'm going.

When I do get off, it will probably be all in a rush, so all I can say is "expect me when you see me!" …

219 Weston Road
Meir
Friday 13th September

My darling Lily,

This, I'm afraid, is the last letter that will be from the above address, for tomorrow morning, at half past eight, I am off to South Cerney in Wiltshire!

I'm really feeling most depressed tonight, for I had so looked forward to a day at home, and now we have got to go straight there without so much as passing through London.

We finally heard where we were going at quarter past five today! I am now feeling extremely relieved that I was put down for 'twins' instead of 'singles', for half of the fellows who are down for fighters are being sent abroad! All the rest of us are being sent either to Little Rissington in the Cotswolds or South Cerney near Cirencester. About twenty-five are going to Little Rissington and the rest of the course – about twelve of us – to South Cerney.

We had our two remaining exams this morning and I should think I passed fairly easily in both of them. The papers were both quite easy and I knew almost all the stuff on them.

I have been looking at the pictures in the newspaper of the damage in Regent Street. My gosh, the city certainly seems to be in a pretty mess now, but I expect Berlin's caught it just as badly. I should think that the majority of Londoners are permanently half asleep now! Don't you feel terribly tired after being kept awake for half the night?

For heaven's sake keep yourself safe, darling one. Don't stand near windows if bombs start falling very close to you.

I'm praying so hard that nothing will harm you, my sweetheart, for I should just go crazy if anything was to happen to you. I'm loving you so terribly much, and longing to be with you again.

My love to you,

Martyn

10

Germany's plan for the invasion of Britain, code named Operation Sealion, was to take place on 17th September 1940; however, the battle between the Luftwaffe and the Royal Air Force on Sunday 15th September, which is now known as Battle of Britain Day, was a decisive victory for the RAF. As a result of this turn of events, Adolf Hitler and the German commanders altered their plans, but continued with the devastating night raids.

Having been posted to the Advanced Training School at RAF South Cerney near Cirencester in Gloucestershire, Martyn began his training on twin-engine Airspeed Oxfords as a commissioned officer.

89 Grenville Gardens
Woodford Green
Sunday 15th September

My darling Martyn,

It seems a long time since I last wrote to you – four whole days! And many things have happened in those few days. However, I'll start at the beginning.

It was Wednesday night when the intensive barrage of gunfire commenced during the night raid. There were many planes over that night, more than we'd heard before, and there were several bombs dropped. The next morning St Barnabas Road was closed so we had to walk down Wansford Road, along Chigwell Road, and up Maybank – it took ages!

In the evening I reached home at about quarter to six and walked up the garden into the dining room to find Mum dressed for going out! She at once told me that a time-bomb had been discovered in Wansford Road and that we were ordered to evacuate immediately. Poor Mum was in a dreadful state and couldn't decide what to do or where to go. But when Les got home he phoned Mr Sutton-Pryce who promised accommodation for at least four. I said I'd find someone who'd take me in Woodford. I knew your mother would if she could – or there was Maisie. So I rushed around trying to phone your mother. This took about an hour as all the phones were messed up, so I gave up trying and walked up to your house. Your mother said at once that she'd take me, so I rushed home again to get my things. I took all the clothes I could carry (I wasn't going to lose them!) – two cases full and some on my arm! I saw Mum and the others into the car and set off for your house. It seemed a terribly long way, my arms were aching. I felt anything but happy and the siren was due to go off at any moment.

However, I reached your house safely and was soon sitting by the fire telling your mother all about things. We had supper and then your father made me a very comfortable bed in the hall. I went to sleep as soon as my head touched the pillow and knew no more until the morning. It was the first complete night's rest I'd had for some time!

Friday was the day of the long air-raid, from about half past nine in the morning till two o'clock. I didn't think it was ever going to stop. Twice when the gunfire was overhead Mr Chapman sent me to the station.

After work I went to Chigwell Row to see the others. They were quite comfortable so I didn't stay long as I wanted to get back before the night raid. It started at about nine o'clock and as the planes and guns became nearer we moved the supper into the hall on two small tables, with your blue lamp to give more light.

Presently the phone rang and I was awfully relieved and delighted to hear your father say, "It's ready for re-occupation."

You seemed awfully near to me all the time I was at your house. I kept expecting you to walk into the room. It seemed strange being there without you. Every time I went into your mother's room you watched me from your photo. You watched me while I undressed – and I felt rather shy! Your mother and father have been terribly nice and made me feel really at home.

I went back home to lunch on Saturday and afterwards I went to Ilford to see Reg and Muriel and, of course, Janet. They are all well and Janet's as adorable as ever – when she hears the all-clear she says, "All gone!" She's really looking quite little-girlish now, less of a baby.

Your flying seems to be all right in spite of your fears. You say you are recommended for 'twins' – I'm horribly afraid that means bombers, doesn't it? I hope that you will like your new post and that you will get comfortable digs.

What are the chances of you coming home – practically nil I suppose. Tell me as soon as you know ...

Martyn used his first day off to return home from South Cerney to see Lily and his parents, and she wrote to him the following day.

My darling Martyn,

I do hope that you had a safe journey and reached the aerodrome in time ... It took me ages to get home. When the train reached Leytonstone I heard the last few notes of a siren, so I thought, that's good, all clear. But when all the lights were turned off I realised that it was the warning for the night raid. By the time we got to George Lane the guns were going merrily. I felt rather frightened, as they were very near and I could hear planes, but I kept on running, and was very relieved to eventually arrive home quite safe and sound.

If I had been many hours later I might have had a nasty time as the line at Coborn Road and Stratford were bombed. There were no trains from Leyton onwards today.

When I reached home last night I was delighted to see your letter waiting for me! It contains the sweetest wishes for my safety. Don't worry, my dearest. I'll be alright – I've got a sort of feeling that nothing is going to happen to me. I do so wish I could feel the same certainty about you. I just couldn't face life without you, darling, you know that, don't you? So please, please don't take any chances, and remember that your well-being is more precious to me than my own.

Sometimes I feel so terribly afraid of losing you, but then I think that God would never have let us love each other so terribly much, if he meant us to part. No, I think the day will come when we shall belong to each other for always, never to have to say goodbye anymore.

And so for tonight I'll say goodbye, and God bless you – I send you all my love – such a lot and all for you, sweetheart.

Yours always, Lily

P.S. Seven air raids today. Eight counting the night one!

RAF South Cerney
Thursday 19th September

Lil darling,

... I have been sitting at my desk, and on the desk in front of me is your new photograph. Every time I look up and see your delightful figure and your sweet face, I feel all warm inside and I smile at you as you stand there smiling at me. As I gaze at you I somehow hope all the time that you will suddenly become real, so that I can run up to you and throw my arms round you, and hug and kiss you ...The only thing of note (at least I consider it so!) is that I went solo on Oxfords this afternoon and made quite a successful circuit. I didn't forget to put the undercarriage down or the flaps up or anything like that, and made quite a good job of it on the whole, even though I'd only done two hours' dual ...

Friday 20th September

... We had an awful night last night, Martyn! The sirens went as I was finishing your letter and at about half past nine, when there was a lull in the gun-fire, we heard an ominous whizzing right overhead. Then there was a noise like heavy hailstones falling. We rushed to the back door and the whole place was lit up by crowds of small fires – incendiary bombs! Les and Arthur rushed out to deal with two in the garden – one on the lawn and another at the bottom. They shovelled earth on to them and soon put them out. Then they dealt with two more, one just outside the fence on the path and one on the spot where we've kissed 'good-night' so often. Meantime I was busy filling pails of water for the A.F.S. who were trying to put out a fire next door caused by an incendiary falling through the roof. Having put that out they raced off to deal with another fire in Wansford Road which was blazing furiously. There were fires everywhere! It was an awful sight. There were sixteen in our immediate vicinity.

After the fires were put out we went back and sat by our fire in the dining room. Presently we heard a plane flying very low – we waited – and then we heard a bomb falling and dived under the table! When it had fallen, shaking the house, we went to look outside. There was a great cloud of dust and earth in the sky and we could hear women screaming. The most terrible sound! We learnt today that a high explosive bomb had dropped in Maybank Road completely wrecking three houses and damaging others. One little boy is dead and one woman is still being extracted from the debris.

Well, after that we decided we'd remain sitting up. Half an hour passed, and then suddenly without any warning there was a terrific explosion which shook the house like jelly and plunged us into darkness! It was the time-bomb which had been at the bottom of Maybank Road for about three days!

We spent the rest of the night as comfortably as possible downstairs with one solitary candle. How terribly relieved we were when the all-clear went at quarter to six and we could go to bed in safety …

Don't talk about the war lasting for years – I'm sure it won't. And even if it did, that's no reason why we should spend all our time just longing for your next day's leave. I know your argument about 'supposing anything happened to you'. But dearest, if anything happened to you before we were married it would be the same as if I was a widow, for I could never love anyone else. Let's snatch at happiness while we can, Martyn! I could stay at the places where you are stationed – at least we'd have the nights together.

But perhaps the war will be over at Christmas. You'll be able to come home and get a good job, and we'll drift back to the old happy days of seeing each other every evening. How infinitely wonderful those evenings seem now! ...

Saturday 21st September

My sweetest one,

Thank you, darling, for your delightful letter of Wednesday. It made me feel so terribly happy and confident that everything will turn out alright in the end, even though we do have a few troubles during this war ...I was most relieved to hear that you arrived home safely in spite of the air raid. Thank heaven you were home before the bombs fell on Stratford and Coborn Road ...

Sunday 22nd September

My dearest Martyn,

This is Saturday and Sunday's letter rolled into one. I meant to write to you yesterday, but it would have been a depressing letter so I'm glad I didn't. Today I find myself saying – it might have been a lot worse!

On Friday night, or rather at about four in the morning, a land-mine was dropped on the Unilever Sports Ground – you know, the one which stretches from Church Fields to the Southend Road. Of course, Elmhurst Drive which faces it got the whole brunt of the blast. Every window was blown in and the tiles scattered like pieces of paper! Every house from the railway bridge up to the Bournes' old house is completely uninhabitable! It's a terrible sight! No one was hurt but of course they all had to leave immediately. Though the damage to property is so awful, one can only wonder and marvel at the providence which caused the mine to fall in a field instead of in a street of houses. I can't help thinking about it – wasn't it a wonderful thing? There were so many places where it could have fallen, bringing dozens of houses to the ground, and killing many people. As it is, the houses can be repaired and all the people are safe and well.

Surely a guardian angel was watching over those people, for here's another wonderful thing. A second land-mine was dropped in Eastwood Road, but by a miracle the parachute and ropes to which it was attached got caught in a tree and held it suspended there! By the afternoon the fuse had been removed and all the danger had passed.

The blast was terrific from the land-mine which did explode. Lots of the shops in George Lane have had their windows smashed. Even the library opposite the station hasn't any glass left! Only one window in the church has gone. Fortunately there were only thirty evacuees in the hall that night and being behind the church the shock was probably lessened a bit. Even a house in St Barnabas Road, just at the top of Wansford, had the bedroom windows broken – so far-reaching was the blast!

George Lane station was closed because of the, then unexploded, mine in Eastwood Road. No trains ran from George Lane to Woodford. Maybank Road was closed to traffic and so were Primrose and Violet Road, and all the people living near were evacuated.

But now the danger has passed and everything is normal again.

We have given up sleeping upstairs now and make our beds in the dining room. So if you stay another night with us I shan't have to leave you! Won't it be nice!

I'm longing to know when you are coming home again – and I'm hoping that it will be this Tuesday. If you do come home during a raid be very careful, won't you? Go into a shelter if it's very bad. And if the guns are firing you'd better go to your own house rather than come right down to me – though you know, darling, how terribly I want you to come. Only I can manage to wait, rather than have you in danger ...

My darling Martyn,

You know how when you were home I asked you to marry me – almost I pleaded with you. (As I've often told you I'm somewhat lacking in that ladylike quality of modesty!) Well, just before you came home I heard a sad story which made me realise how terribly insecure are my chances of future happiness.

A girl at Woodford (you probably know her by sight; I do) became engaged to a fellow soon after the outbreak of war. They looked as much in love when they were out together as we probably do. By about a month ago their plans to be married during his leave were complete. Two days before the wedding the girl received a letter from her fiancé making final arrangements for their honeymoon. On that very same day she received a letter from the War Office saying that he was missing and the chances of him being alive were nil! He was a pilot, last sent on a reconnaissance flight.

Put yourself, as I did, in that girl's place. How terrible was her plight! All the love and longing that she'd had for that boy, to remain for ever unsatisfied. To face a future that could have been so happy with the man she loved, alone and broken-hearted. And worst of all to have to carry on with a smile, pretending she didn't care. (One can outwardly mourn a husband, but not the man one was going to marry.)

If they had only married first – if she had only had a golden memory of even a few days of married life, how very much easier it would be for her to carry on with the memory of the fulfilment of her one great love always in her heart.

Can you understand? I want you – it's as simple as that; I want to be your wife and bear your children and be loved and adored for it every day.

I know you love me – your eyes told me so long ago. Life's so precious, Martyn, so insecure, let's have our happiness while we can ...

Sunday 29th September

My darling girl,

Your letter of Thursday arrived last night just as I was leaving for Cirencester to meet Mum and Dad at the station. I expect you will have probably heard by now that they have come down for a few days, though the final arrangements were made in a great hurry. After hunting right through the town I finally found a possible place for them. The people are very nice and I think that Mum and Dad will be very comfortable.

Really Lil, you must try and get a few days' holiday before the end of November so that you can come down here. Apart from the enjoyment side, I'm sure it would do you a world of good to get away from the raids for a bit.

Try all your persuasive powers on Mr Chapman – but not quite all, we must save some for use on Tuesday week – when I come home again! ...

Did I tell you, Lil, that they have cut our course down? It is now a seven instead of a sixteen week course and we should be taking our Wings exam in little over a month ...

Lily sweetheart,

I have just received your letter containing the tragic tale of the girl whose fiancé was lost on a reconnaissance flight. It certainly was too bad, but that sort of thing happens to so many thousands of couples in wartime and almost every pair of lovers risks that sort of tragedy just now.

I'm afraid that one's loved ones, like yourself and Mum and Dad, always get an exaggerated idea of the risks that one is running. You know, although all of us here quite gaily accept the situation that only a very small percentage of us will see the end of the war, not one of us can visualise himself being the victim of a smash-up!

Crashes are, on the whole, exceptional things for us, and it's a considerable surprise and shock to us when one occurs to someone at one's own station. This has been brought home to me very vividly today, for one of the fellows of the senior course was burned up last night in a night flying smash, with the result that an atmosphere of gloom has descended on the aerodrome today.

We are far less used to crashes actually happening than civilians are to reading or hearing about them! This all seems a very morbid subject, but as you say in your letter, we must face up to the prospect of our future happiness being wrecked in this way, though we mustn't overestimate the possibility.

I say 'our' future happiness, though you would be the only one to witness the wrecking, and you, darling, would have to forget all that might have been and commence to live a new life. I know it sounds impossible now, but it will be the wisest and in fact the only thing for thousands of people to do when this war's over.

I know it sounds sort of callous, but you cannot, you must not, dress yourself in black clothes and try and live in the past.

You are so young, darling – you have only just started your life, and such a thing as we are contemplating would only mean that you had had a false start.

I cannot believe now that I could ever love anyone but you, and I know that you feel that you will never have another love but me. But you are so full of love, my dearest, that I'm sure you would need someone else to love, and I should feel happier now if I knew that, should I be 'written off', you would find someone to love you as much as I do.

I do not think you would find it difficult to discover another boy to love you, for you are so completely lovely, loving and lovable, that any fellow like myself would fall for you just as completely as I did. Should I go, I should certainly not grudge any other fellow the superlative happiness of having you for a wife and I could not forgive you if you tried to deny yourself all future happiness on account of a tragic happening in your youth ...From the way I'm talking you will soon be thinking that I don't want to marry you but you must see how guilty I should be if, for a few weeks of perfect married life with me, you were condemned to a life of tragedy ...

I am afraid to do what you so want me to do – to marry you now. But though all my reasoning and wisdom says, as I have tried to express above, that to take such a step just now, considering all the risks, all the possibilities of tragedy, would be not only stupid, but almost criminal, my heart says: you silly boy, why on earth do you chance losing her forever, when you have every opportunity, but only one great risk? For this war has given me an opportunity of marrying you that I should never have had in the normal way. I mean that I have got a permanent job (though temporary!) with comparatively good pay and would have a most useful marriage allowance, and at the same time should presumably get a gratuity of two or three hundred pounds at the end of the war, if I last that long. ... You say you are willing to take the risk but I'm afraid for you if we lose the gamble. I do wish we could come to a definite decision as to what we should do, for my heart is in turmoil now, with all its hopes and desires and fears ...

Tuesday 1st October

My dearest Martyn,

... The chances of my having a holiday are nil I'm afraid. I doubt whether I, as a clerk of only about two months' standing, would be allowed officially to have even a day off! It's not even as if I shared visible signs of war strain. – No one says of me 'poor little Miss Smith, she is so thin and pale. I'm sure she must be ill!' (Although they did notice that I'd got an awful cold – but that will probably disappear in a day or two, leaving me as 'robust' as before!) So you see my darling, I must resign myself to work such as it is with no breaks, except perhaps an occasional afternoon later on.

What do you think about my proposal to come up to town to meet you? I'm afraid our time will be so short together otherwise. I don't think you ought to attempt to travel down to Woodford during the raid, Martyn – a train is one of the most unsafe places. Please wait in town until the morning. And if you do decide to wait in town, I want to be with you! It seems such a waste of time for you to spend the night waiting for a train and me to spend the night just waiting for the morning to bring you to me. Why, if we were together, the hours would seem like minutes, wouldn't they?

Please let me come. I want to see you the minute it is possible. I long to throw my arms around you and kiss you.

Good night darling,

love, Lily

Wednesday 2nd October

My darling Lil,

… I'm glad to hear that the bomb which dropped near Reg and Muriel's was sufficiently far away to do little damage to their house. I do hope that the bomb or rather landmine in Knighton Woods hasn't disturbed our little rendezvous under the trees, for I'm looking forward so much to being there again with you on Tuesday next!

Now, darling, you have slandered me, cursed me and railed against me (quite unjustly!) because in previous letters I have ignored the question of leave. So now I am going to give you a full statement on this rather delightful, though troubled subject. I'm coming home, dearest, on Monday next, as per usual, for the day!

But, Lily, you mustn't come up to meet me for it is far too dangerous for you to be out in one of the evening raids. If I find that the gunfire is not too bad, I shall come down to your house as soon as I get home, but if things are pretty noisy I shall come down about half past seven in the morning.

Now you know, don't you – and furthermore, you won't forget, will you – that you simply must get a couple of hours off, even if it means bribing Mr Chapman. Surely you can at least persuade the old boy that really there is no point in your returning from lunch till about three o'clock or half past three and then we can have a picnic lunch in Knighton! We should be able to get to our arbour by one o'clock – and then perfect happiness for almost two hours! …

Thursday 3rd October

My darling Martyn,

I read your Monday's letter very eagerly on my way to work this morning – it was a masterpiece in expression! As I read each paragraph I thought over carefully all you had said and at the end decided that most of it was very good logic and common sense.

As I neared the end of the second page, I was afraid that I had failed – failed miserably, for it seemed that you couldn't or wouldn't see my point of view.

But when I got to the third page, I realised that it is only a sweet unselfishness which prompts you to write like this. Up to then I had thought you were quite, quite sure of the stupidity of getting married soon; but when I read what your heart tells you, I felt very encouraged – so encouraged as to write this letter to say please, please stop being so terribly unselfish!

Although at times my outward behaviour is rather below my years, I am not a child, Martyn, and I realise as much as you do the risk I should be taking, and the consequences if the worst happened. As you say, it is I who would be the sufferer, and since I know what those sufferings would be, surely it is for me to choose, and knowing the great risk, yet I am willing, nay eager, to take it!

Just supposing for a moment things were reversed – suppose you said to me, "Darling, you know how dangerous my work is, you know this next year may be my last – you could make it the happiest year of my life by marrying me; will you?" – what a coward

I should be if I refused because of the possibility of you being killed. If you were killed how terribly remorseful I should feel! It would be the sorrow of my life to think I had refused your love.

What you don't seem to understand is that there is no difference whatever in my position if I lost you after we were married than if I lost you before.

Your heart was right when it said, "You silly boy, be brave and take a chance" – but I don't call it 'silly'; I would call it by a nobler name. It's my risk, not yours darling, and I'm ready to take it. I offer you all the love and passion, of which you are the author, that is in me – and you won't take it! ...

I've got courage enough to face anything for the sake of a few months' happiness with you, and you refuse me!

But why all this talk of you dying? What you said at the beginning of your letter has cheered me up no end. And I've got that calm feeling tonight that nothing is going to happen to you. You're going to be alright; I know you are.

Four more days, darling, and I'll be in your arms – oh Martyn, I want to be there so much, so terribly much.

I love you,
Lily

Friday 4th October

Dearest Martyn,

... I'm writing this in rather a hurry as I want to be sure of it reaching you before you leave on Monday. It's to say that I am coming to meet you in spite of what you said! You say I mustn't but I don't have to obey you – yet, darling! So look out for me at Paddington!

I shall wait at our usual place at the top of the Met steps, but if things get very lively I shall go to the air-raid shelter on the platform from which your train went last time. I shall more likely be at the barrier when your train comes in, but if I'm not, wait for me at the entrance to the Met, will you? I may wait on the stairs, the last flight which leaves from the Met to the entrance, so look for me there too. And in an emergency I will go to the air-raid shelter I've already mentioned. I hope I've made things quite clear.

I know you won't be terribly cross to see me waiting for you, will you? Anyway I'm coming, for if you are to be in any danger, I'm going to be with you.

I shan't write to you anymore, as my letters wouldn't reach you in time. So I'll see you on Monday night – I'll get there about eight o'clock and wait until you come. So, goodbye till your arms are around me again – I'm dying for Monday to come.

Bye, sweetheart,

love, Lily

Friday 4th October

… Now, about your proposal to come to town to meet me. I don't really think that you should come up to town if the raids are still going strong, but of course I can't order you to do anything (yet!), so if you do decide to disobey my instructions, there's nothing much I can do about it! In case you intend to be a wicked girl, my train arrives at eight o'clock.

So Lil, I shan't expect to see you there on Monday, but at the same time I shan't be so very angry if you are! …

11

8th October – 14th November 1940

In among the photographs that Lily had kept along with her precious letters were two Great Eastern Hotel receipts dated 8th October 1940 which indicated payment for two rooms for the previous night.

My darling Martyn,

I am waiting eagerly for a letter from you telling of your safe arrival but I suppose it won't come until Friday, so I must be patient.

I caught a train immediately after leaving you on Tuesday but didn't have a very comfortable journey as I had to stand all the way home, along with six others. I was rather disappointed as I had promised myself half an hour's enjoyment with the book you gave me as a consolation.

When I reached home I had to give a detailed account of my adventures – that took quite a time! I've told the story of our night in the waiting room to so many people now that I almost believe it myself! (Almost!) I shall have to guard my diary even more carefully now, now it contains such a precious secret!

After the full and detailed account, I decided the thing I needed most was a hot bath. So, for a delicious three quarters of an hour I lay and relaxed with the hot water caressing my chin. When I got out I felt marvellous, clean and glowing, but so sleepy. The thing I wanted the most was a soft comfy bed with no bombs dropping near, and two strong arms to hold me closely until I fell asleep. But I knew that happiness couldn't be mine (yet!), so instead I took my pillow and eiderdown and, together with the blankets already downstairs, I made up a little bed on the floor in the dining room. At nine o'clock I lay down and was asleep as soon as my head touched the pillow.

A particularly loud crash, when a bomb dropped on the Midland Bank at Woodford Station, woke me up at once, but apart from that I slept right on till the all-clear at quarter to seven when I stumbled upstairs and slept in my own bed till eight o'clock. I didn't want to get up then a bit, I could've slept all day!

The memory of Monday night is beginning to fade a little now – though I'm trying to keep it fresh ...

Officers' Mess
RAF South Cerney
Thursday 9th October

... I do hope that you managed to get home last night before any air-raid started. We ran into air-raids near Reading, but although the train slowed up for a bit, it arrived at Cirencester only about three quarters of an hour late. Dad came to see me off by the way, but I didn't mention the critical subject – I think an application form will be a better method!

I went into Cirencester this evening and managed to obtain my records, so I shall probably be able to bring them home for you to hear on Tuesday. I tried to buy something else for myself. Can you guess? Some chocolate biscuits! But not one shop had any at all! Apparently the trouble is not that there is a lack of ingredients, but simply that the manufacturing plants are busted ...

... Lily darling, I was so terribly happy when I was with you – I think I was happier than I have ever been. I suppose that it's a silly thing to say, but you know I can hardly get over the fact that we haven't got the least scrap tired of each other. I must admit that I expected it to happen – I expected the novelty to wear off, so to speak, but the marvellous thing is that it hasn't at all! Indeed I was thrilled on Monday night, but I was just as thrilled and supremely happy in the train on Tuesday evening!

You are so completely delightful, my dearest, and I am perfectly sure now that I should never tire of your company.

We will be engaged very soon, I promise you, and married too I hope, for I really do want you as much as you want me.

I love you so very much, sweetheart,

Martyn

Friday 10th October

... The enemy was very active last night again, Martyn. Early in the evening we heard eight bombs fall some distance away. One bomb was dropped in Grove Crescent, but the damage was comparatively slight. We had twelve hours of it ...Not tomorrow – not the next day – not the next day – but the next day you'll be coming home again! Isn't it wonderful! I'm getting 'cited already.

But ... I think, Martyn, you ought to wait until Tuesday morning, because of losing your night's rest ... Though two lots of travelling in one day will be very tiring ... So, I don't really think you ought to come home at all. (That's what my conscience says!) ...

Since Martyn had failed to discuss the subject of his wished-for engagement with his father when he had seen him off at the station, he now wrote him a letter and in the concluding paragraphs broached the subject.

Tuesday 14ᵗʰ October

Dear Dad,

... Before I close I want to tell you something that may or may not come as a shock to you.

The point at issue is that I want to become engaged to Lil.

We have known each other for almost eighteen months now and I think you must agree that we should have got to know each other pretty well in that time and our mutual affection would have vanished before now had it been only a passing fancy.

I am afraid that my youth is the one great drawback, but were I twenty-three or twenty-four I should probably be in no better position at the moment and, in the queer position that the country will be in when the war is finished, I feel that I shall probably have as many or as few opportunities as hundreds of men who are now pilots.

And after all an engagement is not binding and in this case it would be doing little more than formalising an existing state.

I should be very glad if you could write soon and let me know how you feel about this ...

My darling girl,

I have just put a call through to you to tell you that I shan't be coming home this evening and before I have finished this letter I expect that I shall have actually spoken to you. (I've just done so!)

It is all a long story and I think I'd better commence with Saturday when the chapter of accidents started.

We had lectures on Saturday morning and the first mishap, which was only a very minor one, occurred during flying in the afternoon. ...

My co-pilot and myself had gone off to practise blind flying and after I had done half an hour of blind flying, with him acting as safety pilot, I went to land so that we could change over. I overshot slightly and as there was no wind we were halfway across the aerodrome before we touched down. I put on the brakes pretty hard as we were quickly approaching the brambly hedge, and at once we went into a glorious, swinging skid, and finally stopped almost facing the way we had come! When I looked out of the window I found that I had completely ripped one tyre off the wheel and I thought at first that I had damaged the undercarriage. Luckily the undercarriage was ok but I had to sit out there in the middle of the aerodrome for almost an hour while the wheel was changed ...

The second mishap, or should I say incident, occurred on Sunday morning. Our squad was detailed to parade at eight o'clock for drill. I arrived about five to eight and found only about four pupils out of twenty-four present! The squad commander, who should have fallen the squad in, had failed to turn up and the deputy commander didn't arrive till after me.

To my great consternation I discovered that the parade was being taken by the station warrant officer, who is an exact replica of the legendary Sergeant Major – a really frightful snarling sort of fellow. By five past eight I had collected about eight fellows together and marched them on to the parade ground. From then on we had an hour of perfect hell with this fellow and were thoroughly thankful when it was over.

Nothing had been said about the scarcity of fellows present, so I thought things were going to be alright – but far from it!

Shortly after we had started lectures, I was sent for by the Chief Ground Instructor, who is also a very grim specimen, and told that I must produce, before four o'clock, a complete report on the appalling attendance on parade.

I obtained a statement from each absentee and made out a report and sent it in by two o'clock.

The Chief Ground Instructor was quite obviously displeased with the pretty poor excuses given and said that he felt the only thing to do was to suspend the day off for the whole course!

Well, this cancellation of a day off was bad enough, but worse was to come. At six o'clock I found a letter in my letter rack telling me that he felt it was all the fault of the squad commander and myself and we three would therefore be awarded two days 'barracks curtailment' which is virtually 'Confined to Barracks'! That really was the last straw and I did feel jolly fed up. Not only was I present on time, but also I have no responsibilities towards the squad. I am not official squad commander or anything!

What was really most annoying was that I was doing night flying last night and so was permitted the day off.

I could've come home this morning and had almost two days!

Of course it was a clever move on the Chief Ground Commander's part for it will mean that the squad commanders and myself will be very careful in future, and all the fellows, who were really most annoyed and apologetic when they found out that I had come off worst, will certainly not slack off parade and/or let me down again ...You told me in your letter about Jack's enquiries regarding trains to Torquay and of your longing to go down there. You know I should like to go down there too – but with something else to admire beside the scenery! How long will it be before I take you on that trip? – Maybe we shall know the answer fairly soon now.

Goodbye my sweetheart till tomorrow. I'm loving you so terribly much and praying for you to be kept from danger.

I love you, dearest,

Martyn

Wednesday 15th October

Lily darling,

I had hopefully expected a letter from you today, but nothing came, much to my disappointment. I haven't heard from you now since Friday, so I'm sure a letter simply must arrive tomorrow morning.

It is just quarter past five and I did not expect to be sitting in the Mess writing to you at this time – I thought I should be sitting beside you in a carriage on the way to Liverpool Street. Still the day is over now and it's no good crying over spilt milk – we must just hope very hard that nothing goes wrong to spoil my trip home next week.

We did fly this morning, though the weather was pretty unsettled. I put in about an hour's solo, during which time I went up above the clouds to about 4,000 feet and practised some steep turns. After I had been up there for about half an hour the clouds closed right up beneath me, so I dived down through them to 1,000 feet and spent the rest of the time with a trip up the Stroud Valley to the Severn.

Incidentally I have just completed a hundred hours' flying – a distance flown of about 10,000 miles – how many times around the world is that?! ...

I didn't quite know how to spend my afternoon off, so I walked into South Cerney which is about two miles from the aerodrome and is a really charming little village of the Cotswold style. I thought, as I wandered down the main street, if such it could be called, how delightfully peaceful the little place must have been before people like myself shattered the stillness with their noisy aeroplane engines!

I spotted the village church hemmed in by grey stone houses, and in my endeavour to reach it, walked down by the river past some most picturesque old cottages whose gardens stretched right down to the opposite bank of the river.

I decided there and then that when the war was over I would say goodbye to the Air Force and retire to some equally delightful cottage in an equally pretty little country village!

It didn't occur to me till afterwards that even if the war lasted for ten years I should be rather young to retire and anyhow, I'm afraid I should never be really happy if I lived permanently far from concert halls and theatres!

Still, it was a very pleasant dream – and a country cottage would be very nice! I walked back from Cerney into Cirencester and there bought myself another shirt. I also bought myself a couple of pounds of chocolate biscuits

– it is so difficult to get them now and whenever I find a shop that has any, I obtain a large supply! ...

That really was shocking news about the bombs in George Lane. They certainly don't seem to have missed the railway by much this time. Is your little coal box still intact? – I suppose there is no glass in the windows now.

I see from the paper that you had worse raids than ever last night, and I'm praying that no bombs fell near you.

Please be careful, dearest, for I don't know what I should do if anything happened to you, for I love you so very, very much.

Goodbye, sweetheart, till tomorrow,

Martyn

Thursday 16th October

Lily darling,

I'm feeling terribly despondent just now, for this morning I received a most disheartening letter from Dad.

After the way you had chastised me on Tuesday regarding our engagement, I felt that I had to write to Dad and state my case ... Perhaps you still feel that my attitude suggests that I don't want to become engaged to you. Please darling, believe that I do, but please remember too that you know my character now, and my characteristics still hold good when making decisions about engagements as about anything else.

You are terribly impulsive, Lily, and rely on your impulses being true. Sometimes I have impulses, and act quickly without thinking, but usually I work things out carefully, counting the cost and taking account of the danger. Maybe you feel that this characteristic is a bad one, but had I been liable to act upon sudden impulses, we couldn't have trusted ourselves as we did on Monday night.

So you see, I wrote to Dad and said that I wanted to become engaged to you, and asked for his advice. I'm afraid you may despise me for taking so much notice of Dad's advice, but please, please don't, darling. I have learnt now that though his advice rarely confirms my wishes, it is always perfectly good advice and in the end his plans are usually wisest. I had a feeling that he would not give me an outright 'yes', though I didn't know why. I had a feeling somehow that the time wasn't quite right, and that, as I have learnt, is Dad's feeling also. You see Dad (and Mum come to that) have, as I have learnt from the letter, rather old-fashioned ideas on engagement.

I spoke of an engagement as a kind of probationary period, but Dad is more insistent that an engagement is a contract recognised by law, and on becoming engaged one binds oneself to be married in a comparatively short period. He considers, and maybe correctly, that on becoming engaged one should have one's plans for the wedding almost fixed up pat. I must admit that I have sympathies with this view, for I should like to feel that once I was engaged to you, the wedding itself was not still 'in the air'.

Dad's other point is, needless to say, and rather understandably, the question of my career.

For some reason he refuses to believe that the Air Force will be my last career and considers my Engineering career as being in cold storage for the duration. I suppose he had high hopes of me becoming a successful B.Sc. one day (though he should know my mental calibre by now!) and I think he still cherishes the hope that I will finish the course on which he started me.

This point is less important though, for I cannot envisage myself going back to college should I survive the war, and if I did continue in the engineering line, I should get a job first and then take my degree at home.

I expect that by this time you will be wanting to know what Dad's specific suggestions are.

He suggests that we work things out and weigh things up during the next few months, and if then we are still set on an early engagement, we make the engagement coincide with either your 21st or mine! Strange really, for I always had visions of announcing my engagement to you at my 21st party!

I know this will greatly disappoint you, as it disappointed me, but I beg you to consider it carefully.

I haven't accepted Dad's suggestions yet and I cannot form any decisions until I have heard all that you have to say. But whatever you do or say, Lily, please remember that my hesitation is not because I love you so little, but because I love you so much.

We may see the end of the war together, darling, but if we do there will be a new life to live.

Please, please, sweetheart, believe me when I say that I love you with all my heart, and I want to make you happy for all time,

Goodbye dearest,
Martyn

There is no letter from Lily in response to Martyn's description of his father's opinions, but presumably it was the main matter under discussion when they met, and in a subsequent letter to Lily he adds one more pertinent point.

… This is what Dad says – "I leave the major question at issue entirely to your own discretion, hoping that you will beware not to allow your heart – right though I am convinced that it is – to run away with your head."

And that, I think, completely dispenses with the question of whether Dad objects to us being married! …

Monday 3rd November

Lily darling,

I was really most annoyed to read that you had had no letter from me on Thursday, for I had made a special effort to catch the quarter past four post on Tuesday. I think they must clear the box any time they fancy. The other day I walked down the hall at quarter to seven in my pyjamas to catch the seven o'clock post and when I got there the box was quite empty. Dashed annoying.

Yesterday I had the most exciting flight so far.

There was a wind of about 50 mph, driving rain, and one could hardly see across the aerodrome but at three o'clock we were detailed for a cross-country to Liverpool!

We took off (I was navigator, a fellow named Tate was my pilot) and set off on our way. It was so misty that when we got up to 1000 feet we could hardly see the ground and we bumped about all over the sky. It was so terribly bumpy that Tate found it impossible to steer a decent course, so I was feverishly map reading, and trying to locate our exact track over the ground. We reached Cheltenham alright and went on towards Worcester, though the weather was getting still thicker and still bumpier and we were pitched about like a cork in the ocean. I was clinging on to my seat with one hand and my map with the other, with my head out of the window as the streaming rain made it impossible to see through the cabin windows.

We got to Kidderminster and then found we were running into low cloud below 1000ft. Tate said he was turning back, and I thoroughly agreed that it was the wisest thing to do.

So we turned round and ploughed homewards arriving at Cerney just before the visibility decreased to nil!

Since writing the beginning of this letter we have had another shot at the trip to Liverpool – with not such a successful ending!

We set off at about half past ten, Tate being pilot again and myself navigator, though the weather was again pretty duff. It improved as we went north however, and we reached Liverpool on time. We turned round, and started on the return trip and everything went swimmingly as far as Cheltenham. But at Cheltenham as we crossed the ridge of hills we ran into a very thick bank of clouds. We were up at 2000ft and imagined they went down to 1500ft, so we flew blind through the middle of them.

When we estimated we were over Cirencester we went down, but instead of breaking through at 1500ft we got down to 500ft and were still above them! We saw Cirencester through a break in the clouds, and made direct for the aerodrome, which we also sighted through a break. The clouds were down to 200ft though, and we only had glimpses of the aerodrome as we came round in the circuit. Tate tried to land, but couldn't see the aerodrome till we were too close, so overshot and had to go round again. On the second attempt we had another shot, but this time lost the aerodrome while making the circuit! We flew around, barely over the treetops, for about 10 minutes, and then all of a sudden spotted another aerodrome through a gap in the clouds. It was Kemble – about 5 miles away.

Tate made a very low circuit, extremely near to the aerodrome as he was afraid of losing it, and tried to land after turning in almost over the boundary. There was hardly any wind though and we went sailing across the field at a terrific rate. Tate then seemed to pull the nose up to try to get her to sit down, but the next thing I remember was that the nose was pointing acutely towards the ground, and the ground was very rapidly coming up to meet it!

A wing dropped suddenly, hitting the ground and tipping us onto the other wing and ripping half of it off. The undercarriage collapsed and we went pitching along with a shower of bits of wood, fabric, propeller and goodness knows what else!

Well, to cut a long story short, the machine finally stopped, or should I say subsided, and we found to our surprise that neither of us was even bruised. Had we been ten feet higher it would probably have been a different story, for the nose would have hit before the wing and that would've been most unpleasant. As it was we were both quite undamaged, though the machine was well and truly wrecked.

We were fetched back by car to Cerney, and then learnt that two other fellows had done almost the same thing at Cerney – only they didn't come off so well; one had a broken arm and the other was pretty well bruised all over.

Well, I seem to have wasted a lot of paper telling you of my adventures, while I expect that the main thing you want to know about is when I'm coming home. I'm afraid it will be a disappointment this week, for we have exams on

Monday afternoon and in addition I shall be night flying unless the weather is too bad.

So, goodbye till then, sweetheart.
You know I am loving you such a lot,
Martyn

Wednesday 5th November

Lily my dearest,

I have just managed to get through on the phone to Mum and have learnt to my great distress that you came up to meet me last night. I feel that I can't forgive myself for ever suggesting that you should, for there was always the possibility that I should be suddenly detained as I was yesterday.

I really did think that the telegram would reach you in time, and I was awfully annoyed when I heard that it hadn't reached you till this morning. Although I think it is terribly sweet and grand of you to come up to meet me and although I am so very delighted when I find you waiting for me when I arrive, I really do think it would be wisest for you not to come up ...

Thursday 13th November

... We had a bad raid here last night, Martyn. There were about eight bombs dropped round about, one in Oakdale Road, one in Chase Road, one in Bressy Grove, and one on the riverbank near Chigwell Road. Your mother said the house shook when the bomb fell in Bressy Grove. I do so hope that no more bombs fall near you. I'm so afraid for you. It seems that you are never out of danger.

The little clock that you gave me has been reposing in my drawer ever since it gave up working, but on Sunday I got it out and told it sternly that you were coming home and would be very cross if it didn't go! – And it promptly started and has been going quite gaily, until this morning, when overcome by sorrow at your return to your beastly old aerodrome, it's stopped and all my persuasions to make it go are useless! ...

Friday 14th November

My darling girl,

Today we practised finding the drift of the aeroplane, and hence the speed and direction of the wind by means of a piece of apparatus known as the Course Setting Bomb Sight. It is mounted in the nose of the aircraft and one has to be full length on the floor to operate it. Whilst I was flying the aeroplane and my co-pilot was finding the wind, I completely lost the aerodrome. Luckily I recognised a Cotswold village that I knew, Bourton-on-the-Water to be precise, and so was able to get home safely.

But just at present I am suffering from that grievous malady which at times you have pretended to suffer from. The symptoms are that one's head fails to fit in one's hat without the application of considerable pressure, and the trouble is, as you have no doubt guessed, a severe attack of conceit!

The reason that my head has swollen so rapidly is that the results of the exams are out. Needless to say I haven't really put up a good show, but considering the disadvantage I am at, owing to scarcity of grey matter, it isn't really too bad.

Putting it briefly I got 92% in Navigation Theory (1st incidentally), 90% in Navigation Practical, 90% in Airmanship,

87% in Signals Theory (also 1st), 90% in Armaments and 82% in Practical Signals. All this, for some obscure reason, gave me a total of 82.6% in the whole exam, and so sixth-place out of 50.

So that is that, and my 'Wings' should be a dead cert. ...

12

20th November – 25th December 1940

While Martyn was completing his pilot training Lily began to contemplate Christmas.

At this time the air raids and the escalation of war continued. Coventry suffered two days of concentrated bombing which caused devastation to the city and two weeks later Southampton was heavily bombed, followed by Bristol.

89 Grenville Gardens
Woodford Green
Thursday 20th November

...Mr Chapman has taken himself off to the Wanstead office this afternoon and I've no knitting to do! I was wishing most intently that I had brought a book to read when I had the happy idea of writing to you... I am getting quite excited about Christmas! Brother Reg, Muriel and Janet have promised to come to dinner on Christmas Day – raids permitting. I do hope they can. It would be nice if you could come to dinner – but I mustn't be selfish. I expect your people will want you at home. I don't care really, as long as we are together! ...

Lily sweetheart,

I'm afraid I'm feeling just a little bit dopey at the moment ... The reason for this is, as you have probably guessed, that I was night flying last night and did not get to bed till six o'clock this morning – the time I am usually just getting up!

I did one dual circuit and then three solo ones, all of which were quite successful. Then at about two o'clock I had to go and do a couple more solo, and I must admit that I quite shook myself while doing these two.

It had become very bumpy, was raining, and the wind direction had altered so that the flares were cross wind. I took off and went round in the circuit, falling all over the sky, and then tried to land. I was almost down when I found I couldn't see the ground because of the rain, and at the same time I was drifting in towards the flares. I opened up and went round again, and this time got a red signal which meant I wasn't allowed to land because of another machine being in the way. I went round once more and got another red, and then third time lucky, got a green. I was bumping so much that I couldn't keep a straight course and zigzagged in. At last I landed, not at all sorry to be down!

I gather that my antics shook the people on the ground more than they shook me, though I was quite sufficiently shaken for one evening!

Some days ago we had a night vision test in which we had to read faintly illuminated figures in a pitch black room. I was told by my instructor yesterday that, on our course, a fellow named Bevan and myself had both been classed as 'exceptional', and that, I have a horrible fear, means night fighters. I hardly feel that hurtling around in a Hurricane from dusk to dawn is my 'meat', but I suppose I should get used to it.

I've just been into the Mess to investigate my letter rack. Sure enough there was a letter from you – you really are an absolute brick, sweetheart. I don't think you have 'let me down', if one can put it that way, once.

I was very pleased to learn that you reached home before things warmed up.

You know, darling, I had a feeling that you would make rather a charming speech about not letting your pleas override my judgement! I adored you for it, darling, but it could not conceal that your whole letter breathed the same words as you yourself whispered on Tuesday: "Martyn – Christmas!"

I know that your heart is perfectly right when it whispers those words, for my heart echoes 'Christmas' in an attempt perhaps to persuade my head to finally decide. But my silly head is still not dead sure, though events of the near future, plus your delightful tempting, will no doubt produce a discussion before Christmas comes!

In spite of my silly head, believe me, dearest, that I love you with all my heart and long for you to be mine ...

Saturday 22nd November

My darling Martyn,

Your letter has made me feel so anxious and unhappy about your future, for the thought of the danger that may be in store for you is an awful one! Night flying seems to me about as hard, as hazardous and dangerous, as it would be to shut one's eyes and walk into the road at Oxford Circus! I can only hope and pray that for some reason you may be spared such an awful task. Why, when your life is so precious, so terribly, terribly precious, are you compelled to risk it so often! My only hope is that God will take care of you. When I think about the terrible possibility of losing you, as I'm afraid I often do, I am quite comforted when I remember how very, very much your mother and father love you, for I feel sure that God wouldn't ruin three people's lives.

If only you are spared till that wonderful day when all our waiting and longing is over – I can face anything after that.

I object to you calling your head silly – it's not a bit, it's the darlingest head that ever was! And its thoughts are as dear and precious to me as its outward form.

Although it would be complimentary to me if you begged me to marry you each time you came home, I would very much rather see those qualities in you which cause you to consider carefully and be quite certain first! I think you'll make a grand husband, Martyn! – So don't blame that careful, wise head of yours – I love it.

You are coming home on Tuesday – aren't you? ...

Till Tuesday then, all my love,

Lil

Thursday 27th November

... You know, Lil, we have had some marvellous luck, haven't we, darling? I think we are the luckiest pair in the whole Fellowship. We see each other almost every week and then not just for a few hours in the evening but for a whole afternoon – or usually a whole afternoon at best! Thank heavens we are so lucky, sweetheart, for it is so terribly hard to wait more than a week at a time to see you ...

... This afternoon, Martyn, I bought two Christmas presents – a jar of face cream for Marie and a box of bricks for Janet, which I have just finished playing with – they're fun! I also bought some wool for a jumper which I've just started. It's pink – the colour of crushed strawberries and cream! It's rather a strain knitting it because I keep wishing it was blue! – But I'm being firm with myself ...I'm already deeply interested in the adventures of the people in James Hilton's book *Lost Horizon* – it's awfully good! You are a darling to bring me these presents! You know I think of the things you give me as being 'ours' rather than mine – because one day I hope we'll share everything, and you'll belong to me and I'll belong to you. I want that day to come so very, very much.

Good night, precious one, take care of yourself for me,

I love you so,

Lily

Friday 28th November

My dearest Martyn,

I haven't yet received a letter from you, so I am a little disappointed! I expect you arrived too late to write, but as long as you arrived safely I am content to wait.

I finished *Lost Horizon* – and enjoyed it very much. I do wish I'd seen the film. If ever it comes round again I'm definitely not going to miss it. I think the greatest surprise I got, though, was when I read at the end of the book, where the story ended, 'Woodford Green 1933'! Isn't it strange? James Hilton must have lived here whilst writing it.

It's icy cold here – ugh! How I hate it! I expect it's even colder at Cerney though. Mind you wear your overcoat!

I shall feel very envious tomorrow when I think of you waiting at the station for your people, for already I'm longing to see you again …

Martyn's parents stayed once again in Cirencester with Edith Townsend and her mother who had become firm friends. Martyn doubtless travelled back with them to Woodford for his Tuesday off.

Wednesday 3rd December

My darling Martyn,

I'm thinking of you now, speeding along in the train – at least, I hope you're speeding so that you reach Cerney and bed as early as possible, for I'm sure you must be tired.

For myself, I feel absolutely exhausted! It's a funny thing but I always do on Tuesdays – the Tuesdays you come home! Arthur attributes it to an afternoon off, Mum says it's excitement and Dad says it's love! I think my tiredness is caused by a combination of these three. Of course all those strenuous 'hugs' I give you are bound to make a difference. But I think that an early night and sweet dreams of someone to hold me tightly will remedy this.

In these, my saner moments, I can see how unwise was the request I made you at lunchtime. It was born of the deep desire that your nearness and dearness always arouses within me. You awake such an urgent want for your love, your physical love, that I feel I could go to any lengths of abandonment to satisfy it. – Keep me from this, Martyn. You are wiser, less impulsive than I, dear – they are traits in your character which I admire very much, which I rely on. I'll accept your decision.

When, as in this case, I feel in my heart of hearts that I am wrong I'll be honest with myself and let you decide. But when,

189

as in another case, my heart, my head, all of me, tell me I'm right, I'll say with all the temptation I'm capable of, "Martyn – Christmas?"

And now good-night, my own, my darling one – the dearest boy in the world to me.

Keep safe,
Lily

Thursday 4th December

My darling Martyn,

I've finished James Hilton's *The Passionate Year.* I started it this afternoon when I read two or three chapters at work, and by that time I was so completely enthralled that directly I'd finished tea I just had to go on and on until now, at quarter past nine, it's finished! It was grand, I loved it! Thank you so much for several hours of intense enjoyment! I'm not very good at describing or explaining why I liked it so much. You must read it yourself. You definitely must read it. We'll discuss it then.

I tried to listen to the *Choral Symphony* tonight, partly for my own enjoyment and partly so that I could imagine you sitting listening to it too. But even if the story hadn't claimed my whole interest, it would have been impossible to hear it as our wireless gave up the ghost, as it were, at a very early hour, owing doubtless to the disturbances outside. By which I mean that the raid tonight was such as is usually described by the BBC 'as heavier than of late'! ...

Friday 5th December

My dearest Martyn,

This afternoon I phoned your mother while she was at your Grandma's to tell her that you had arrived safely. It's a weekly arrangement of ours ... I was pleased to hear about Ken. I hope he gets his commission. He'll look marvellous in officer's uniform! (Though of course not quite as nice as my darling looks in his!)

I am being very careful not to get excited about your leave, in case it doesn't come off! All I ask and pray for, is that you have Christmas at home. It seems too awful to think about Christmas without you. I shall want you so much then.

There's a delicious smell in our house – do you know what it is? Christmas pud!! And, oh boy, does it taste good! I'll say! I stirred it and tasted it and wished! Now there's four of them bubbling away in the saucepans. So you see, you simply must come home at Christmas or you won't be able to have any...

Thursday 11th December

Lil dearest,

... I went down to the Townsends to say goodbye tonight, staying to supper, and while I was there the windows rattled violently all of a sudden as three bombs were dropped. Soon afterwards another lot came down, then the alert sounded and this was followed by a few more 'sticks'. Quite an excitement for the sleepy old town, though I doubt whether they fell nearer than a couple of miles!

It is a perfect moonlight night and now we are experiencing another air-raid! ...

Unofficially we have heard that we shall finish flying tomorrow and get our clearance forms for leaving Cerney completed on Friday ...

Finally, on 14th December, the momentous day came when Martyn was awarded his 'Wings'. Even during the war this was an event of major significance to a pilot. The simple woven cloth 'Wings' brevet – a recognition to Martyn, the RAF and the rest of the world that he was now a fully-fledged pilot – would have been presented by a senior officer to him and other successful members of his flight at a formal parade, which in peacetime it would have been possible for Lily and his parents to attend. There was always a (sometimes very short) period of leave after the end of pilot training, and Martyn would have been intensely proud to go back to Lily and his parents with his new wings sewn onto the left breast of his uniform. But the wings were only an indication that he was now a pilot – further training in a specific role had yet to come. So after less than a week's leave, he went off to his next posting at RAF Squires Gate to be trained in navigation and reconnaissance as a first step towards becoming a pilot in the RAF's Coastal Command.

Red Court Hotel,
South Promenade,
Blackpool
Monday 22nd December

... This hotel seems to be pretty good on the whole, though there is a shortage of hot water and absence of heat in bedrooms. The grub, so far, has been pretty good, and I think it should be extremely pleasant and comfortable here.

I am attached to No. 3 School of General Reconnaissance and shall be spending three months here doing little else than Advanced Navigation. Apparently one flies as navigator the whole time, and doesn't pilot the machine

at all. (I'm sure I shall have forgotten how to fly when the course is over.) If one comes through pretty well, it seems fairly certain that one gets on to flying boats! So it looks as if all my highest hopes and wishes are about to come true!

We apparently have Saturday afternoon and Sunday off but that hardly gives one a chance to get home when the train journey is ten hours! But darling, we have a long weekend about once a month apparently, from Friday evening till Monday morning, and that will just suit me down to the ground. I am afraid that once a month would be as much as I could manage anyhow, now that the fare is little under two pounds ...I really can't get over how lucky I am to be posted here, for all the fellows from Cerney, not posted here, seem to have been sent to either Hull or Manchester prior to going abroad.

I feel that it is very probable that we shall go abroad after leaving Blackpool, but that's three months off yet and at present the main consideration is weekend trips home!

I think I'd better close now, so goodbye for the present, sweetheart, and happy Christmas to you if this letter reaches you before the day. I love you so very much dearest one – this last week has shown me so clearly that I love you more than ever ...

Monday 22nd December

My own dearest Martyn,

I wanted to write to you last night, but my heart was so full of love and longing for you, that I did not attempt to put my thoughts on paper for the tears were pricking behind my eyelids and I knew I should cry. So I waited till this morning, as I shall still post it at the same time and this morning I don't feel quite so sad and lonely.

Although I know it's silly, I'm hoping and praying still that on Christmas morning I shall be able to kiss you under the mistletoe and wish you a 'Happy Christmas'!

I expect you're quite resigned to the worst, so that you will have a gorgeous surprise if you can come home, but that as you know is not my method. If it was, this paper would be wet with tears and by tonight I shall have almost convinced myself that you'll be coming home in time, and be getting quite excited!

I have always thought that some guardian angel must have been appointed to watch over you and to arrange any special little happinesses he could for our benefit – so wonderfully fortunate have we been so far. And though my faith in him was shaking on Friday, it still persists and keeps me expectant and hopeful. So much so, that when the postman knocked this morning I rushed to the door with a wild beating in my heart and a smile already on my lips! – Silly wasn't it?

I arrived back yesterday at quarter past one and looked in at Shadrack's but Mr Chapman had gone. After lunch I went up to Fellowship and found the parcels. I took your Pop's parcel down to Albert Road. On the way back I met Jack and Joan on their way home from the station. Jack looks awfully fit and well and very nice in his uniform.

Prissie then went home so I played badminton with the boys. We had some jolly good games. But they were very disappointed to hear that there wasn't going to be a party! They quite understood though when we told them that the star Master of Ceremonies had had to make a hurried departure!

We played on till the siren went at six o'clock, then we too made a hurried departure. Maisie had come by this time, so I walked down with her and decided to call in for *The Wind in the Willows*. By the time we reached her house the guns were going merrily so Mrs Hatton insisted that I stay to tea. So I did, and at about seven when the first lull came I decided to run for it. However, I had only reached the Southend Road when the plane came over and all the guns absolutely 'let go'! I ran as hard as I could for home through the worst packet I've ever been out in, listening intently for shrapnel. It was very much worse than Sunday night! But I eventually reached home safely.

What a mercy it was that we didn't have a party! For we could hardly have continued with such a barrage, and it kept it up all night until five o'clock this morning. It was the worst night we've had for a long while. How singularly strange that it should have come the night you left us! ...

This time last Sunday we were in Knighton, Martyn! Oh, if only you could be calling for me this afternoon and we could go to Fellowship together. I was so happy last Sunday – so terribly happy! ... Last week was so wonderful, wasn't it? I loved every minute and though I thought it impossible, I loved you more than ever before. You are so sweet to me, Martyn, so infinitely loving and kind – I loved you with all that was in me ...And now goodbye and keep safe, dearest,

Lily

Tuesday 23rd December

Dearest Martyn,

... It seems horribly dull to be just staying in tonight, after my evening spent with you and wandering about. I'm afraid tonight is not the night, though, for wandering, or even for fish and chip picnics, for there are several planes about and the guns have been firing steadily for the past hour. The welcome lull in the activities last week was obviously only in honour of your homecoming!

Arthur is very busily decorating the dining room with paper chains, balloons etc. I am supposed to be helping him, but I can't work up any enthusiasm for Christmas now – it's all gone, like a pricked balloon! – But oh, how quickly it would come to life again if you could come home, my darling. You must, you simply must – I'm hoping so hard! ...

Tuesday 23rd December

My darling girl,

Well, I've almost completed two days in Blackpool now, and I really think I'm going to thoroughly enjoy myself! No, I don't mean that I'm going to run riot in Blackpool, though there is every facility for doing so!

This is a veritable metropolis of amusements. In addition to three theatres, a dozen or so cinemas, crowds of dance halls and a skating rink, there are heaps of miniature circuses, waxworks and automatic machine booths. One could easily visit a different show every night and spend all one's pay into the bargain! Admittedly there is a play I want to see – Diana Wynyard and Rex Harrison in *No Time for Comedy* and a couple of films, *Lucky Partners* and *Night Train to Munich*.

Nevertheless I haven't the slightest intention of treating this as a long holiday, and anyhow I shall soon have plenty of work to do in the evenings.

I really do think I am going to enjoy this course though, and now there is no importance about getting one's 'Wings', it should be fairly easy to settle down to the three months without anxiously waiting for the weeks to go by. You will no doubt be pleased to know that we only do two and a half hours of flying a week here, and all of this as navigator.

The lecture syllabus is pretty large – it includes Advanced Navigation, Meteorology, Theory of Instruments, Coding,

Ship Recognition, Reconnaissance, and heaven knows what else.

We have lectures every day from 8:30 till 12:15 and 2:00 till 4:30. Pretty short hours really, and then of course we have a day and a half off every week. We do our flying during lecture times whenever the weather is good. It'll need to be good, for nearly all the flying is done over the Irish Sea!

We shall be working on Christmas Day but will have Boxing Day off. Personally it wouldn't worry me a bit having no days off at all, as it is impossible to use them to come home!

I am afraid it will be about a month before I see you again though, for apparently it is unlikely to be less than four weeks before we have the long weekend.

I'm very pleased to say that my pal Gary Williams from Cerney, the musical fellow, is also on the course so I am looking forward to going to some concerts with him, though at present there are no concerts because of an abundance of pantomimes!

I'm looking forward so much to receiving a letter from you, my sweetheart – I know you will have written at once, and expect there will be something for me at the aerodrome tomorrow.

Goodbye till tomorrow, Lily darling.
I'm loving you so very much,
Martyn

Christmas Eve

My darling Martyn,

I was terribly thrilled to receive your long letter, for though I'd been hoping it would come today, I was afraid it might be delayed owing to the Christmas rush! The post hadn't been when I left this morning but Dad, who has the day off, has just brought it up to me.

I was so glad to hear that you are happy and comfortable in your new surroundings. I'm afraid my highest hopes and wishes have nothing whatever to do with flying-boats (I 'ates em!) but as yours apparently have, I'll try and be glad for you!

Mr Chapman has just gone – he's going away for Christmas so I'm left in charge, with permission to shut the office at four.

During my lunch hour I popped in to see your mother. I always have a mood, half sad, half expectant, when I go to your house when you're not there. I always feel that perhaps you might come downstairs as I enter, or be standing by the fire and come forward for my hat and coat. Your presence seems to be everywhere in the rooms. This afternoon I almost saw you in the glass, looking so dear, so handsome! Oh, if only it was the real you!

But I am beginning to feel sad, as I do now if I think of you for long – and months to wait seems an eternity! ...

Christmas Day

My precious darling,

It's Christmas night – the family are having a belated tea, but I felt that a slice of cake was quite sufficient, so I'm taking this opportunity, the first today, to write to you.

This has been my unhappiest Christmas ever – I just couldn't stop thinking about you, wishing so terribly that you were here – it seemed all wrong without you. I've been horribly miserable all day! I shall be very thankful when Christmas is over and I don't have to pretend a jollity that I don't feel. Besides, I want to start living the next month as soon as ever I can because I want it to go quickly! (You can probably guess why!)

Janet is even more adorable than ever and runs in and out, beaming at everyone and saying "Happy Chw'mas."

Janet with her mother Muriel and her grandmother Christina

13

27th December 1940 – 3rd January 1941

Martyn redeemed himself by appearing at Lily's house last thing on Christmas Day and staying until the evening of Boxing Day.

89 Grenville Gardens,
Woodford Green
Friday 27th December

My precious darling,

It seems ages since I kissed you goodbye! I can hardly realise that it was less than twenty-four hours ago. I do so wish we could have Boxing Day over again. I can't really feel terribly sad today because I'm so thankful that my Christmas was a happy one after all – the happiest I've ever had! I don't think I've ever felt quite so overwhelmingly happy as I did on Christmas night when suddenly your arms were round me and your lips on mine. It has quite restored my faith in your guardian angel – I thought he'd forsaken you!

We're playing Monopoly, but I've gone bankrupt, so I'm writing this by the fire, amid the noise of tinkling dices and gunfire outside! Yes, with your departure has come the return of the air-raids.

When I left you last night I found the carriage which looked the warmest and had only just sat down as the train started.

For a little while my thoughts wandered caressingly round you. I thought about our marvellous day, about the things you'd said, about the comfort and contentment that was mine when I was sitting beside you with your arm around me. I was so happy just to feel you there, and to be able to look into your eyes sometimes, to see you smile. My love for you seems to increase with every hour spent with you – I pray that it will always be so! I thought then what a paradise our life together will be. We'll be so happy, Martyn, so divinely happy! I'm so longing for that day to come.

Muriel and Reg met me at the station – they enjoyed the walk. It was quite a treat for them!

I was late to bed and work was just the tiniest bit irksome this morning, but I'm so eager to live the days which must pass before we are together again because I can hardly bear to wait for you to come, my darling. Do come quickly. I love you so much, so very, very much.

Goodbye, sweetheart,

Lily

Red Court Hotel,
New South Promenade.
Blackpool
Saturday 28th December

My darling Lil,

Although it's not yet half past eight, I have gone to bed in an attempt to work off the effects of last night!

I'm afraid there were no sleeping berths left when I reached Euston, and anyhow they were all first class, so I toured the train until I found a nice comfortable compartment, then settled down on the seat for a few hours' sleep. … At Preston I had to change on to a slow train, and this I think was even colder than the first. It stopped at every station between Preston and Blackpool and finally reached the Central Station at about seven o'clock. I got to the hotel in time for breakfast and on arriving there was delighted to find two letters from you awaiting me. After breakfast I set off for the aerodrome, feeling none the worse for the journey ...

Oh Lily, darling, why is it that we seem to love each other more and more every day? I used to feel sure that the thrill of loving you would wear off as we got to know each other more intimately. I felt that at least we should only be thrilled by kisses and embraces, but my heart still beats fifteen to the dozen when I hold your arm or face you across the meal table.

I sometimes wish we didn't love each other such a terrible lot, for it is so awfully hard to live apart, and saying goodbye is almost torture now.

I have just been reading your letter – how you had lost interest in Christmas – but wasn't it a marvellous Christmas after all? I can hardly believe that I ever contemplated not coming home – and I know well enough that I shouldn't have enjoyed myself the weeniest bit, had I stayed in Blackpool.

Darling, I did so enjoy myself, though 'enjoy' is a perfectly inadequate word. I was delighted with the surprise I gave you on Wednesday night – delighted to find how happy I had made you by coming home.

The supper that night, and the lunch next day at Les's were so truly Christmassy and homely, and I forgot all about the war, and Blackpool and everything else.

As we were in each other's arms in Knighton, I was thrilled as I always am and shall be, but as much as anything I enjoyed those few hours before I left, when we sat by the fire with my arm round your shoulders and your head against mine. I felt so peaceful and contented then – as if it had been our own fire that we were sitting beside – with no cares or worries of being parted, but a long happy future ahead.

Maybe there is a long happy future – but maybe not. Perhaps I'm not sorry that we do not know.

I'm just going to start on my new box of biscuits!

I feel I want to reproach you for giving me so many presents – for wasting so much on one who deserves so little – but oh my precious one, it was so very, very sweet of you.

Talking of presents, I have just spent some of my present money on a recording of *The Bartered Bride Overture*. I have a feeling I shall probably buy some more records before long!

Well, my sweet one, I must close now or I shall never get the letter posted. So goodbye, darling, till tomorrow.

I'm loving you such a lot,

Martyn

Sunday 29th December

... On Saturday, Martyn, I rushed over to Ilford to spend my Christmas ten shillings. I knew what I wanted – some material. Yes, it's blue of course! Quite nice, I think, but wait till you see it, then I'll know!

I got back at about two o'clock and had dinner with Janet chatting to me most of the time. Then I washed and changed in preparation for going up to the Fellowship. I kissed Janet goodbye – how I wish she was still with us! – and arrived at Fellowship at half past three.

We had three or four games of badminton and then decided to start the party by ourselves as your Pop hadn't yet arrived. We all sat around the fire, only about nine of us, and tried to solve George's converted proverbs. When your father arrived we had the refreshments – some cakes and watery ale. Well, it was supposed to be raisin wine and tasted marvellous neat, but Tony diluted it rather generously, too generously in my opinion.

We passed the evening very pleasantly playing various games. I won in Musical Chairs twice! But the part I really enjoyed most was when we played Murder and I had to scream, being the murdered person! They all knew who it was!

We stayed until about half past nine as there were no sirens and I was escorted home by friend Clifford.

This morning I caught the train to Paddington to meet Nora. She is just the same as ever!

You remember hearing about Jack? – The pilot in training that she met last summer? Well, a week or so ago Laura was reading a list of 'Killed in Action' and saw his name on it. But Nora has three other latest attractions now, so I gather that the tragedy hasn't caused her many sleepless nights. We had a good chat and then Marjorie arrived and we went to the platform. The train was a Pru special so I met a lot of my old friends.

It seemed so odd to be standing on the platform waving goodbye. But it was absolutely marvellous to know that I was going home to dinner and to the Fellowship and to bed in my own little room, instead of away from everything and everyone! It was well worth going up there just to experience that delicious thankfulness and relief that I haven't got to go to beastly old Torquay! – And to think that if it hadn't been for me, clever little me, I might still be there!

At Fellowship, just as we were about to commence, E.J. put a packet on the mantelpiece and said to me, "You'll probably want to look at those later." It was the photographs of course. Wasn't it tantalising of him? You know how impatient I am! I kept looking at them longingly and wishing I could have a peep …

Lily darling,

When I posted my last letter I was on the way to see *Lucky Partners*. I never saw that film though, for when we reached the cinema there was a terrific queue, and we decided to try and get into something else. Can you guess what we finally saw? – *Waterloo Bridge*!

And really, Lil, it was a very good film indeed. Vivienne Leigh, incidentally, is a ballet dancer, and Robert goes to see her dance. And can you guess, ducky, what she appears in? – *Swan Lake* of course! …

This evening I went to the local Methodist Church, but was not particularly impressed with the service. In fact I really enjoyed it just about as much, and in the same way, as Jane of *The Water Gypsies* enjoyed her visit to Fish Street! I think I must have enjoyed the hymns and singing in just the same way, for it gave me the same feeling that "they were all jolly good chaps one and all!" And the sermon – well, it really was like the "unconvincing third act of a promising play".

In fact I'm afraid I looked round the congregation once or twice and thought to myself, "What on earth are we listening to this stuff for?" I came out, like Jane, with a peaceful, comfortable feeling, but far less emotionally stirred or satisfied than by the previous night's entertainment!

I feel somehow that these cynical thoughts are rather wicked, but I do think that the majority of preachers are producing the most appalling drivel, which helps no one at all, especially in times like the present.

But I must stop preaching to you now, for it is getting late and my eyes are drooping, and I must leave space and time to tell you how much I love you, dearest one, and how much I'm longing for you to be with me for always.

Bye, sweetheart,

Martyn

During the night of 29th December 1940, London experienced its most shocking bombardment yet. More than 100,000 bombs fell on London. High explosive bombs caused massive building destruction whilst incendiary bombs, though small, caused devastating fires covering an area greater than that of the Great Fire of London in 1666. The City of London, London's historical heart, suffered catastrophically and many of its renowned buildings were destroyed or severely damaged, including the Guildhall, eight Wren churches and three hospitals. St Paul's Cathedral alone, although damaged, still stood tall amongst the rubble and flames.

30th December

Darling Lil,

... Yes, we really have been marvellously fortunate – as I have so often said before. I can't believe somehow that this good fortune will last forever, but I know you will reproach me for such a pessimistic outlook!

The queer part is that you are so unduly optimistic and yet all these optimistic hopes nearly always materialise! ...

When I arrived back at lunchtime today I found your letter and also a parcel from Auntie Clarrie – a Christmas present, needless to say. And can you guess what the present was? A butterfly box of chocolate biscuits!!! I have three butterfly boxes here now – but one is empty and the second has been started!

We had a warning at lunchtime today, but the all-clear went ten minutes afterwards and nothing exciting happened at all.

You, though, seem to have had a pretty awful time last night with the storm of incendiaries. I do hope that Woodford escaped the worst of the business.

As it's past eleven I think I'd better close down till tomorrow.

So goodbye, sweetheart, and heaps of love to you,

Martyn

Unbeknown to Lily, Martyn wrote a letter to her father and Mr Smith duly replied, with Lily's mother actually writing the letter.

30th December 1940

Dear Martyn,

I received your letter this morning. In this as in most cases I am father's secretary. This is his reply.

It was indeed a great surprise to us, as of course you are both rather young to take such a step in life and we had no thought of losing Lily so soon.

We trust neither of you will decide to do so without thinking the matter over very carefully, and praying to be led to do the right and best thing.

We, Lily's parents, will give you our consent providing your own parents are quite agreeable.

We are confident that you have given this matter your fullest consideration and our acquaintance with you so far has given us every reason to believe you to be worthy of our trust. We hope that this trust in you will ever continue.

With this we send our good wishes and hope you will be spared to each other and enjoy many happy years together when you settle down.

Yours very sincerely
Christina and Frank Smith

My dearest Martyn,

... I expect you too know now that the all-important answer was 'Yes'!

Isn't it grand! I think so. I hope all your qualms have gone now, and oh, I do hope that my impatience hasn't led you to do something you will regret. You are <u>sure</u> now darling, aren't you?

I'm so proud and happy to think that I'm really going to belong to you for always – and so terribly excited! It's the most wonderful compliment you've ever paid me. I do wish that you were home now so that we could share our happiness – but it's not very long to wait is it? Have you heard any more about the actual date of your weekend? Do let me know as soon as you can won't you, so that I can get excited! As though I wasn't that already! ...

1st January 1941

Lily darling,

I was very sorry to read that, after my careful and elaborate efforts to prevent it happening, you had managed to discover so easily the origin and contents of my letter to your Dad.

I had hoped that I should have been able to weigh up and consider his reply without you knowing what it was or even of its existence. But the deed's done now, so I shall have to let you into the business and you'll have to grin and bear it.

As you anticipated, the answer was not a direct 'no', but no stretch of imagination could class it as a definite 'yes'.

Of course, it is not a question of 'we two' (I'm glad to say) but of 'when to' (oh, horrible pun) and your people, as mine, seem to feel that, though they've seen some young marriages, this one would really be the limit.

I suppose that to our parents we must seem absolute infants and I can imagine the shock to them must be as great as if Janet started riding a motorbike.

I cannot see though that the present position would be the slightest bit different if we were three or four years older. My position anyhow would be just as good – yet bad, and just as safe – yet unsafe.

I do however appreciate the wisdom of waiting until we are older, for no doubt in four or five years' time we should know definitely whether we were destined for a long span of happy married life, or no married life at all.

These days I am living in two worlds – half in the South Woodford world, where one plans for the future, considers things carefully, and decides what is the 'done' thing to do, and the other half lives in the Service world, where one takes things as they come, lives in the present and marries as soon as the right girl comes along, regardless of age or anything else!

Believe me, these two worlds are miles apart, as different as the wartime from the peacetime world and it is terribly difficult to steer a middle course.

When I'm speaking to my pals here, I just can't think why I'm hesitating and yet when I'm at home or corresponding with your people or mine, I can't think what ever could have made me contemplate the fantastic idea of marriage!

I suppose in theory I should take advantage of the two uncertain conditional 'YES's and whisk you off to the jewellers to buy an engagement ring before they'd recovered from the shock.

But somehow I can't do that. If I'd had two definite 'YES's I should have been delighted, while definite 'NO's, so disappointing, would at least have relieved the tension.

But these indefinite answers make me more undecided than ever.

Maybe if I survived the war and we were married now, a worse tragedy might result than if I didn't survive and we weren't married at all.

This is all a bit morbid, perhaps a little cynical, but really, darling, I don't know what to do, which way to turn.

I'm sort of waiting for a sign, and yet I know I somehow shan't get one, and shall have to make a decision which will be about as sure as if it had been decided by the toss of a coin.

Oh darling, darling, I do wish I could see the right way, for I love you so very, very much, and want you with me for always.

Martyn

Thursday 3rd January

My darling,

I was bitterly disappointed to receive your letter, for when you wrote to my father I thought that all your doubts and fears had gone at last. I thought that your people, though not eager for our marriage, were at least resigned, and I thought that you yourself had reached a definite decision in favour of our immediate engagement. I expected an ardent, eager, impatient letter from you in reply saying, "Name the day!"

— And now, imagine my distress, my disappointment, to learn that you are still as undecided, as uncertain as ever you were!

Forgive me if my feelings lead me to say things that I should repress, but honestly darling, this is a beastly position for me to be in. For you is the danger, the adventure of your flying career, and when you come home on leave I'm always there to love you, to look at you with adoring eyes. Then comes the goodbye – I'm very weary of them – and you go away again and I'm so unhappy, wondering if there will be a next time!

If I thought you didn't love me my pride would prevent me from saying "Marry me" – but I know you love me. People as fine and as straight as you are don't lie. – But you will say it's not a question of loving you, but the risk of our marriage not being a success. But I still insist that it's my risk entirely – I know what that risk is and I am willing, eager to take it. I've said that so often, I'm tired of saying it. Then why? – Why your hesitation? The worst that can happen is your being killed. I'm not running away from that possibility – I'm facing it. But I can't face it unless we are married first.

Would you then willingly give me a broken heart, a dull despair, a wish to end my life? For that is what you are doing.

The prospect of your being without a job at the end of the war doesn't frighten me in the least! I don't see why it should you. Where is your pluck, your faith? If you are alive and well that's all that matters.

I'm sorry if I was to remain in complete ignorance of the subject of your letter to my father. But we are a very 'family' family, you know – and Dad never has letters which are so private that the family may not know the contents. His letters are, without exception almost, addressed to Mr and Mrs Smith so just that 'Mr' aroused curiosity. The question of our engagement has been discussed quite openly and freely by Dad and Mum, Arthur and Les. I'm sorry but it has. (I'm more sorry now – it's rather an anti-climax!)

You will be very surprised I expect when I tell you that I have seen the answer to your letter. – I am sorry, but I did. And I must say that I read it very differently to what you did, for I took it to mean a definite 'yes', providing that your people were agreeable. From the subsequent remarks I have learnt that my people are quite prepared to give me to you, are quite sure of the suitability and do not hold our youth as a serious drawback.

Oh my darling, each day is precious – life is so <u>uncertain</u>, our love is so certain. I'm trying to catch happiness and you're running away from it – afraid of the shadows that lurk by the way. If anything happened to me would you still say "it was as well we waited"? I think the 'yes' or 'no' of your answer would be better than tossing a coin.

Goodbye my lover.

I'm yours for the taking,

Lily

14

6th January – 12th March 1941

The RAF base at Blackpool was expanding during this period to accommodate not only the pilots training in reconnaissance and the air mechanics receiving technical training, but also the large number of new recruits receiving their basic training. This is probably why Martyn was required to move from the Red Court Hotel to Saint Anne's Hotel at Saint Anne's-on-Sea which was to the south of Blackpool and nearer to the aerodrome.

St Anne's Hotel
St Anne's-on-Sea
6th January

My darling girl,

When I read through your last letter I realised that in reality I had already made up my mind and tonight I have written two other letters in addition to this one!

Perhaps what most decided me was the last paragraph in your letter – it made me realise exactly how you must feel by showing me so clearly how I feel myself ...Only one thing matters now, my darling, and that is that I have decided, at last – and so only one thing remains to be done and that is to buy the ring!

Oh Lil, darling, I'm so glad I've decided at last, for it has been so very difficult, and even if I am still rather afraid, I feel quite steeled to meet the future now.

It is so cowardly of me to fear, when you are so confident and courageous, but sweetheart, it is for you that I was (perhaps I still am a little) afraid, or for us after the war – for myself I don't care a damn ...Darling, I love you with all my heart and soul and being – you know that, don't you, and please believe me that I shall go on loving you for always, my little sweetheart.

I love you so much, Martyn

89 Grenville Gardens
Saturday 12th January

Dearest Martyn

... I like the sound of the zircon rings you described in your letter. I should think they're just the sort of thing I'd like.

There was no badminton yesterday afternoon so I decided I'd like a good walk and rang up Muriel. It wasn't a very nice day – damp and windy, but I walked all the way.

I played with Janet for a little while and then Muriel and I sat by the fire and talked romantically about engagements and marriages and honeymoons! I'm getting to be very fond of Muriel – she will certainly be a great help now. I shall be able to ask her advice about lots of things. We had quite a long confidential chat, and then Reg came in, so we had tea. I left soon after tea and Reg walked to the Savoy with me.

The siren went soon after I got home, and we had a very noisy three hours ...

... I sat with your mother in church today and went round to your house with her afterwards, with the idea of having another look at the photographs. Your mother asked me to stay for tea and we talked about you and how you would be coming home next weekend and I told them the latest news.

As I sat at the table, I kept thinking that next week (if I'm invited) I'll be able to look up and see you sitting there and love you with my eyes!

After we'd finished we sat around the fire, but alas, not for long: at about half past six the sirens started to wail, so I made a somewhat rapid departure!

I reached home before the gunnery started but it's been very noisy since ...

Finally, Martyn took Lily to buy the ring and they became engaged.

Wednesday 16th January

My darling Martyn,

... It was torture saying goodbye to you tonight – even worse than before. When you'd really gone and I opened the front door I felt an awful lump rising in my throat and I thought I was going to cry.

But when I walked in and took off my glove there were eager exclamations about my ring! They all like it very much indeed and were most interested to hear about our experience in getting it.

In telling them about the day's happenings, my awful longing to run away and cry subsided ...

Now that you have gone all the light and warmth in life have suddenly vanished – but the one bright spot (literally!) is my darling little ring ...

Sunday 19th January

Dearest Martyn,

... When your father wrote his talk for this afternoon's Fellowship, I think he must have expected you to be there, for several remarks seemed as though he had intended to address them to you – to us. But he was definitely on our side. For instance, in one place he said, "What would have been wrong for a boy of 21 to do, ten years ago, would be quite right and sensible today." And further on, towards the end, he said, "Don't always be held back by the fetters of age-old customs and principles."

I wish you had been there – I'm sure parts of it were meant for you.

All the girls noticed my ring! (It was just the wrong day to be chairman!) They all examined it afterwards and thought it lovely ...

I'm now listening to the musical biography of Grieg. You know the more I hear his piano concerto, the more I like it – I'm so glad you've got the records. Of course, you know I'm only marrying you for your records, don't you?! ...

Tuesday 21st January

Dearest Martyn,

... I really had almost given up trying to get a new diary and I thought I'd have to give up writing my autobiography! I was getting quite worried about it! But today I succeeded in getting one, so I have been very busy copying out the contents of the past three weeks into my new one. I turned idly to the clean white pages of April, May and June and I wondered what I should be writing on them. If only we could know. I wish it would hurry up and come to an end, this longing and suspense.

Muriel rang me up this afternoon to ask me to come to Janet's birthday party on Saturday. Don't you wish you could come? – I do. She was very interested to hear about our engagement. She thinks I've 'picked a winner'! Honestly though, she added, "Reg and I like him very much." Of course I don't think I'm meant to tell you – but then, I tell you everything, don't I. So I won't leave out the nice things ...

Wednesday 22nd January

My darling Martyn,

... I was delighted to receive this morning a very pretty card from your Grandmother and Auntie May congratulating me on our engagement. It says – 'May the joy which is yours today, keep increasing for many, many, happy years!'

Wasn't it nice of them? – I don't think we need to wonder any more what they think about it! I feel terribly pleased that they have accepted me so kindly as being worthy of their darling. I'm so glad they like me ...

Thursday 23rd January

... How curious that Dad should have made those seemingly pointed remarks in his talk. Do you really think he was 'on our side' or was he trying to excuse the irresponsible actions of his offspring?!

I was most shocked to learn that you were only marrying me for my records – but it gratifies me to realise that I shall always be able to keep your interest alive by the simple expedient of buying new records! ...

Tuesday 4th February

My dearest girl,

... We did a Dead Reckoning exercise today over the Irish Sea, flying to lightships and sea positions.

We started off very well, flying correct courses and arriving at our objectives slap on time. But on the last leg of the flight the wind veered right round through 180 degrees, with the result that instead of striking land at Blackpool, we found ourselves over Barrow-in-Furness!

Luckily we spotted where it was and soon got back on track to the aerodrome. We couldn't see Blackpool when we were almost on top of it, but perfectly clear in the distance were the snow-capped Pennines and mountains of Wales. The sea was as calm as a millpond and the Isle of Man looked most attractive in the sparkling sunshine ...

Sunday 9th February

Lily dearest,

Today I really have got something to tell you, for this morning I had one of the most exciting flights for months!

We were detailed to do an ordinary four-legged flight, but when we took off we found ourselves flying straight into thick fog that was slowly coming in from the sea. While we were still climbing up to the correct height for the trip, we decided that it would be stupid to attempt it, so the pilot endeavoured to go down and land.

We were up at about one thousand feet so he put the nose down and made a shallow dive through the stuff, hoping to break through it. We went down and down and down and all of a sudden, through a break in the mist, we saw a road, with houses and a tram car rushing up to meet us! We couldn't have been more than a hundred feet above the deck as I could clearly see some people who were getting on the tram staring up at us! I guess they were as scared as we were, for you can imagine how much it would shake you to see an aeroplane hurtling towards you out of the fog!

I needn't tell you that we shot up again with considerable rapidity and were soon on top of the fog layer. But before we had had time to get over this, we suddenly saw the top of Blackpool Tower come charging towards us like a buoy on a sea of cloud. As we swung away in a steep turn, it came horribly close and then vanished into the murk.

For ten very anxious minutes we circled round and round and every now and again the tower appeared, shot past us and then disappeared again! Just as we were getting quite dizzy watching the antics of the tower, a radio message came through telling us that the visibility was nil at Squires Gate and instructing us to fly up to Carlisle and land there.

When we got the radio message we hadn't the slightest idea whether we were over the land or the sea! Luckily we found ourselves crossing over the promenade a few minutes later and were able to swing round and creep up the coastline for eighty miles or so until at last we reached Carlisle.

We landed there, waited for an hour or more until a message from Squires Gate informed us that the weather was clear, and then set course home again.

There was still some mist about when we landed at Squires Gate but we got down alright and so ended the trip – but it was fun while it lasted!

I was most amused to read in your letter of Thursday that Janet's bow-wow had been christened 'Raf' as RAF was written on the box. I was also awfully flattered to hear that she had recognised my photo! ...

Wednesday 12th February

My darling Martyn,

... It's been a marvellous day here; as mild and sunny as spring-time. So, as soon as I'd left the office I went home to see whether there was a letter from you, and then set off for my walk. I went up to Horn Lane and along the Green to Monkhouse Lane where I met Reg and Muriel, who were just going home. I persuaded them not to and we walked on into Knighton Woods. Dear Knighton! You seemed so close to me tonight when I was walking along the familiar paths – sweet memories of you were thronging into my mind all the time.

We went down the lane until we came to the end and so out into Roding Valley. We crossed the new bridge and then walked straight along until we arrived at Woodford Station – and so home. It was a gorgeous evening and the sky was perfect.

I had some more congratulations yesterday and they think my ring is lovely ...

With a rare weekend off, Martyn went home; but this time, rather than being buoyed by his visit he became very despondent.

Lily my dearest girl,

I felt that I must write to you at once to tell you how sorry I am that I was so moody in the train last night. I don't know how it was, but as I stood on George Lane platform, I suddenly had the wretched feeling that all these trips home were monotonously futile. I felt angry that I was always having to leave home again and that probably for the remainder of my life I should never spend more than a day or so at home.

I felt jealous of your good fortune on being at home. I had a sense of a feeling that has been haunting me for some weeks; a feeling of aimlessness, uselessness, futility. I feel disorientated in some way – yet I don't know why or what with.

Some months ago I was absorbed in the church, in the Fellowship and the Fellowship Circle. I had something to think about then, ideas of ideals to get my teeth into, a philosophy to work out and a better world to plan for.

But now I've really lost all interest in these things. I've quite lost faith in the church in its present form and although the Fellowship is still going, and I delight in seeing all my friends in it when I am home, it seems to be doing nothing worthwhile.

Up here of course there is nothing to inspire me. We live entirely in the present, with little or no thought for the future – which is the national theory after all.

But I feel at a loose end now. I lack an ambition and I need one dearly.

I wish sometimes that I could live in the more immediate future, that like yourself I could regard marriage as my immediate aim and my nearest goal. I wish I could place the importance on it that you do – that all girls do – but somehow I'm unable to ...I wish I could throw all my enthusiasm into carving myself a career but a career seems a rather futile, selfish thing and as long as I work now with a reasonable amount of diligence, that career will take care of itself, as far as it is possible for a post-war career to develop from a war career.

No, I want something else to strive for, something else to aim at and just at present I don't know what my goal is, nor do I know where, when or how to start.

So I am feeling all confused and despondent.

My moodiness spoilt the journey to town for me. I felt that I had somehow wasted the time with you and when I got on the tube at Liverpool Street I wanted to rush back to you and cover you with kisses!

I just had to tell you all these thoughts, darling – I hope I haven't shocked you and I hope you'll be able to sympathise with me, but if it's hard to do this, please believe one thing, sweetheart. Believe me that I love you with all my heart and soul, my dearest darling.

I do love you so much,

Martyn

Tuesday 18th February

Lily, dearest,

... This afternoon we had organised games. No, we didn't sweat our socks off with soccer – we went skating! Needless to say I could hardly stand up at first, but by the end of the afternoon I had passed the wallflower stage and was making short trips across the floor. It really is great fun and I'm quite stung by the 'skating bug'. I feel that after two or three more afternoons I ought to be able to navigate the floor without difficulty.

One of our instructors, a young fellow, brought his wife along and oh, I did envy them skimming over the ice. Girls look so delightful as they slide over the ice in their tight, short-skirted dresses with high-topped skating boots, and I visualised you on the ice and dreamt how perfect you would look. When I've learnt how to skate I'll teach you, darling – I'm sure it's even more thrilling and delicious than dancing! …

Friday 21st February

Lily, darling girl,

I was so glad, so very glad to receive your letter today, for it just gave me that shake-up that I'd been needing awfully badly. Heaven knows that my whole life pivots on these trips home to see you, that from the very moment that I left you at Liverpool Street I was dreaming and longing for the minute when I should see you again.

I love and wonder at your sweetness and devotion in braving bombs to meet me and in waiting for hours for my train to come in.

I don't really regard marriage as indifferently as I inferred in my letter. I've been putting off our wedding just because I'm scared – dead scared.

I don't want to be morbid but I can't believe for a moment that I shall survive the war and then, if I did and we were married, we should probably be in the most terrible state. There will be an awful slump after the war and useless people like myself will just have to scrape a living by snatching any odd cheap job that comes their way. We should probably be absolute paupers and isn't it perhaps a rather foolish thing for you to jeopardise all the happiness of your future life by tying yourself to me for a spell of happiness that might last less than a year?

Lily, believe me, please believe me, that I love you now more than I have ever done, and it's because I want so much to be with you and love you in the years to come that I'm so moody and mad and hysterical about my position now.

But I see even clearer now that I just cannot live without you – darling we must get married in the summer ...

Sunday 23rd February

... We flew again yesterday morning, and as the Bothas had once more been banned from flying over the sea we were sent up to make position fixes by taking sights of the sun. For this purpose, we had to go above the clouds and did in fact go up to eleven thousand feet – the highest I have been! I got violent earache on the way down because of the large pressure change, but I'm glad to say that it very soon went off. Just as we were coming into land we noticed another Botha on the beach! Imagine my surprise on landing to learn that its occupants had been Guy Holdsworth and Mike Young!

Both the engines had cut almost as soon as it had taken off and the pilot had to force-land at once. The machine hit the sea first and then careered along on to the beach until it finally stopped with its nose dug well into the sand. Being lucky enough to come down in shallow water, they got little more than a shaking and a wetting, though the aeroplane was a wreck. Guy has some whacking bruises and Mike had to have a gash on his head stitched up but apart from that they're ok.

Just as we were landing, two Defiants in front of us got rather too close together and one chopped the other's tail off with his propeller. The first landed quite safely, though with a bit of a bump, but to our amazement the tail-less one took off again, hopped over the house tops and also landed on the beach!

Two machines on the beach in one afternoon – and a Sunday afternoon too! Didn't that give the inhabitants of Blackpool a thrill! ...

Tuesday 25th February

Lily darling,

... I was very sorry to hear about Jack, although I'm really not a bit surprised. More and more pilots are being trained abroad and most of the Flying Training Schools are being moved, one by one, to Canada or to Africa. Cerney was due to go early in the spring as it was proposed to station a Bomber squadron there instead of the flying school. If Jack is trained in Canada, he will probably come back to England for operational work but if he goes to Rhodesia I'm afraid he will go out east.

Then of course I was most thrilled to hear about the dancing on Saturday night. I'm just longing for you to teach me the quickstep – the whole prospect of dancing with you again makes my blood tingle with delight!

The discussion on Sunday afternoon sounded most profitable, though I was rather shaken by Prissie's idea of Dressmaking, Cookery and Carpentry classes for fellows as well as girls! I shall need some cookery lessons if I get on to flying boats though, for the second pilot is also chief cook and has to produce delicious dishes of boiled eggs and kidney soup!

I should love to see you digging the allotment, Lily dear. It was very noble and energetic of you to volunteer ...

...This afternoon we flew again going down to Hereford by way of Northwich and Wrexham and on the way back we did another photographic reconnaissance of Fleetwood harbour.

The last leg from Fleetwood to Squires Gate was quite amusing though, for we 'beat' up the seafront right down the coast, flying about ten foot off the sea and 'hurdling' any piers that came in our way! I should think it gave the people on the front quite a thrill – from the way they were staring and waving at us anyhow! ...

Thursday 6th March

Lily dearest,

... I read with considerable interest – and a certain amount of amusement! – about your enthusiasm for the allotment and all the hard work you're putting into it. Jolly good show, darling. Let me congratulate you heartily on your efforts! Keep on persevering with the digging until I am able to give you a hand.

How dare you have another lover without my express permission – though perhaps on this occasion I'll excuse you! No, darling, I'd really rather have George play Robert

Browning than do it myself, for I know I should go all coy playing love scenes with you! ...

I have just come back from a performance of Mendelssohn's *Elijah*. When I agreed to go I hardly expected the performance to be a particularly good one, so I was agreeably surprised when it turned out to be quite excellent.

It's now about half past eleven. I've just consumed a cress roll and an apple tart and I'm writing this letter in bed! But Orrocks is trying to go to sleep, so I think I'd better say goodnight now and turn the light out.

Darling, I'm thinking of you and just longing for Saturday week.

Goodbye dearest one,
Martyn

Friday 7th March

Lily dearest,

... I've been swotting again tonight, so once more I'm writing this letter to you in bed.

Today we had a Reconnaissance exam and it turned out to be quite an easy one. It was a three hour paper and it took me every minute of my three hours to complete it. Even then it was a bit of a rush, for the questions were all very long ones, requiring extensive tabulated answers.

Tomorrow we've got Patrol and Search and though I can't say I feel that I know so very much about the subject, I reckon that I should be able to concoct some suitable answers!

Our Ship Recognition exam is on Tuesday and our Met exam on Wednesday, so I reckon I'm going to have a busy time over the next few days ...

… After flying for about half an hour today we ran into such thick soupy clouds that we decided to turn back. We felt our way back by map reading, for we were only flying at about 800 feet and there were too many high hills and balloon barrages around us to be pleasant! Anyway, we got back alright, only to find that some red-hot news had just been received.

Our Group recommendations had come through and these have only to be approved by the Air Ministry to become definite. I am, as I expected and hoped for, going to Silloth on Hudsons!

Five chaps went on boats after all, lucky beggars. About eight fellows are going to Barnstaple on Ansons – Roy Orrock and Mike Young are amongst them, and all the rest of us are off to Silloth. I should have liked Barnstaple of course, but I must admit that I should have been pretty fed up if I had missed Hudsons – as you know I'd always wanted to go on Hudsons if I couldn't get flying boats.

But I know what you're thinking – what about leave?!

Well, unless anything is altered, I shall be having eight days commencing on Saturday next! Grand, isn't it. I'm getting frightfully excited now! …

Darling, won't it be marvellous to be able to see each other for eight days in succession! I'm longing to be with you again, for I do love you so much, my little sweetheart ...

Sunday 9th March

Lily darling,

I've just arrived back at the hotel after a very enjoyable day in Manchester ...

Mr Thompson and Grandpa Thompson came to meet me and they greeted me with the surprising and delightful news that Ken was home on forty-eight hours leave! Wasn't it an extraordinary coincidence and a remarkable spot of luck? Ken is staying at Shrivenham for only a fortnight more and then he has five weeks leave and proceeds to his next station as a brand-new officer. I guess he'll look frightfully smart in full regalia!

Ken and Iris are getting engaged when he has his leave. They were apparently ring-hunting yesterday but Iris couldn't find one she liked. Iris was most keen to know what your ring looked like and I tried to describe it – but not very successfully.

I gave them a detailed description of your allotment activities and they thought you were very plucky to tackle the job, though they were naturally pretty amused when I told them that you had to stand on the fork to get it to penetrate the ground!

Do you realise, darling, that next Sunday evening I shall be with you and, posting permitting, on the following Sunday evening as well!

I can hardly wait for the next five days to go by – I am so longing to see you.

Goodbye, sweetest, till tomorrow,
Martyn

Martyn beside a Blackburn Botha

Monday 10th March

... Today I actually flew the Botha for the first time. Yes, the pilot suggested that I flew the kite for a while whilst he stretched his legs, and so I took over. It's really a very nice machine to fly on a steady course – I hardly had to touch the controls at all.

I do hope that these raids quieten down again during next week and I hope too that the weather keeps fine – I want so to help do a spot of digging on your allotment ...

Tuesday 11th March

Lily dearest,

... You must spend more time writing to me than you do writing out coal bills, for by this morning's post I received three letters from you! Not of course that I want to deter you from writing!

I was extremely sorry to hear that the raid on Saturday night was as bad as the papers said it was. I do hope they'll use up all their bombs by next Saturday. Still, you managed to have a very enjoyable ramble by the sound of it, followed by a good spot of dancing, before you had to face the music. You make no mention of bombs dropping close to you. I only hope you haven't had any more narrow escapes.

In spite of Dad's timing miscalculations, I was glad that *The Barretts of Wimpole Street* went off successfully and according to plan and I was awfully pleased to hear that Prissie had now found an old woman to help and that everyone had volunteered their services in unison. I know how keen she's been to try and get this sort of work underway and I do hope the efforts are successful ...

Wednesday 12th March

My dearest Martyn,

This will be the last letter I write before seeing you – it's great to be able to write that!

I'm only expecting you to be at home until Friday – as a precaution against disappointment! Last time, you remember, I was so sure that you would have the whole week, and was bitterly disappointed when you had to go. On Friday, when you're still here, I shall be rewarded!

Your letter has been a cause of great disturbance in our house! When I reached home Mum informed me that there were two letters for me. I snatched the first eagerly from the mantelpiece, then looked for the second – and it had disappeared! It had slipped down between the wall and the mantelpiece. Of course I was most upset. It was so tantalising – so near and yet so far. We tried all sorts of methods for getting it up – a saw, a bread knife and a piece of wire – but in vain. At last we decided that nothing could be done until Arthur came home, so I went off to my allotment, wondering very anxiously why there should be two letters and what was in the second one!

I was the only one there tonight but George came later and chatted to me and escorted me home. When I reached home I found that Arthur had unscrewed the wooden framework and lifted it out, thus disclosing your letter! It was a relief to get it.

I was terribly pleased to hear that it might be Friday – I hadn't dared to hope for that, I do hope it is. I shall come and meet you of course, so be sure you let me know in time. If there is a bad raid I may find my way to the nearest shelter at Euston, but I shall most likely come out in time for your train. So look out for me!

I'm looking forward so eagerly, so impatiently to see you – longing for our week of happiness! ...

Bye-bye my dearest, till Friday (or Saturday!).

I'll tell you how much I love you then,

Lily

Wednesday 12th March

Dearest Lily,

...This, darling, will be the last letter that you will receive from Saint Anne's and I'm very sorry that I can't tell you exactly when I shall be coming home. I probably shall not be finished till Friday evening and in that case it will be Saturday morning or afternoon before I reach Euston. So, I'm afraid I can't ask you to come and meet me – but I shall be at the 'coal box' as soon as I can! ...

15

After their eight days together, Martyn set off to the RAF station in Silloth on the Cumbrian coast, west of Carlisle, while Lily continued working for the coal merchants and immersed herself in various other worthwhile activities.

From the outbreak of war, the Silloth airfield was used for training pilots and in November 1939 No 1 Operational Training Unit of Coastal Command was established there. By the spring of 1941 Lockheed Hudsons, which were used by the RAF for reconnaissance, were the main training aircraft. The difficult and dangerous training involved low level flying and gunnery practice using a target towed by another aircraft.

My dearest girl,

... Now let me tell you about Silloth.

It is a much larger place than I had imagined, but don't get the wrong idea, it is by no means a big place. It is a very bleak little holiday resort, presumably frequented by the people of Carlisle. There is no 'front' but the street which is nearest to the sea looks out on to a strip of green which borders the lower cliff. The street is paved with cobblestones and short knobbly trees line the pavements. The hotels have flat, geometric, un-decorative fronts painted in the drabbest colours of grey, dirty white, and brown. In fact the place looks just like a tiny French seaside place – a miniature Dieppe!

I should think the town boasts as many shops as Theydon Bois and every shop sells everything, from soap to sardines!

There is one cinema, which is rather smaller than the Lecture Hall, but the programme is changed three times a week.

Silloth is actually a small port and is handling quite a lot of traffic, now that places like Bristol and Glasgow have been bombed.

But, darling, the one great snag of the place – we have one day off a week and never a weekend. The thought of two months without seeing you is the one thing that has depressed me since coming here. But I'm not going to let it, for if in three or four weeks' time there seems no chance of forty-eight hours leave, then I shall come home for the day!

The whole of the aerodrome is built on the hut principal. The officers' mess is a series of huts, as are all the offices and classrooms too.

From the outside it looks pretty rough, but actually it's very comfortable and homely. Both the lounge, or anteroom, and dining room are about the same width as the Fellowship room but twice as long. The bedrooms are quite small but hold two beds, a wardrobe, washstand and table. I'm sharing with Jimmy Richards. I've fixed up my radio, set out my pictures (need I say who of!) and there is a stove in the room which pleasantly warms it and which one can sit by and read.

This morning I have done my first one and a half hours' flying on Hudsons. I think I'm going to like these aeroplanes very much, though at present I am quite bewildered by the masses of instruments, levers, knobs etc. with which the pilot is surrounded. It takes quite a time to get used to them apparently; in fact, we spend the first month of the course just learning how to use them to fly! The Hudson's got a lovely roomy interior, there's even a bed or couch on which the navigator can recline when he gets a bit tired or fed up.

The Hudson is one of the few machines in the RAF with automatic pilots and these really are a treat. You just switch on 'George' and then go to sleep or tuck into your sandwiches! If you want to turn, climb or dive you simply turn the little knobs like those on the radio set – it is all too, too simple! …

A Lockheed Hudson

Learning to fly the Hudson

Lily my darling,

I am just sitting by the fire in my bedroom listening to *Carmen*. My radio is working particularly well tonight and I am thoroughly enjoying the performance and wondering whether you are listening too?

Your letter was waiting for me when I came into lunch today – I felt terribly ashamed when I found that you had anticipated that I had not washed my hair yet!

I have had such busy evenings since coming here, though – writing letters, swotting up notes on handling Hudsons and doing another important job. Can you guess what it is? I have just finished editing *Dear Brutus* [by J.M.Barrie] for the Fellowship play reading. I have cut out three characters entirely and shortened it down to approximately three quarters of an hour.

It's rained continuously all day today and the aerodrome was just a large mud swamp. I think we must've been having the weather that you had on Monday night – how annoying that you weren't able to get down to your seed sowing. Still, this weather seems to have spared you from raids. I see that London has had no raids for five nights in succession.

I imagine that your excursion to the Majestic was undisturbed by blitzes. I do hope that you enjoyed yourself and that George took care of you, and didn't let you get out of hand! I wish I could have come too.

Darling, I'm just gazing at your photo and wishing so much that the face could pop out of the picture and ask me to kiss it.

Goodbye, my little sweetheart,
Martyn

My darling Martyn,

... It's twelve o'clock on Sunday morning, and I'm in charge of the culinary preparations, so I've got one eye on the dinner, one eye on the clock and both ears to the wireless from which are issuing the strains of *St Matthew Passion*! Do you remember hearing it two years ago? I remember so well meeting you on the steps of St Paul's. I remember what you wore too and thinking that you looked nice! I can still feel the thrill I got from the beauty of the singing and the atmosphere of the loftiness and ethereality.

We had quite a nice ramble yesterday in spite of the April showers and bitter east wind. We were only four in number! – George, Maisie, Tony and myself. We caught a bus to Loughton garage and then turned into Epping Forest at the top of the hill. I believe it's reputed to be the prettiest piece of forest in Essex. It's certainly very lovely, perhaps you know it. In my own mind I was planning a little picnic there for you and I, next time you come home. It would be delightful. Shall we?

We made a kind of circular tour keeping to the forest until George said it was time to go home, so we struck off in the direction of Loughton and subsequently caught a bus home. I had tea, changed, read your letter (three times!) and reached the Fellowship room at quarter past seven.

I was in time for the first game but I only had one other for by that time dancing was in full swing and though partners were rather scarce (George, Tony, your father and Don) we had quite a good time. Your father was delighted with your version of *Dear Brutus* and I copied out your cast list and gave it to him. These two factors encouraged him to tackle the task of getting people to take part last night and the rehearsal is fairly certain for Thursday. I have bagged a book to read it through – I'm taking the part of Margaret as you suggested.

We had an alert last night at nine o'clock but the all-clear went within half an hour to the great delight of everybody! George and Maisie walked home with me.

It's such a lovely morning – deep blue sky with big cotton wool clouds. The sun is smiling and frowning alternately! Oh darling, if you were only here – things seem so incomplete without you. What's the good of a lovely day if you are not here with me to enjoy it?

I shall want you here this afternoon too, when I go to the *Messiah*.

Do make 'them' let you come home soon. ...

Monday 31st March

My dearest Martyn,

I meant to tell you in my last letter that on Saturday morning I rose at twenty to seven and at five past seven I was on my allotment raking, and drilling seed holes! This work completed, and the ground quite ready, I then sowed three rows of parsnips. I felt very pleased with myself!

This morning I had intended to get up at the same time and sow some carrots, but to my extreme annoyance there was a heavy frost, so I shall have to wait till tomorrow morning as tonight I shall be otherwise engaged.

You'll be most amused to hear about my engagement for tonight – no rudeness please! Ethel Tulloch has asked me to assist her in the management of Reg's cub pack! So I'm going along tonight to see how I get on. I must admit that the idea rather appeals to me – but we shall see. Do you think I'm capable?

There was a gorgeous programme on the wireless yesterday that I must tell you about, in case you didn't hear it. It was called

The Enchantment of the Ballet. It commenced with quite a large chunk of *Les Sylphides*, including all the nicest parts – and to me, who have no gramophone to play it whenever I like, it was a great treat. Then we had Stravinsky's *The Firebird*, *La Boutique Fantastique*, *Prince Igor* and a very familiar piece which the producer referred to as Stravinsky's *Ragtime*. I'm sure I know the piece but under another name.

I couldn't turn myself away till the end of the program at quarter past two and I was due to meet the others at the Castle at twenty-five to three, to walk to St John's. Of course, I was late and missed them, so when I arrived at the church they'd just gone in. However, I had quite a good seat, though near the back. I thoroughly enjoyed the *Messiah* – it was lovely.

At my suggestion we walked home through Knighton, down our little lane, and on to the Green. We reached home at about six.

After tea the six of us who are to be in *Dear Brutus* went up to see your father to get him to fix a rehearsal. We went in and – you know how it is! – stayed there till half past nine! I think we talked more gardening than *Dear Brutus* but the cast is settled and also the rehearsal for Thursday, so all is well ...

Monday 31st March

My dearest girl,

I'm feeling pretty weary again this evening, for I've had quite a bit more dual flying this afternoon and the strain has rather fogged me out. I was doing very nice take-offs today and fairly good circuits, but oh the landings were so rotten!

I was getting to a state of utter despair, but my instructor bade me not to get worried and assured me that the knack would come all of a sudden.

This evening I've stayed in and have been playing over some of the records belonging to Jimmy. The case that I had sent on from Squires Gate still hasn't arrived so I haven't any records of my own at the moment to play.

You say do try and get some exercise – I'm afraid that I'm going to get some without trying!

Yes, tomorrow morning we arise at the fantastic hour of quarter past seven in order that we may participate in half an hour's P.T. before breakfast! This sort of thing really goes against the grain – we just don't like suffering from the indignity of shivering in shorts and it really is so very cold these mornings! Still, I guess I shall endure it ...

Tuesday 1st April

... It's delighted me so much, Lily, to read that you had been listening in to the performance of the *St Matthew Passion* and that it brought to you too the memories of our meeting on the steps of St Paul's and the awe-inspiring experience of hearing it in that solemn and majestic atmosphere that only St Paul's can afford.

I think that we must be blessed with some mystic telepathy for not only did we both listen to *Carmen* and *St Matthew Passion* but also to *The Enchantment of Ballet*! Yes, by sheer chance I happened to switch on my radio and heard to my delight strains of the *Les Sylphides*. Needless to say I tuned in at once and stayed to hear *The Firebird*, *The Fantastic Toyshop* and the *Prince Igor* dances ...

You make me so envious when you tell me about rambles, and dances on Saturday nights, but don't stop telling me! I long so much to be walking through Epping

Martyn and Jimmy Richards

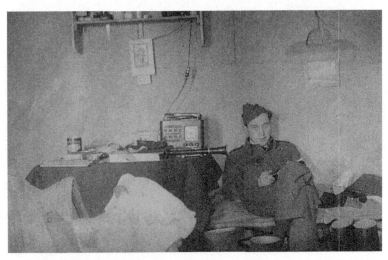

Writing letters in the room at RAF Silloth, shared with Jimmy Richards

Forest with you or dancing with you in the Fellowship room but I'm afraid it will be many more weeks before I'm doing that again.

Congratulations on your first efforts at seed sowing. I hope that there was no frost this morning and that you have been able to sow some carrots as well.

Congratulations – hearty congratulations in fact – on your proposed activities with the cub pack! 'Do I think you're capable?' you ask. Well, I certainly find it rather hard to imagine you keeping in order a crew of mischievous young boys! But I certainly think you'd be doing an excellent job and it would be good experience – if you see what I mean?! ...

Wednesday 2nd April

My precious darling Martyn,

... I've been having the wildest, awfullest dreams all night about you! But now I can forget them for I have received your letter by first post this morning ...I was filled with delight to hear about the P.T. I'm so terribly glad. Mind you go every morning! It's just what you need. You baby – I thought you liked the cold?!

Marie's been to tea and I have just been up to Woodford to see her on to the train ...

… I'm sitting in the Mess as it pours with rain outside and I've read in your letter that rain has prevented you from sowing your parsnips – or was it carrots?! Rain, rain, rain – that seems to be the only thing that one can depend upon these days!

So in addition to Smithy, Dopey, Piglet and all those names that you have so innocently acquired, you are now blessed with the name Bagheera! I don't quite appreciate what it means but I hardly feel that it is as descriptive as the others! But joking apart, I'm so glad that you managed to deal effectively with your little band of rowdy urchins and they certainly are rowdy from what I've seen of them. … You're really going to have your time cut out these days – what with Scout work, secretarial work and the allotment. I think it's a jolly good thing, as long as you still find time to write to me! And I know you will! …

Thursday 3rd April

… I am glad, Martyn, that you heard both the programmes that I enjoyed so much on Sunday. If only I had known at the time that you were listening – they would have seemed even nicer. We must arrange to listen in to the same programme one day, and then we'll know we're both thinking of each other at the same time.

I hope they don't let you skip P.T. I want you to be fit and strong so that you can stand the strain that you will surely get.

I am so glad that you approve of my new role as cub mistress! Yes, I think I know what you mean by it being good experience! Sort of practice? …

Friday 4th April

Dearest Lily,

… I'm afraid that I have some rather bad news for you. When I leave Silloth I shall either go to Ireland or Iceland. All the Hudson squadrons have now been transferred to one of these two places, though the chances of going to Ireland are infinitely greater than Iceland. No weekends at all then I'm afraid, though it certainly doesn't seem as if we shall get any weekends while up here at Silloth.

Can you bear another disappointment? – Because I'm afraid that I've got to tell you that we're having no weekend at Easter, only just our usual day off which happens to be Sunday. It is an awful curse isn't it – though I must admit that I was never very hopeful of being granted an extra day. …

Sunday morning 6th April

My darling Martyn,

Saturday was a horrid day. The clouds were so low and heavy as to have the appearance of fog. It was rather cold and there were frequent showers. Not very pleasant for a ramble, you will say. – So did I, and thinking we should play badminton instead I wore my blue shoes (the ones you gave me) and sauntered up to the hall. However, when I arrived I found George, Tony, Maisie and Betty just about to start on a ramble.

So I went with them, of course, up Grove Road, across the forest to the Kingfisher and through to Friday Hill via marshes and ditches and swamps! When we reached that old, old tree on the way through the forest towards Chingford Mount (do you remember in the summer we all climbed on to it and had a photograph taken?) my feet were so wet and muddy I decided that I really didn't want to spoil my shoes entirely and the only way to prevent that happening was to retrace my steps. So, I said goodbye and went back alone. I walked right along the High Road and whilst I was looking in that dress shop at the top of Snakes Lane the others went by in a bus! ...

I went up to the hall again at about seven o'clock and played three or four games of badminton and had a few dances. But I didn't really enjoy it. I felt very gloomy and sad last night. The others were all making plans for Easter and it kept reminding me that you wouldn't be here.

Florence went to see Muriel and Janet last night and had a very amusing story to tell of one of Janet's private conversations with herself. It seems that she'd accidentally sat on the box in which you gave her Raf and she was filled with remorse about it. So much so, that at night after her bath Muriel heard a little soliloquy which went like this:

"Janet sat on box! Poor box!
Poor Raf not got a box!
Uncle Martyn's box – what will Uncle Martyn say?
Uncle Martyn tell Auntie Liddy!"
Wasn't it clever of her? I bet she knows a lot! ...

Sunday evening 6ᵗʰ April

... I think that I may say without boasting, Martyn, that the play reading of *Dear Brutus* was a success. It went off without a hitch. We each had a book to ourselves so we all came in at the right time and in the right place. We had a real stage composed of a few chairs arranged at the far end of the room, by the gas fire, and the audience facing us. There was a good crowd present – quite a lot in fact.

Your father was really excellent. He really got his part over and in my opinion was the star of the performance. He was a treat to act with. Maisie was good as Mrs Dearth and so was Joan. Prissie and Stella both have rather soft voices for play reading but still I think they could be heard ...

Oh darling, this longing for you gets more intense every day – how can I bear it for another month? ...

Tuesday 8th April

My dearest girl,

... I needn't tell you how pleased I was to read in your letter that Bob Jacobs is now off the danger list. It is a great weight off my mind though we are all feeling a bit gloomy today for we've just heard that one of our pals from Cerney was missing on Thursday in a Berlin raid. Still, he may still turn up alright.

I was also very glad to hear that *Dear Brutus* did really go off well. I'm sure you made an excellent Margaret – I should have loved to have heard you doing that part ...

Tuesday 8th April

My darling Martyn,

I've had a most successful day! And I'm feeling most excited and pleased with myself! If you could only see what I can see – something that's propped up on a chair in front of me ... but I'll start at the beginning.

Taking my courage into both hands this morning I informed Mr Chapman that I had a very important date with the Medici Society [who sell the painting reproductions] and suggested that this afternoon would be a good opportunity for fulfilling it. Well, I didn't quite put it like that – I was slightly more diplomatic, but that is the gist of what I told him. He muttered something about 'calls', but he finally gave in.

I caught the train from George Lane and arrived at the Medici Gallery in Grafton Street at about ten past two. Then I proceeded to enjoy myself. After I'd had a good look round I started the difficult task of choosing. It was extremely difficult! I picked out the ones you'd noted, all except one, and then I saw it! And without more ado I said, "I'll take that." Immediately I saw it I felt that you would like it best of all. Aren't you just burning to know which one it is? No, I'm certainly not going to tell you. You'll have to wait till you come home. But it's lovely, Martyn – it really is – I'm sure you'll love it. I can hardly take my eyes off it to write to you! (You know what I'm like when I've got something new – how I must stop all else to look and admire and get excited.)

Well, I told the girl that I'd return for the picture and then I wended my way back to Oxford Street with a gleeful beam on my face!

'The Landmark' by Edward Seago – a painting of Blakeney windmill

Somehow – I don't know how it happened – I suddenly found myself in C&A's! Wasn't it extraordinary? It was good to be back again. But I had so little time – twenty minutes before I must be back at Grafton Street to collect the picture, for I should have told you that I'd arranged to meet Marie at the bank at ten to four. So I simply had to take just a quick look at everything and tear myself away. I rushed back to Grafton Street, collected the picture and walked to Oxford Circus tube and so to the bank. I felt most conspicuous for it's quite big and was rather heavy. But I managed to get it to the bank safely. And then it suddenly occurred to me that I hadn't had any lunch! I'd had such a rush and been so busy thinking of other things that I had completely forgotten about it! However, there was no time for such trivial things, for just as I reached the appointed place, Marie arrived.

We walked towards Liverpool Street – and on the way came to Etam's. Do you remember what Etam's is? The shop which sells delicious lingerie! I went inside – and don't be cross! – I bought some gorgeous pyjamas. Trousseau ones! They're a very pale delicate shade of blue. All soft and slinky! You'll love them! I can hardly wait!

And that's not all. You know I told you that Marie suggested giving me something to wear for a wedding present instead of a set of saucepans or something which will not be of immediate use? Well, as silks and satins will soon be unobtainable, she's bought me her present this afternoon. It's a set – do you know what a 'set' is? (A petticoat and you know what goes with it!) Such pretty ones they are too! Both in pale pink with wee flowers embroidered here and there. Really charming. And of course I'm dying to wear them too! Aren't I a lucky girl?

So as I told you I'm feeling all excited and pleased inside not only for what I've got myself but mostly for what I'm waiting to give you, my dearest dear ...

This letter may be the last to reach you before your birthday. If so, I wish you all the best things in the world. Everything that you desire, and above all, that your future may be happy and carefree.

Bye, my precious darling.

My love to you,

Lily.

Wednesday 9th April

My dearest darling Lily,

Your lovely letter made me realise how much I too was aching to be with you again – how often during the day I am dreaming of you – and how greatly I am dreading being posted away from you for months at a time. Yes, it seems far, far more than seventeen days since we last kissed goodbye. I simply can't wait much longer. I shall just have to dash home for the day to see you.

I've had a massive mail today – six letters and one parcel in all! The parcel was my birthday present from Auntie Clarrie – a silver propelling pencil, just the right size for my jacket pocket and engraved with my initials. I needn't tell you that I'm feeling very pleased with it. ...

Wednesday 9th April

... Muriel and Janet have come to stay for the weekend. Janet and I had a most exciting game with 'Raf' until Janet was carried protesting to bed!

Then I went down to the allotment and tackled the remainder of ground still to be dug. And darling, wonderful news! Some of my parsnips are coming up! Isn't it grand? They're only weenie, tiny little green shoots at the moment but they're certainly growing in rows. So I shall be the first to boast of seeds coming up – for even Harold's haven't put in an appearance yet!

I haven't told you yet about the proposed excursion to the theatre to see *Dear Brutus* on April 19th. I've been longing to see it, but I wish very much that I was going to be seeing it with you.

Is there any hope at all of your coming home soon? I seem to be always asking the same question but it's the thought that is with me the whole time …

10th April Maundy Thursday

My darling Martyn,

… No more work till Tuesday morning! Isn't it grand! And right up to this afternoon at five o'clock I had resigned myself to working on Easter Saturday. Mr Chapman has been moaning all the week about having to open on Saturday, so this morning, since it didn't matter to me, I suggested to Mr Chapman that he needn't come in, as I could do all the work quite easily. He said he'd think about it – and then late this afternoon he suddenly decided to close down until Tuesday so that neither of us will have to go in. It's a lovely feeling – no work for four days – but what a waste. Four days which could be just heaven if you were here! …

There is a ramble to the zoo on Saturday, led by George, but I'm not going. I'm not very keen for one thing and I can't afford it for another. (I can't buy slinky pyjamas and go on expensive rambles!)

George and Maisie are on the verge of falling in love! Yes, I'm quite, quite sure. George used to come down to the allotment alone, you know; now Maisie comes too. They blush when they meet unexpectedly and they think out all sorts of reasons for meeting to discuss various things. In fact they have all the symptoms! Aren't they lucky to have each other and to be able to see each other whenever they want to? Those happy days with us were so short.

I am finishing this letter by candlelight as the siren has just sounded. The others are in bed and Janet has been wheeled into the dining room, so we've had to turn the light out so that she may not be disturbed ...

12th April Easter Saturday

My darling Martyn,

After church yesterday I went home and changed and then went down to my allotment. I viewed my parsnips with great pride and then set to work on some more digging. I dug laboriously till lunchtime. Then left Prissie in charge of my tools and went home to lunch. I went back again at about two and worked until quarter past three. Then I dashed home, washed and changed, and set out to meet Prissie as we had arranged to walk to Loughton where the *Messiah* was being performed. We had quite good seats on the side at the front and I enjoyed it very much. Three of the soloists were from our church choir including Alice and Joan. They sang very well indeed.

Prissie and I walked all the way home – pretty good, wasn't it? We wanted to get in trim for the ramble on Monday.

So – Good Friday and your birthday are over. I was thinking about you all day, wondering what you were doing, and how it felt to be twenty-one. It's a strange Easter, isn't it? It must seem even queerer to you! Did you hate it very much – having to fly on Good Friday – on your birthday? But if you were actually flying I expect you enjoyed it! ...

On Easter Sunday, 13th April 1941, Martyn's maternal grandmother, Eliza Nickerson died.

16

Having been unable to spend Easter or his 21st birthday with Lily or his parents, Martyn travelled back to London on the evening of Monday 14th April. After spending Tuesday at home, that same evening he caught night trains to make his way back to Silloth and was out flying at six o'clock the following morning.

89 Grenville Gardens
Woodford Green
Wednesday 16th April

My dearest Martyn,

I was awfully pleased to receive your letter this afternoon. I'm always relieved to know that you've had a safe journey …George (and Maisie!) came down to try and persuade me to go to *Dear Brutus* on Saturday (the romance is flourishing in leaps and bounds!) but they're having four-and-ninepenny seats, so my expenses would be about seven shillings and sixpence. I just shan't have seven and six this week, unless I borrow, which I dislike doing, so I think it will be wisest not to go. Don't you? There'll be another opportunity, won't there?

I'm so glad you really liked your picture, Martyn. I adored giving it to you. I was as thrilled to be giving you something that would please you as if it was something for myself. I would give

255

all my possessions (not much but my all) just to have you beside me now.

But four weeks will pass, Martyn. They'll be long and lonely, but they'll pass – and then – oh wonderful, happy day, the day that brings you back again! ...

My darling Martyn,

Please excuse pencil – I know you will when you know the circumstances in which it is written!

Don't be alarmed. I'm quite safe and well, but last night, Martyn, at quarter to four in the morning we had three bombs – one on the opposite corner and two in Wansford Road opposite our turning. It was horrible! But though we are shaken up rather, we are feeling so thankful to be still alive. There were six people killed in Wansford Road.

I think our house is repairable, though all the ceilings, doors and windows are down. When the all-clear went at quarter to five Arthur and I left Mum in a neighbour's house and started to clear up the mess. Oh the dust and the dirt, the plaster and soot, the pieces of glass and wood – my poor hands are no longer fit to caress your cheeks – but I'll soon mend that!

I've been hard at work the whole day shovelling plaster, sweeping, moving furniture, and now at nine o'clock I'm absolutely deadbeat! So, though I know you will want to hear all there is to tell, I can't write any more tonight. For if I think about it I shall cry, and that will never do. So don't worry about me, dearest. I'm alright. I am still your darling little girl, I can still laugh and be gay – houses don't matter, only people! ...

Good night sweetheart, I'm loving you more than ever,

Lily

My darling Martyn,

Well, tonight I'm feeling a little more cheerful and a little less weary and dispirited than I was yesterday.

I slept under the table last night on a mattress on the floor. I was so absolutely exhausted that I slept through two alerts without waking. Wasn't it good? Frankly I should have been pretty scared to hear the warning. I felt so thankful to have been spared that. As a result of a good night's rest, though still very tired this morning, I felt considerably better and able to start another day.

When I went home after work at the end of the morning, in order to go to your Grandma's funeral, I was delighted to find that our front door, though scarred and broken, had been put back in its proper place. The front windows had been filled in with felt stuff and the dining room made fairly comfortable again.

I put on my black costume and white blouse which were quite unaffected except for dust which I brushed off. I caught a bus and arrived at The Homestead at half past two. I was introduced to various people and when everybody had arrived we assembled in the dining room where the coffin was laid for a short service. The flowers were very beautiful; forty wreaths altogether. Ours, which was laid on the coffin with those of the nearest relatives, looked very lovely; there was a foundation of fern and green stuff, and an outer ring of narcissi, and inside that, white carnations with mauve tulips and violets. I felt pleased with my choice of flowers.

After the service we went by cars to the City of London Cemetery. It started to rain on the way and continued while a few words were said as the coffin was lowered. We stayed a little and then went to the cars and started back.

In the meantime a meal had been prepared so I was soon busy helping people to cups of tea and food ...

All this time the rain was absolutely pouring down and I was hoping for all I was worth that our roof had been repaired. As soon as the rain eased a little, I borrowed a mac and set off for home. My hopes about the roof were in vain – they said it was too big a job to tackle this afternoon so we are flooded out upstairs! However, it'll help to lay the dust ...

RAF Station
Silloth
Cumberland
Saturday 19th April

My dearest Lily,

I can't tell you how relieved I was when I learnt from today's letter that you were quite safe after your horribly narrow escape on Wednesday night. I was hardly at all surprised to hear what an awful time you had and how narrowly your house had escaped the bombs.

Oh my dearest darling, how terribly grateful I am for your escape. I simply cannot express it in words.

I know what an awful shock it must've been to you – all of you – and how heartbroken you must have been to see the shattered glass and broken wood. I do so wish I could be at home to comfort you. Don't cry, sweetheart. You're safe and all your family are safe and they're the only real things that matter ...

Sunday 20th April

My dearest Martyn,

Well, here is my usual Sunday after lunch letter, written in the most unusual and uncomfortable circumstances. But at least we've had a cooked dinner, and not many people have had that, for since last night's blitz the gas is off.

I'm sitting in the dining room – our one habitable room – and the wind is howling through the roof trying to tear down the curtain which we have up in place of a door. There is the constant noise of falling tiles as the men are up on the roof – they've just started to repair it.

We had an awful night – too scared to do anything but crouch under the table while bombs seemed to come nearer every minute and we wondered if morning would ever come. The all-clear went at five, however, and we then managed to get to sleep.

This morning I've been over to Wanstead to claim for damaged clothing. I found them most sympathetic. They promised to pay me three pounds.

We knocked some of the kitchenette ceiling down this morning as it was dangerously cracked – more mess! But we thought ourselves very fortunate when Florence brought the dinner in, cooked in her electric stove.

By the way, *Dear Brutus* was cancelled as there was an unexploded bomb outside the theatre. So we're waiting for a later date ...

My darling Martyn,

... The siren has just gone so we'll be making preparations for the night in the safest place we can find. I sleep under the table. We've only had distant guns up to now, so we are hoping and hoping that we may have an early all-clear. If you receive this letter you'll know that everything is alright. ...

Today I have to report on a very important development in the new romance! This afternoon George and Maisie walked down with me and they were holding hands! (Though not as we do, with our gloves off. It's much nicer like that, isn't it?) But tonight coming home, they were holding arms, as we do. How's that! Pretty quick work I thought – nearly as quick as you and I! Maisie is bemoaning the fact that now she's going to Torquay for a week. But I could tell her that going to Torquay is absolutely fatal for falling in love! Absence makes the heart grow fonder. I look down from the height of my experience and knowledge and smile condescendingly at these two children!

Oh, wonderful, heavenly sound – the all-clear! It's just gone, so, as I'm very, very tired after last night's lack of sleep I'll leave off here and say good night, my dearest darling. I'm simply living for the time when you will come and hold me safely in your arms and take away all my worries and troubles and kiss me and tell me you love me.

This is what I long for all the time.

I want you very much,

Lily

My sweetest darling,

I can't tell you how glad I am that you went to Grandma's funeral on Friday especially after your heart-breaking experiences on Wednesday night

Why I'm so glad I don't quite know – whether it's because I know how proud and happy Grandma would have been could she have known you were there – or whether it's because I'm so pleased to feel that on such an occasion my fiancée could go as part of the family – or whether it's because I am so proud to have such a perfectly sweet and able person to represent me. I do wish that I could have been there with you, though; that I could have seen all the wreaths that you say were so beautiful and especially the one that was your choice.

You say 'don't worry about me' but how can I help worrying when you have to sleep on a mattress beneath a leaking roof in constant danger of more bombs. You must remain safe and sound, my sweetheart, for you mean more to me than anything in the world.

I finished off the first month at Silloth by flying for six and a half hours yesterday and now we have left 'A' Flight and gone over to 'B' Flight.

Today we have flown for the first time as a permanent crew. I have Jimmy Richards as my co-pilot and we have two wireless-operator air gunners. We did a couple of cross-country flights today but over at 'B' Flight we also do such things as dive-bombing and harbour reconnaissance ...

My dearest Martyn,

... In your letter you mention your relief at receiving a letter from me that was written on that fateful night. I wrote it as usual and propped it on the sideboard for Arthur to post in the morning. It was just after five o'clock when I returned to the house that morning from the warden's house in Wansford Road where we had spent the rest of the night. I groped my way into the dining room from the garden and there in a bed of soot by the fireplace I dimly discerned something white. I picked it up and blew the grime off. It was your letter! Some of the dirt still clung, but I had no clean envelopes to use, so I posted it when I went to phone Mr Chapman to say I wasn't going to the office. Did you notice its filthy state? I kept the news of our night from you as long as I could.

That paragraph you wrote about going to 'B' Flight and the horrible, dangerous things you're going to do, strike terror into my heart. Do, do, be ever so careful, Martyn. What should I do if anything happened to you? Don't take any chances, or needless risks, will you? I'm so afraid.

That week's holiday from May 17th, which I thought so impossible when you were here, is gradually becoming my one aim and wish! And when I set my heart on a thing ... I usually get it! By hook, or by crook (whatever that may mean?)! So, somehow I must set my woman's wiles to work on Mr Chapman for I am determined to have it!

I'm afraid that when you heard my news you must have been terribly distressed, but don't be any longer, dearest. I'm alright.

My darling sweetheart, I adore you! – More than ever!

Lily

... The cubs are still behaving quite well and we had a successful meeting last night. I took them for plasticine. By 'took' I mean I kept them well employed and interested while Ethel taught two of the more advanced boys how to obtain their next badge.

I told them to model an aeroplane! They were all jolly good, ten times better than I could've done. And the things they discussed among themselves! Talk about technicalities! There's nothing they don't know about planes – British and German. I've learnt quite a lot!

I don't feel at all like dancing at the moment and anyway Maisie and George will be able to have more dances together. There'll be more than enough girls as it is.

I've been down on my allotment this evening. I've sown a row of radishes and three rows of beetroot. Don't you think that's a good effort?

Gosh it's cold in here! We've still got a patch of the dining room, by the French doors, open to the sky and though we've got a roaring fire the draught is terrible ...

Wednesday 23rd April

My darling girl,

... This morning five of us went up with one of the instructors and had a demonstration of a new wireless device used for detecting ships at night and in bad weather.

This afternoon I flew with my usual crew and the air gunners were firing from the air at a target on the ground. For this I had to fly at only 300 feet and as it was very bumpy and the swinging turret makes the machine wobble all over the place, piloting was really hard work.

Jimmy, Guy and Geoff have gone to the pictures tonight, but I am duty navigator today and have to stay in the camp in case a machine has to go up to look for a ship or effect a rescue somewhere ...

Thursday 24th April

... We've managed to block up most of the draught holes now, and I'm keeping tolerably warm beside a huge fire.

I was glad to hear that your night flying had been cancelled. How I wish you never had to do it! Do, do be terribly careful, dearest. I can never tell you enough how very, very precious your life is to me or how my every moment is spent in longing to see your dear face again and feel the comfort of your presence.

Is May 17th still definitely the end of your course? Oh I do hope so. If you knew how I am counting the days, how I am longing and yearning for the day when you will come home to me again.

I love you with all my heart, Lily

Thursday 24th April

My dearest Lily,

... So glad to hear that you're still managing to keep the cubs in order – I was most amused to hear about the plasticine aeroplanes! Maybe they'll have more success in arousing your interest in aeroplanes than I have had!

I am simply longing to see your allotment – at least I'm longing to see it in a few weeks' time when all those rows of beetroots, parsnips and radishes are proudly boasting small green shoots. Or maybe they will be big ones by then.

Talking of coming home – don't definitely fix up for the May 17th week, for I don't guarantee getting leave then. Some of the last course got twelve days, but some got none. Not that I want to dissuade you from exercising your woman's wiles on Mr Chapman – there will certainly be no harm done! …

Friday 25th April

My darling Martyn,

The hour is late, so this letter will have to be fairly short I'm afraid. It takes such ages to get all the bedding down and everyone settled for the night.

We've had a most enjoyable Fellowship evening at Mrs Tullock's. Joan, Stella and Maisie sang, George did a monologue and I read two of Stephen Leacock's stories. Maisie sang extremely well, I thought; she's got a real deep, husky contralto voice that I found most pleasing.

My reading was received with some amusement and as an encore I read the story about Hoodoo's Christmas stocking but though I'd read it before, I became so convulsed with laughter that I had to hand the book to George for him to finish!

After the entertainment we had refreshments and then George and Maisie walked home with me. They are both feeling very sad tonight, as Maisie goes to Torquay tomorrow. I wonder if he'll kiss her tonight! What do you think?

Well, it's getting late so I'd better say goodnight and lie down on my little mattress and dream of that happy, happy day when I can lay in your arms.

Bye-bye, my own sweetheart,
look after yourself for me,
Lily

Friday 25th April

Lily my darling,

… Tomorrow morning we fly at six o'clock again and although it's very unpleasant dragging oneself out of bed at half past five, it's very nice to get up into the air really early and to be streaking down the Irish Sea whilst most people are just thinking about getting up!

Thank you for today's letter, though it does seem to contain a spelling error. You say 'we are beginning to get slack at the office' – don't you really mean 'slacker'?! But all the same I'm very glad to hear that you're getting such a lot of opportunities to write up the Fellowship Council minutes.

I've no more news for you today, darling, so goodbye till tomorrow,

I love you so very much, sweetheart,
Martyn

P.S. Auntie Clarrie wrote today, and said how very much they appreciated you being there for the funeral on Friday. Mum has also written and said the same …

Saturday 26th April

Dearest Martyn,

Directly I'd had dinner I went down to my allotment and set to work, determined to finish digging the last strip of grass or die in the attempt! At last at half past five I decided that the wee, tiny piece that was left wouldn't matter and I went home to tea feeling exceedingly pleased with my afternoon's work. There's only a patch, say about two-foot square, left to do, so I feel that my real labour is over.

Whilst I was working, or to be more correct, just as I was lying on the grass having a much needed rest, Prissie and George and Tony appeared. It seems only three people turned up for the ramble so they decided not to go, so we all stopped and had a little chat.

Oh, I must tell you what George said. I've no doubt you'll be amused. When he arrived, he said, "I was looking for you, and from a distance I identified Prissie as your sister-in-law and yourself as Janet! I was wondering where 'Auntie Liddy' had got to!"

It appears that I was bending down at the time, disguising my real height. So, I'm afraid there must be some resemblance after all!

George was trying to persuade me to go dancing. He promised to see me home, teach me to foxtrot and offered several other inducements, so that I finally promised to go. But when I reached home I felt so absolutely weary that I just couldn't summon up the energy. Instead I had a gorgeous, wonderful bath with the water lapping the edge – though the wind howled through the top tiles and I had to keep a wary eye on the few remaining oddments of plaster – but it was worth it.

I do so hope that you will definitely get leave on May 17th for I am absolutely pinning all my hopes on that date ...

Sunday 27th April

... It's possible, Martyn, that when you do come I shall be living at another house. At least I hope so. We've decided that this one is too uncomfortable to live in and a very frail air-raid shelter! There's really no point in us staying because we were only renting it, you know. So, just as soon as we can find somewhere suitable, we shall go. The bedrooms are quite unusable for there is no ceiling at all, only laths between the tiles; and the council won't tackle re-plastering till after the war. Downstairs we can't use the front room, firstly because all the bedroom furniture and bedding is stored in there; secondly, because we've only got felted windows which necessitates a light on all the time; and thirdly because a lot of the wall plaster is down and a slight crack in the bricks is showing. The crack is on the dining room side causing a bulge this side. These unpleasantnesses have a very depressing effect on me.

Oh, I do hope we get to somewhere else. It's awful to turn the corner of Wansford Road and see the blind windows and the destruction on either side. Our front door no longer has a lock – you just push it and walk in! ...

Although Lily's parents spent some time looking for another house to rent in the area, they were unable to find anything suitable and, in the end, repairs were made to 89 Grenville Gardens and they remained there.

Monday 28th April

My dearest girl,

... I was amused by your observation that George and Maisie were feeling sad because of Maisie's imminent departure for Torquay. How awfully nice to have only a week to wait. It seems an incredibly short space of time when one has to wait a month or more!

I don't know whether you have the makings of a scheming matchmaker or whether you are just curious about Maisie's reactions to a thrill you once felt yourself – that first exciting and daring kiss; at least, it was daring for me!

I've done about five hours' flying today – three hours doing firing from the turret at a target towed by another plane and two hours practising a procedure for landing in bad weather ...

Thursday 1st May

My dearest Lily,

I am sitting in the Mess, feeling a little weary. I did an hour's dual flying and then was certified as ready for solo. Jimmy was ready for solo at the same time so we started looking around for an aeroplane. By the time we had found one and brought it over from the far side of the aerodrome it was about half past midnight and we were detailed to fly for a couple of hours from then.

There was a stiff crosswind along the runway we were using and we swung off onto the grass whilst taking off and bogged the machine! But the control office had noticed the crosswind and after they'd changed the runway and our plane had been dragged out of the mud we finally got off the ground at about two-ish.

We flew till about half past three and then we both felt rather tired so we chucked it up for the evening ...

I wish I could tell you something about the 17th but I'm afraid I know nothing as yet. All I know is that I'm just longing to be with you again, sweetheart. ...

Sunday 4th May

...You'll no doubt be pleased to hear, Lily, that my usual flying luck held up last night when we had a crack-up in night flying.

Unfortunately I was the pilot when the crash occurred but to my relief we none of us received more than slight bruises and we managed to get well clear of the wreck before the flames spread ..

Monday 5th May

My dearest girl,

I think I hardly need to tell you what the enclosed piece of silk is from. There was not much left of my parachute but I managed to retrieve one or two pieces and I thought you might be able to make a couple of handkerchiefs from the pieces sent herewith ...

I had a letter from Mrs Jacobs about Bob. He was the only one in the crew to be saved. He was at Athens then but has now presumably been evacuated. He must've been on his way from Egypt to Greece or something like that, for he lost all his kit except his camera which was hauled out with him. He's now suspended in a wooden frame with weights on his left leg and his arm in a sling but they tell me he's recovering rapidly ...

Tuesday 6th May

My dearest girl,

This afternoon we all became budding film stars as some men from Fox films came down to take sequences for a new film called *A Yank in the RAF* which stars Tyrone Power!

Three of our machines flew in close formation up and down the Solway whilst a fourth, which carried photographers, cruised around us and took pictures from various angles. I was in the leading machine of the formation and in case you ever see the film, this was aircraft Q.

The Lockheed Hudson labelled 'Q'

I'm glad that, although the warning spoiled your dancing, the raid on Saturday night did not develop. I am so afraid that you will be having more bad raids now that the moon is waxing. ...

Wednesday 7th May

My darling girl,

As I write this letter I am listening in to Beethoven's 7th and I'm wondering whether you are listening to it also. It must be about a year since I last heard it played at a concert and it's certainly a treat to be enjoying the delightful melodies again.

Today I've been flying both this morning and this afternoon doing low-level bombing and practice attacks on another aircraft. Quite amusing, though the steep turns and dives rather play havoc with one's tummy ...

Friday 9th May

Lily my darling,

I can hardly believe that this time next week I shall have almost finished my stay at Silloth.

I'm afraid that even if I do get some leave, I shan't be home on the Sunday, for only on that day do we start getting our clearances. But I expect by the middle of next week I shall know where I am going and also when I really do get away from this station.

Last night we were flying again and it all went off quite successfully. In fact I was doing really good landings yesterday. This afternoon we were up for a couple of hours and did some more low-level bombing of a fixed target.

By the way, in regard to your enquiries, I can assure you that I am perfectly ok – not in the least bit injured and not in the least bit unnerved either. I must admit that I was a wee bit apprehensive last night, but when we got into the air I felt quite at home again. ...

Saturday 10th May

... It was very sweet of you, Lily, to go along and read to Mrs Bernard and then, if you're able, to get the entertainment party to visit her. You're doing a fine job of work.

Today we spent two and a half hours beetling around the Irish Sea, taking photos of all the ships we saw, and we saw a deuce of a lot!

I seem to be having a spell of bad luck at the moment, for during the trip I suddenly heard a sharp crack. We could find nothing wrong however, and cruised on without worrying, but when we landed, the machine sagged down on one side and started swinging to the left. The port tyre had burst!

Luckily I had landed very slowly and made a very soft landing too, so I was able to pull the aircraft up before the swing developed or the undercarriage collapsed. ...

... Only a week to wait now, Martyn! Perhaps by this time next week you will already be on the train speeding south. Oh how I am longing to see you!

Do tell me directly you get any news at all about leave or what time you will arrive, and please do try and wire me so that I can come to meet you. You will, won't you? ...

Tuesday 13th May

My dearest Lily,

I was very relieved to find in today's letter the news that, although Saturday night's raid was bad, you had not been directly affected by the bombing. I've had a letter from Mum today and she tells me that some bombs fell in Roding Lane – they must've been the ones that sounded pretty close to you.

I can't say I am at all confident about getting any leave. I shan't know where I'm going next till Saturday, or probably Sunday, and it will be on Sunday that I shall know if I'm getting my leave. So I'm afraid there is no hope of us going together to Fellowship on Sunday.

I hope that the powers that be decide to be merciful. It would be a pretty shocking outlook if I'm condemned to the wilds of Scotland or Iceland without even a glimpse of home ...

Martyn successfully completed his flying training on Hudsons and was now all set to join a Coastal Command squadron. Sadly, many young men were not so lucky and lost their lives whilst at RAF Silloth. In fact, so many accidents occurred over the Solway Firth that the area became known locally as 'Hudson Bay'.

In April 2018, as part of the centenary celebrations of the formation of the Royal Air Force, a permanent feature of a replica Lockheed Hudson was erected on Silloth Green. At the unveiling ceremony the actor Tim Barker read his moving poem entitled 'Hudson Bay'.

Hudson Bay

When the Nazis threatened Europe all the world was called to arms
And an aerodrome was built here, among the peaceful farms;
It was not a combat station, just a work shop and a school
Where men came for instruction, and machines came for renewal.
And the town was full of guests as it had never been before,
Guests who travelled from around the world to exercise for war.

Men learned gunnery and bombing, navigation and the skills
How to hunt for submarines and when they found them, how to kill.
But to exercise for battle is to sit a lethal test
And failure claims the lives of both the weakest and the best;
And sixty heroes lie in graves beside the Solway Shore
Who saw the face of death before they ever faced the war.

Flying low over the wave tops, flying blind on moonless nights,
Sitting cold in lonely turrets, peering over cannon sights,
They flew many types of aircraft but the name that still survives
Is the fatal Lockheed Hudson, for it claimed so many lives
In the waters of the Solway, and so many went astray
That the waters of the Solway were re-christened "Hudson Bay".

Some were instantly recovered, some were never seen again
And many sank or drifted to be cast up now and then;
And many were so damaged that their names could not be guessed,
Flayed and broken by the ocean; and its creatures did the rest
For the creatures of the ocean take whatever comes their way,
And they reaped a royal harvest in the years of Hudson Bay.

Now when strangers bring their caravans to Silloth by the sea
They're looking for a holiday with peace and harmony,
And driving into town they seldom cast a second glance
At the little blocks of factories and light electric plant;
But those buildings have a history and where tourists camp today,
Other strangers came to Silloth who have never gone away.

Flying low over the wave tops, flying blind on moonless nights,
Sitting cold in lonely turrets, peering over cannon sights,
They flew many kinds of aircraft but the name that still survives
Is the fatal Lockheed Hudson, for it claimed so many lives
In the waters of the Solway, and so many went astray
That the waters of the Solway were re-christened "Hudson Bay".

Tim Barker

17

On leaving Silloth, Martyn was posted to RAF Wick near John O'Groats, to join Coastal Command's 269 Squadron, but as he was also granted two weeks' leave, he had time to spend beforehand back in Woodford with his parents and with Lily.

Two days before his leave ended, Lily met him by chance in the street, and she was alarmed to see how crestfallen he looked. It transpired that this wasn't simply due to anticipating his imminent departure but because he had once again been worrying about whether it was morally right for him to hold Lily to the commitment of marriage. He was aware that 269 Squadron would be moving

276

from RAF Wick to Iceland and it could be many months, or even more than a year, before he would have more leave, and that was presuming that he wasn't killed in action.

Lily succeeded once more in allaying his fears and assuring him that he was the only one that she wanted to marry and she would wait for as long as need be.

While Martyn was at RAF Wick the squadron was changing over from flying Ansons to Hudsons, so through the month of June he was involved in ferrying aircraft to different aerodromes. Once the transformation was complete, 269 Squadron established its base at the newly created Kaldadarnes aerodrome in Iceland to take on its role of reconnaissance and anti-submarine patrols between Iceland and Scotland, as well as the vital escorting of convoys as far out into the Atlantic as the Hudson's limited range of five hours would allow.

Lily celebrated her 21st birthday on 13th June 1941.

RAF Station,
Wick, Caithness
Friday 13th June

My dearest darling,

I've been thinking of you more than usual today, and that, Lily, is a terrible lot, for every day my mind is feverish from morn till night with dreams of you.

But today is your birthday and I'm wishing so intensely that I was at home with you now and able to share the happiness which I know you must be feeling.

Somehow I can't imagine you seeming any more grown-up. In fact, I'm totally unable to imagine you ever being any more serious or sophisticated than you are now! ...

You know darling Lily, I'm hardly surprised that everybody seemed to think you a most amusing spectacle when you marched down the aisle with the cubs on Sunday morning! I can hardly believe that you look particularly glamorous under the expanse of Reg's scout hat! Especially in the severe cut of a cub mistress's shirt and shorts!!

But after all, the main consideration was that the cubs should take you seriously, and as they did – well, I shouldn't worry ...

89 Grenville Gardens
Friday 13th June

Dearest Martyn,

... Your watch arrived safely and I wrapped it up and put it away till this morning. Then the first thing I did when I woke up, before opening my other presents, was to put it on – and admire it! I love it!

It was really quite exciting this morning as I had six parcels to open and about five cards which Mum had kept back as they arrived yesterday. I had another five cards and two letters by post later on. Your mother gave me the badminton racquet last night – it's a beauty! I'm terribly pleased with it. It makes a lovely 'pong' when you hit with it. I'm sure my play will improve!

The six parcels consisted of:

A wine-coloured handbag from Maisie – awfully nice!

A box of stationery (this is a sheet of the paper) and a wire hairbrush (no steel comb now!) from Betty and Arthur.

The tennis racquet from Mum and Dad.

The undies-set in pink that I told you about from Marie – it's terribly pretty!

A blue sports bag from your Auntie May. Wasn't it nice of her? I was terribly surprised. Just what I wanted for my two racquets!

A pale green satin dressing gown from Les and Florence. It really is awfully nice – I'm sure you will like it. Florence tried to get blue but couldn't. This is a lovely shade though and has a faint coloured spray design.

And I've been given money for a case from Reg and a book token from Prissie...

Monday 16th June

... How many more times am I to tell you that I do not wear shorts for cubs! Much as I should like to. I'm sure you would like me to – by the number of times you mention it, but unfortunately, it's not allowed. I've got a frock made by myself – rather short, to allow for free movement – with two stunning pockets (which don't open – I stitched them up by mistake) and short sleeves with very square shoulders to make me look tough!

But it's definitely not a skirt, ducky. Girls would look an awful sight in straight, pleat-less, corduroy shorts. We are somewhat cushioned you know! Hence the pleats! ...

Wednesday 18th June

My darling Martyn,

It's one minute after you phoned and all my senses are tingling with joy at the sound of your dear voice, so I thought I would write straight away while I feel so close to you and it seems that if only I looked hard enough I would see you! It was just wonderful to speak to you, Martyn, and gave me the most exquisite thrill. It was just lovely hearing you say 'ducky' again! – But I did so want it to last longer. I could have cried when I heard your receiver go down and I thought of you walking away, soon to fly hundreds of miles away from me ...

Tuesday 24th June

... Last night we took the cubs to the forest. We had quite a good time and I ran the games. We ended up with 'hide and seek' and finally we lost the whole pack and had to set out ourselves to look for them! We were late back – but still it was fun. On my way home I popped into your place and chatted, and collected the chocolate, and some pea sticks for my allotment. Then I went home, and feeling rather exhausted, to bed ...

Wednesday 25th June

Marie came to tea yesterday and we went to the Kingfisher to go swimming. It was rather crowded when we got there, but people gradually drifted away and it was gorgeous in the water. A bit fresh at first – but even you wouldn't have thought it cold! We swam, and sat out, and swam alternately till we were completely exhausted ...

I'm getting so impatient to know where you are going! It's very tantalising – all these secrets. And I can't make out why it will take you so long to get there? Unless you are going by boat – and I sincerely hope that is not the case.

I took the negatives into Boots yesterday. They're going to take a fortnight! I hate waiting for snaps – don't you? What a lot of things there are to try my patience! You make me more impatient than anything else, though. You make me fall head over heels in love with you, then you're whisked off to the North Pole, or somewhere exciting, while I have to sit quietly at home! Longing to be with you, to look after you, to love you. But you will take me with you soon, won't you darling? Or I shall die with longing for you!

Bye-bye dearest, keep safe,

Lily

RAF Kaldadarnes, Iceland
Friday 27th June

My dearest girl,

Well, here I am in Iceland at last and not exactly thrilled with the prospect of spending a year or more out here!

I am writing this letter just after lunch but I expect you are already thinking about tea. Of course the time of day cannot be guessed by looking out of the window. It is quite light day and night. In fact it never gets any darker here than at eight o'clock on a June evening in London. No lighting at all is needed, and the electricity is rarely switched on.

Flying goes on through day and night without a break but of course I've done no trips as yet. The visibility up here is marvellous and whilst we were still 80 miles from land we could see the snow-clad peaks of the giant mountains that tower to 5000 feet.

The first sight of Iceland was a lovely spectacle as the white streaks of snow and glaciers merged into indefinite layers of white cloud which lay around the horizon. Above the clouds the sky was a clear, brilliant blue and seemed to be glittering in the light of the blazing sun.

But this beautiful vision sent a chill shiver through my whole being for I realised that I was now 1000 miles from home and I was suddenly gripped by a feeling of intense loneliness.

I'm still feeling lonely but the thought of the exquisite delight of seeing you again and the intense happiness of being home inspires me to resign myself cheerfully to the long months ahead.

You said that you would willingly endure all inconveniences if you could be with me. Well, you would have to be a pretty tough girl to enjoy yourself up here. Last night I slept in a sleeping bag on the floor of a corrugated iron hut and washed in the morning in a canvas pail with water out of a petrol can!

Already we've set to work to make ourselves furniture from packing cases and soon our primitive quarters should have quite a homely atmosphere. All this improvisation and makeshift should be quite good fun but I must admit that at first it comes "rather 'ard" after the comfort of a proper Mess!

We get some compensation though – an extra fourteen shillings a week field allowance and a saving of seven shillings a week on Messing. But heaven knows what we shall spend money on here. There is absolutely nothing to do or buy on the camp and we're five miles from the nearest village. Of course, we have a two day stand-off once a fortnight and are then able to go into Reykjavík which is about a three hour journey from here by road.

Guy came up here with me yesterday and we have spent today getting the place weighed up and our hut made comfortable. We have drawn our 'aircrew suits' from the stores. Gumboots are also provided and believe me you need them.

I'm hoping that Geoff will come up soon, for in his aeroplane, which was delayed by engine trouble, is my camp kit. When that arrives I shall have a camp bed to sleep on.

I don't expect that Jimmy will be coming over for a week or so and I'm hoping that when he does come he'll bring over a lot of letters from you. Apparently the mail comes in about once every ten days and presumably leaves Reykjavík with the same frequency. And as you can see by the envelope there is no charge for mail from Iceland to England – so I shall make yet another saving!

Well my dearest, I'll be closing down, for I've got quite a lot of jobs to do before tea. I've got to write a letter to Mum and I've also got to drive a nail into the wall somewhere – can you guess what for? – to hang your picture on of course! ...

My darling girl,

I am sitting on my camp kit chair and this writing pad is resting on a packing case table. I am wearing my new aircrew suit which is battledress made of the same cloth as my sergeant's uniform and my legs are encased in huge socks, which if extended would reach to my hips but at the moment are rolled down to the tops of my gumboots. But I'm afraid that however well I describe the scene, you could not form a true mental picture in your mind. I have to be seen to be believed!

I've been collecting more kit today and I shudder to think how I shall be able to take it with me if ever I leave this place. They've given me a stiff black oilskin raincoat, a huge and very heavily padded overcoat, which weighs decidedly more than my great coat, and an Irvin jacket, which is a waist-length jacket for flying, lined with warm soft fur. I've also been issued with a few more oddments such as these four-foot-long socks and special anti-snow glare goggles. At the moment it's not quite cold enough for all this equipment but when the winter comes it'll certainly be very, very useful! ...

Sunday 29th June

My dearest Martyn,

How I wish I knew where you are! I think you must be in Iceland by now as I've had no letter. But still no telegram has come and I'm getting rather anxious – though I'm trying not to worry. ...

After Fellowship yesterday we went to Maisie's for tea. Seven ladies and George! But needless to say, he didn't mind! Tea consisted of lots of things carefully saved up for the occasion and now unobtainable, including a birthday cake with candles. We went out into the garden and spread ourselves over the lawn. It was so lovely lying out there in the sun and we stayed until church time but I'm afraid it was too long for me, for today I've got a slight touch of sunstroke and feel horribly shivery and headachy.

I need hardly say how terribly I shall miss your daily letters, for I know you will understand how I feel and realise that your letters mean just as much to me as you say mine do to you. It is hearing from you every day that keeps your image so much alive in my heart, that brings you near to me; and often I read them over again in bed so that the lovely things you say are echoing in my ears, bringing your voice to me.

But, darling, shan't we have a lovely lot of letters when they do come. In five weeks we should have about thirty! You will write every day just the same, won't you? But not of course if you are working hard and your hours of recreation are cut down. Don't neglect sleep and rest, darling. You must keep fit and well ...I have completely given up the idea of a white wedding. I don't want any carnival or pageantry now. I should really like just you and I and our families – no one else. But I suppose that can't be. Of course I should hate a registry office; I shan't feel married unless it's at a church. From regarding our marriage as a 'wedding', I think of it now as just the tie that will bind us to each other for always. Naturally, when I knew how much you disliked all the fuss and bother, I tried to persuade myself that perhaps a simpler wedding would be nicer, and now I honestly think as you do, and though white weddings are very lovely and pretty to watch I don't want it for us, Martyn. All the trappings don't matter now darling – it's only you and I – and you have suddenly become so terribly dear to me, so essential for my happiness, so very, very precious that I don't care for anything except that ...

Wednesday 2nd July

My precious Martyn,

Please excuse pencil and what is going to be rather bad writing, I'm afraid, as I am in bed with an extremely painful attack of sunstroke. This morning I really couldn't get up so we sent for the Doctor who says it's definitely sunstroke and I'm to stay in bed and only drink fluids and he's coming again tomorrow ...

Thursday 3rd July

My darling Martyn,

I had my first visitor today – your mother. I see her, or phone, pretty often, so she soon found out. It's nice to feel that one's presence is missed in society! ...

I'm happy to say my head pains are much less than yesterday but I'm afraid I make a bad invalid! I do hate lying here when there's so much to do outside, and the thought of them playing badminton tonight is very tantalising.

It seems that I've picked just the wrong time to be ill as far as Mr Chapman is concerned ... Coal is to be rationed (only to one ton a month – that's very generous!) but it will make more work. So you see, I am cursing my misfortune in more ways than one.

There are two nice prospects to look forward to though, when I'm better! The first (you'll probably laugh!) is that I shall have to purchase a large shady hat, for the Doctor says I'm not to go out without one! You wouldn't call any of my millinery large, would you? If they'd sheltered the right part of my head I wouldn't be where I am now! (Oh, vanity, thy name is woman!) So I can buy one without any twinges of conscience, and anyway my turn-out for the rummage sale depleted my stock considerably. I hope I didn't get rid of any of your favourites. The blue bonnet had to go!

And now perhaps my most important news. I have practically bought a bike. Dad saw a Rudge Whitworth in the shop in Woodford Bridge and, after considering it for a day, I decided that it was absolutely futile waiting for a second-hand one, and new ones are almost as rare, and anyway, I could always sell it again and through your sweet generosity I already had nearly half the price – so I have paid a deposit on it and it's as good as mine! Of course, if it hadn't been for your lovely present, I wouldn't have had it at all, so I'm even more terribly, terribly pleased with it …

Friday 4th July

My precious darling Martyn,

To my great surprise and delight I received two letters from you this morning! It was so lovely to hear from you again for I've missed your letters sadly even though I've only been three days without. But those three days were full of anxiety for me and it's simply grand to know that you're safe and well.

I have read them many times already and through the things you say, and your dear familiar writing, I have managed to bring you very close to me, for now I can really picture you in your new surroundings. I did, though, find the 'aircrew' suit and long stockings a little hard to imagine after thinking of you looking so smart and debonair in your dress uniform!

Have you unfolded your camp bath yet? No, I knew you hadn't! Well, try not to get too dirty, won't you ducky. Are there any women in camp? If not, who does your washing? If there are – are they WAAFS? And do tell me about the Icelandic girls! Have you met any? What are they like? …

Yes, I must agree, conditions from your description do sound pretty primitive! You didn't say anything about the rats though, or haven't they put in an appearance yet? But in spite of all these disadvantages I still feel tough enough to thoroughly enjoy being there myself. Oh, I'd just love to come, Martyn! I've always had a spot of wanderlust in me you know, and I really feel quite jealous to think of you seeing all these new interesting places – while I stay quietly at home. I do so want to come – those mountains they sound so lovely! Anything cold appeals to me at the moment – that wretched sun has turned enemy and I used to love it so much! ...

Saturday 5th July

My dearest darling girl,

... Our trip last night was a rather long convoy escort and after making the usual reports on the flight I set course for my hut for a few hours' sleep, but when I opened the door, lo and behold, on my bed was a large pile of letters, all just itching to be opened!

The one from Dad said that he felt my arguments for getting married on my next leave were very sound and even suggested that he could add more to those I had mentioned. To my amazement he remarked that I should leave the question of a post-war job until the time came and not worry about that now.

And then, after expressing his conviction that you have all the virtues that go to make a good wife, he concluded by saying that if we do decide to marry, we shall have the 'warmest benediction' from himself and Mum!

So do we make the big decision, darling? I can hardly imagine you saying 'no'. In fact I shall take it as a certainty that you will shortly become Mrs E.M.A.!

Darling, I'm feeling so terribly excited now and I simply can't imagine how I shall endure two, or three, or four months here with such a marvellous leave to look forward to!

Of course there are going to be one or two snags, you know. One is the possibility that I may have to wait a fair time for leave and that when it does come it will be granted on the spur of the moment.

We must have all things cut and dried, Lily. We must have everything fixed to the smallest detail so that final arrangements can be made a few days beforehand.

Another snag is that it seems pretty unlikely that you would be able to join me up here yet awhile. By next year the place may be more civilised and officers' wives may be allowed but for the time being I'm afraid there's not much hope.

What would you do for the present? Would you stay on at Shadrack's if they would still employ you? That will be entirely up to you, of course, but I should imagine that you would find it rather lonely if you had no little office in which to write your letters to me! And would Mr Chapman consider granting you a week's holiday without pay, do you think? We must have at least a week's honeymoon, you know! ...

When I do get leave it should be about fourteen days and I suggest that the wedding takes place about three days after I have arrived home. Do you know if it is possible to fix up weddings at such short notice?

I'm wondering how you are going to choose your wedding dress, in view of the fact that it may be summer, autumn or winter when you are actually married! Do you still propose to attire yourself in blue and wine?

The wedding breakfast question is going to be rather tricky now that food rationing is so comprehensive and taking into consideration that the whole affair will have to be fixed up on the spur of the moment. Do you think a 'slap-up' tea (or dinner) should be attempted or do you feel that some kind of buffet meal would be most convenient in the circumstances?

I've just been looking through our list of people to be invited and I must say that sorting them out is going to be a very difficult business.

At the moment I can hardly believe it's true that we shall be married in a matter of weeks – even yesterday such a possibility still seemed very remote.

I can just imagine how excited you will be when you receive this letter. I can imagine you planning your wedding dress and thinking about brilliant schemes for the wedding day and honeymoon! ...

Monday 7th July

My dearest girl,

... You are so keen to come to Kaldadarnes that I hate to tell you that coming up here will be off at least for a few months after we're married. In fact you might have to wait until I'm posted home again before you'll be able to come and live with me. Would you rather postpone the wedding until you're able to live with me? I can hardly believe you'll say 'yes' and I'm certainly hoping that you won't!

No, ducky. Jimmy wasn't hurt in either of the crack-ups that he had whilst staying at Wick. He didn't tell me much in his airmail. He only described how, after a 600 mile trip, the starboard engine seized up and caught fire and then unable to reach a clearing they crashed into trees and caught fire. Actually, six were killed and five others were unhurt. He's writing to me though, so I should hear some more gen in a month's time.

Martyn at the controls

We had some fun this morning, for whilst patrolling around the convoy we saw a line of spray and a long green shape beneath the water! At once we prepared for anti-submarine action – bomb doors open, bomb switches on etc. etc. and we wheeled round in tight circles trying to keep it in view. We lost it for a minute or so and then we saw the long shape again – it was coming to the surface! Breathless, we stared and stared and then it appeared on the surface – a huge whale! You can imagine our disappointment as it blew and then submerged again. Subsequently we saw two or three more of them and huge things they were too. …

Saturday 12th July

My dearest girl,

… It rather shook me when I saw what a lot of questions I'd got to answer for you, but I'll try my best to give suitable and tactful replies. No, there are no bathrooms but I have unfolded my canvas bath and already used it three times. It is less than four foot square so you can imagine bathing is a little tricky to put it mildly!

No, you'll be relieved to hear that there are no women on the camp – though we are hoping that they'll send us some WAAFs pretty soon!

The Yanks are certainly here in full force but they're not taking the island over completely – at least as far as we know. Their troops will apparently relieve ours but though some of their squadrons may operate from this country, it's extremely unlikely that we shall be sent home. Oh dearest one, I do so wish you could come up here too, but that also seems to be a very remote possibility at the moment.

I am awfully glad that you've asked Mum to go with you to the Prom. I know she'll enjoy the Grieg concerto and Beethoven's Eighth. Talking of the family, I was delighted to hear that Mum and Dad and Auntie May had all been down to see you on your birthday and that Auntie had brought you such a grand bunch of roses.

There was a considerable 'flap' on here today, for the commander in chief of coastal command – Air Marshal Sir Philip Joubert de la Ferté – visited the station. I've got a deuce of a swelled head, for I was second pilot to our squadron leader in the aircraft that took him back to Reykjavík! So, if you read of the Air Marshal's return to England you can remember that but for your fiancé's steady hand on the throttles, he would not have made such a safe journey from Kaldadarnes to Reykjavík! …

My darling Martyn,

... It has been so terribly hot! On Saturday I set off on my bike for the Kingfisher pool and was very soon enjoying the coolness of the water. After having quite a good swim I sat out and sunbathed. I'm beginning to get quite brown but not painfully so - I'm being careful about that. By the time I'd cycled home the clouds were very black and a few minutes later a storm broke. It's quite exciting during the storms but it's a good job they don't last long for there are one or two tiles that got dislodged on our roof and now, if we have a heavy rainfall, the water absolutely pours into the dining room. They're supposed to be coming to repair it, but in the meantime, directly it looks like a storm, we have to move the furniture and get a bath in position.

On Sunday I cooked the breakfast and dinner. We had some peas from my allotment and some from our garden that Dad sowed and I carefully kept mine separate. And do you know, everybody said mine were best! They certainly were jolly nice. I do wish you could sample them.

We are very slack at the office just now (no laughter please!). We shall be very busy in the winter if a stricter rationing comes in but this morning there was nothing doing and I kept on seeing girls go speeding by on bikes and wishing that I could be on mine. I really am awfully glad I've got it, now that I'm used to riding. I just love it! I can't think why I haven't wanted a bike before! But I'm very grateful to you for arousing that desire – you are certainly entirely responsible you know ...

Your last letter was written on the 2nd July – twelve days ago. It seems such a long time and I'm simply longing to hear from you again. Have you any more hopeful news of leave? From the little bits of news one reads or hears I've realised that you will have to stay in Iceland in spite of the USA measure. In a way

I'm glad because I do feel you're a bit safer out there. But oh, darling, I do long to see you! You are in my thoughts the whole time and every minute is spent in longing for you.

I love you so, Lily

... This morning, Martyn, I got up early and cycled down to the allotment. I picked about a pound of peas, a bunch of carrots and lettuce. Then I thinned my cabbages and savoys and did a spot of weeding. By that time it was half past eight so I mounted my steed and went home to breakfast. Certainly, if I didn't have any more produce at all from my plot, it would have been worth cultivating, but when I look at my sturdy parsnips, carrots, beetroot (all about a foot high) and the bulging pea pods etc. I'm jolly glad I toiled and dug last spring! It gives me no end of a thrill to think I did it all alone.

I shall always have to have an allotment now, Martyn, until the time we have a garden of our own. Oh, that'll be a lovely time, won't it, darling!? We'll probably quarrel as to who's going to sow the lettuce! Just a little friendly quarrel, so as we have to kiss and make up. We'll never quarrel seriously, will we, Martyn? We love each other too much ...

Thursday 17th July

... Jimmy, Geoff, Guy and myself are all installed together in one hut now. We've scrounged a lot of nails, wood and compressed fibre boarding and commenced making the hut really luxurious!

Shelves for washing and shaving tackle and packing case cupboards have been produced, whilst the 'pièce de résistance' is a wardrobe which is large enough to hold all our coats and which stands the length of one wall! ...

Martyn fooling around with Geoff

My dearest girl,

Still no more letters from you have arrived and I am finding it increasingly difficult to concoct material for my letters to you.

The routine is more or less the same here from day to day and I have no delightful Proms or exciting rambles to tell you about, so it's a great help when there is a letter from you to reply to!

Today I have been with the Wing Commander on a sightseeing tour of the island. That is rather an overstatement – actually we flew almost the entire length of the south coast taking a good look at the coastline. For the first time since I've been here I flew quite close to the glaciers and they really are a fine sight from the air. The ice presents a very different appearance from snow. It is speckled and seems to flash and glitter in the sunlight whereas the smooth snow glistens a bright, even white. But why should I describe glaciers to you? For after all, you are an experienced Swiss traveller and know far more about glaciers than I do!

On the way back the 'winco' wanted fun and games so he flew along the jet black lava beach at 40 feet, scaring all the sea birds that appeared as white flecks against the ground. There were seals too by the water's edge but their dark bodies were pretty hard to distinguish ...

I seem to be doing an enormous amount of amateur carpentry these days – making washstands, tables, cupboards and goodness knows what else. My latest effort is a folding chart board for navigating on and this has occupied my time for the last couple of evenings. Personally I think it is a milestone in the history of navigational

Martyn with his air crew

instruments, but because it is not as rigid as it might be, and because I have dividers and protectors attached to the ends of elastic bands, Guy and Geoff accuse me of pinching Heath Robinson's ideas and are themselves continually suggesting additions and embellishments!

It's Tuesday evening at seven o'clock. What will you be doing now, I wonder? Maybe you've just met Maisie and George and Tony and Joan and Prissie and Alice – maybe you're just on your way up to the Kingfisher! I can just imagine you walking up Grove Road and I envy you very, very much. At least it's not so much you that I envy but those who are with you – I envy everyone who has the pleasure of even seeing you when I am denied such happiness ...

Wednesday 30th July

My dearest girl,

... I had expected to spend a fairly quiet day but at eleven o'clock I was told that in half an hour's time I should be taking off on quite a long trip. We were, in fact, going to have a look at Greenland's icy mountains and I need hardly tell you that I was delighted with the opportunity of such a unique bit of sightseeing.

The visibility was astounding and the Greenland coast could be seen when we were still almost 100 miles distant. And then, as we got closer, we saw the most amazing and terrifying coastline that it is possible to imagine.

I expected smooth, snow-covered hills and I was not a little surprised to see a land completely covered with steep, pointed, jagged mountains of utterly bare rock.

When at school you first read about mountains, you visualise them as very high cones rising straight out of the ground. But when you see the mountains of Wales or Scotland, or Iceland for that matter, you find that the ground slowly rises until one point is higher than the rest of the ground and this point is termed the mountain peak.

But the mountains of Greenland surpass one's wildest dreams – they are as steep, rough and pointed as those flint arrowheads that one sees in museums and from afar the coastline appears as a string of gigantic, black, dog's teeth!

All the mountains are capped with snow but it almost seems as if they are too steep for the snow to cling to the sides. Between them, glaciers run like huge rivers down to the water's edge. We must have seen dozens of glaciers as for three hours we flew down the coast. Yes, it was certainly an amazing spectacle – a sight that I shall never forget.

The icebergs too were a sight for sore eyes, for some must have risen to almost 500 feet and were over a quarter of a mile in length. As you know, they are wider beneath the surface than above and all the border of ice beneath the water appeared a brilliant bluish-green colour in the sunlight. It was just as if the bergs were surrounded by green neon tubes and I was spellbound as we passed directly over one of the largest. Its flat, oval shape glistened white in the brilliant sunlight, bordered by a ring of brilliant blue-green and the whole was sat in a sea of deep Mediterranean blue!

It was a long trip, but one that I wouldn't have missed for the world – a real consolation for being so far from home! ...

When I arrived back I found that a letter from you was waiting for me and I was amazed to find that it had only been five days in transit. I do wish though that the intermediary ones would come. There must be almost a dozen on their way somewhere and they are like the missing pieces in the jigsaw puzzle ... I want to hear your reactions to the letter with my ideas about our wedding, for by the timing of this latest letter I feel sure you must have received it. But I must just wait patiently and look forward to that pile of envelopes that must come soon! ...

Friday 1st August

My dearest girl,

... For the last ten minutes I've been sitting pen in hand, trying to think of a way of commencing this letter!

Today I seem to have even less news for you than usual, but it's been teeming with rain all day and I've done nothing but eat meals and moon around the drome. I've done a little reading and fixed up a rather unsuccessful apparatus for pouring water from a petrol can into our wash-basin, but I'm feeling pretty browned off at present and can't settle down to do any useful work. A glance through the window is enough to dampen the highest spirits and I'm also particularly gloomy because the long-awaited mail has still failed to put in an appearance. I understand that there is a chance of it arriving tomorrow but I am so impatient for it to come that I can't settle down to wait for it!

And then I've been further depressed by some new gen about leave. We are to have twenty-eight days per year, though we are actually entitled to fifty-six, and it will all have to be taken at one time. Furthermore it is inclusive of travelling time so, if I come by boat, I shall have no more than fourteen days at home.

Heaven knows when I shall get it, though. One has to have been up in Iceland for at least three months before leave is granted and of course there are crowds of other fellows who will be due for it before I am. Still, one never can tell. Maybe this rather gloomy outlook will brighten and I shall be seeing you sometime before Christmas after all.

Fancy, over nine weeks have passed since I was with you. I don't think we have ever been apart for so long before. Sometimes I can hardly believe that over two months have elapsed since I was last at home, yet at other times, and this very moment is one of them, it seems ages since we said goodbye at Euston. When I do come home I shall hardly be able to remember what Euston looks like but I shan't be long in recognising a certain girl if she's waiting there to meet me!

When censoring letters, I often find airmen complaining because their girls have got tired of waiting for them to come home and have found other attractions who are more frequently within reach! It makes one so happy when one knows that one has a girl who waits patiently, or should I say impatiently, but faithfully for one's homecoming. I know you'll wait for me, darling one – maybe you won't have to wait so long.

Oh, my sweetheart, I'm just aching to be with you – to claim all those kisses that you're owing me now.

Keep loving me, Lily,
I'm loving you madly all the time,
Martyn

Dearest Martyn,

... I wasn't a bit amused by your account of the flight with the 'winco'! In fact I was most apprehensive. I'm referring to the fun and games of course. I disapprove entirely and completely of such dangerous showing off and you just tell him next time to go off and have his fun and games by himself without subjecting my beloved fiancé to such unnecessary danger! I hope you don't do that sort of thing – or that your prowess will tempt you to indulge in such hazardous pastimes. I think you've got more sense and I hope that you haven't forgotten your promises not to take any risks. You won't forget, will you, Martyn, not for a minute even, how precious, how terribly, terribly dear, is your life to me.

Although I shouldn't know a folding chart board for navigating if I saw one, I have no doubt it is a very useful instrument! If you say so, I will agree unconditionally that it is a milestone in the history of etc. etc.! ...

You said such lovely things about me, Martyn. I feel very flattered! Did you really mean them, darling? Am I really as nice as that? I can hardly believe it.

I often think of that day, your last but one day at home, when I met you suddenly returning from Wanstead. I remember the thrill of pleasure I got when I saw you walking towards me – until I saw how woebegone you looked. I remember how very frightened I was when you said we ought to break. How, suddenly, the world looked very, very bleak to me and seemed to crumble before my feet. How terribly relieved I was when I knew that you hadn't stopped loving me after all – and that was all that mattered! How crazy it was, Martyn. Do you think we could ever forget the happiness we've given each other? Do you think we could look into each other's eyes and not feel the passion rising? No, darling, we are not the sort of people who love lightly. Of course we must never break – we were just made for each other. And were we not friends before we were lovers? Our love will last, Martyn, I'm sure of it ...

Wednesday 13th August

My darling Martyn,

The last letter I had from you was nine days ago! So I'm beginning to hope for a letter each time the postman comes ...Last night Tony handed me a little book and said, "The Fellowship wish me to present this to you, hoping you will study it carefully, as they consider you a danger to the public!" I looked at it. – It was the Highway Code! (I'm not really as bad as that!) ...

When are you coming home to marry me, Martyn? I'm getting very, very impatient! It's eleven weeks tomorrow since you went. That's an awful long time and I'm pining for the sight of your dear face. Will it be soon? ...

Friday 15th August

My darling girl,

... I was called out to fly last night and was in the air until after midnight. We'd a rather important job concerning a certain gentleman, whose trip or trips across the ocean you have no doubt read about in the papers. I wouldn't know much about his activities, as papers are so irregular up here and I am not often able to hear radio bulletins.

All went well until we arrived home in pitch darkness and then an unlucky landing – not by myself this time! – resulted in another crack-up!

Fortunately, it was not nearly as bad as the Silloth business, though unpleasant whilst it lasted. My only injury was a large bruise sustained in the haste of getting out quick, so don't worry about it. I have a charmed life! ...

18

On 9th August 1941, the British battleship HMS Prince of Wales transported Winston Churchill across the Atlantic for a secret conference with President Roosevelt. This culminated in the signing of the Atlantic Charter which was a statement of shared ethics and intent between the United States and the Great Britain alliance.

In a BBC broadcast that Churchill gave a few days later, he explained the significance of the charter and also thanked the Navy and RAF for providing him with protection.

Communication between Lily and Martyn was very difficult and haphazard at this time. Although they both continued to write to each other almost every day there was a time lag of between seven and ten days between a letter being written and received, and mail sometimes went missing altogether.

Martyn also had the added frustration of having to abide by the need for secrecy concerning his flying activities.

My precious darling Martyn,

I wonder what you are doing now? Perhaps you are flying across a wide expanse of ocean. That's a frightening thought, though, so I think I'll imagine you safely on the ground in your hut – possibly writing to me. Or maybe you're at Reykjavík? It seems about time for you to have another two days off. Wherever you are, I hope you are thinking about me, for I am wanting you desperately just now and it helps a little to know that you have the same longing. The same ache in your heart.

Do you remember that evening last August when, having reported at Sevenoaks, you eventually arrived back home? I was crying over the letter I was writing to you, quite unaware of the lovely surprise coming to me. I was saying how much I was going to miss you and how I'd give anything to have you back. And miraculously – you came! I was so happy that night – as if you'd been away a month, instead of a few hours!

Then there was Christmas Day. Lots of presents, everyone having fun, everyone except me! I hated the presents and the games. I hated Christmas because you weren't there. How could I live through the rest of the evening with tears smarting behind my eyes because everything seemed meaningless without you? And then came your knock at the door! How I did hug you, didn't I?! I believe I even cried a little – foolish little girl! But you came just when I needed you most, just when I couldn't carry on without you.

Oh, I know it's foolish – but I'm listening for your knock now! I know it's quite impossible – but you always come when I want you most and when I want you desperately, as I do tonight nothing seems impossible.

This is all very silly! I'm sorry. It's Sunday night, you see. I don't think I'd better write any more on Sunday evenings. I'm finding it very hard to keep back the tears. If you knew, you would say 'Poor little girl, I will do without a letter rather than you should make yourself so unhappy!' Would you say that, Martyn? Will you forgive me for leaving off here and starting again tomorrow to tell you all the things I meant to? I'll be better in the morning ...

Sunday 24th August

My dearest Lily,

This evening, after going to church, I had dinner and then listened to 'Winnie's' speech. It was encouraging to hear that, if we do win the war, it is no longer proposed to adopt the policy of crushing Germany's economic life – the main blunder of the last peace ...Do you remember me saying in a previous letter that I had escorted a notable personage on an important trip? Well, you'll know now to whom I was referring! In his speech he mentioned how a Catalina was watching overhead. Well, our aeroplane relieved the Catalina just as the *Prince of Wales* steamed slap through the middle of the convoy!

We hadn't been warned about this little review and it shook us considerably when the battle fleet suddenly altered course right through the line of cargo boats! Close examination revealed that the convoy was gay with bunting so we realised then that the sudden meeting was not wholly accidental.

When at last we sent 'returning to base' to the *Prince of Wales* it replied "Cheerio and happy landings." Most ironically we cracked up when we did get home! ...

My dearest Martyn,

... We have heard a great deal about Churchill's trip and I dare say you have by now. I must say that the Atlantic Charter has given me a good deal of hope in the possibility of right being done at the end. We shall see. Of course I was most thrilled when we heard about his visit to Iceland. Did you see him?

I was very relieved to hear that once again you've got out of a smash lightly. Thank God you weren't hurt. Whose fault was it? Do be ever so careful, darling ...I had the greatest thrill I've had in entertainment for a long time yesterday at the last night of the Proms. It was simply grand. I enjoyed every minute. Have you been to a last night Prom? I never have before so it was my first experience – a grand one at that!

We arrived at the Albert Hall at quarter past five and queued for a quarter of an hour before the door opened. We had a good pick of the seats – it was M section again – the wrong side for the soloist but to our delight when he came on he walked straight to our side as he was being accompanied on the harp.

The *Rebus Overture* by Frank Bridge was quite new to me and was only performed for the first time in February of this year. Its original title was *Rumour* and it starts off with a little tune that gets magnified as it goes along.

Henry Wendon sang the 'Faery Song' gorgeously, but though we clapped and shouted for more there was no time for encores apparently.

It was great fun stamping one's feet to the tune of the 'Sailor's Hornpipe' in the last item. The place really shook with it! And people promenading were trying to dance. But the biggest thrill of all was at the end when we all rose to sing 'Rule Britannia' and then clapped and shouted and stamped for Sir Henry Wood; we sang 'For He's a Jolly Good Fellow' and

'Britannia' a second time, and then 'God save the King' – but still we kept on clapping until, Sir Henry having appeared for the third time with his hat and coat, our hands were too sore to clap any more and we subsided!

Once there was really no likelihood of Sir Henry appearing anymore we put on our macs and went out into the rain. By the way, the party consisted of Tony, Clifford, Alice, Joe, Prissie, your father and myself. We came out of the Albert Hall at ten past eight, and as we should've had rather a rush for the train, we decided to miss that one and spend the interval of an hour in the Lyons Corner House. So, we walked down to the station and went by tube to Charing Cross. We rushed along to the Corner House expecting to see long queues, but no, we were able to walk straight in and your father found a friendly head waiter who piloted us to a table for six. It was so nice to be there again with all the bright lights and gay chatter and the band playing serenades. We had a good old traditional Corner House help yourself hors d'oeuvres with brown bread and butter, and coffee which your father insisted on paying for! Yes, Martyn, I had coffee! And I liked it! True, there was only one lump of sugar and I should have like three, but in spite of that I enjoyed it. An accomplishment which you may take all the credit for! I only tried it to please you, you know, and I'm most grateful to you now for persuading me. But don't try and make me drink tea, will you?! I really couldn't, Martyn, not even for you! ...

On 27th August Martyn experienced one of the most eventful days of his RAF career.

Thursday 28th August

My dearest darling,

As I have absolutely no news of my own for you, I'm going to start straightaway and answer some of your letters. You're very lucky, you know, doing such a lot of things every day and having so much to talk about! I envy you tremendously when you write on, page after page, telling me about Proms, badminton, Fellowship outings, allotments and heaven knows what else!

And I sit down, feverishly searching my mind for some scrap of news to tell you – some incidents or experiences from my life of which fifty per cent is quite uninteresting and the rest must be kept secret! …

On the morning of 27th August a U-boat had been detected by an aircraft from Kaldadarnes so a second 269 Squadron Hudson, flown by Squadron Leader James Thompson, went to investigate. The captain of the U-570, who had climbed out on to the bridge, heard the approaching Hudson's engines and ordered a crash-dive but Thompson's aircraft reached the U-570 before she was fully submerged and dropped its four 250-pound depth charges. One detonated just 10 yards from the submarine. The U-570 resurfaced and ten of the crew emerged. The Hudson fired on them with machine guns, but ceased when the U-boat crew displayed a white sheet. Most of the crew remained on the deck of the submarine as Thompson circled above them. He radioed for assistance and Martyn and his crew, who had been flying a Hudson from Scotland to Iceland, diverted and helped to guard the U-boat until a Navy vessel came to capture it and take it in tow. They also took photographs of the submarine with the crew clustered on the conning tower. This was the first occasion in which aircraft alone had succeeded in capturing a submarine. The

U-570 was a newly built submarine, on her first war patrol, and hence of invaluable interest to the Admiralty. Subsequently the submarine was put into Navy service as the HMS Graph.

Monday 1st September

Dearest girl,

... I'm afraid that I must advise you not to buy your wedding dress as yet, unless of course they are becoming increasingly scarce and expensive. I can now hold out little hope of getting home before Christmas. In fact I've resigned myself to the idea of seeing nothing but Kaldadarnes for the next four months and am hopefully planning for leave in the early New Year. So, if you do decide to buy some articles now, I suggest that you choose those suitable for spring wear.

I'm just gazing at the photo where you're wearing your pale blue dress, and what memories that brings back! Dances and doorsteps – dimmed lights, romantic atmosphere and my arm around you and then kisses and a long embrace when we reached home! Darling, won't it be marvellous when we can enjoy such ecstasy again – till then I shall dream contentedly of the past and long for an even more perfect future.

I'm loving you with all my heart, sweetheart,
you know that, don't you?
Martyn

Lily in her blue dress

My precious darling,

... I had a lovely time last night! There was nothing arranged for Fellowship, tennis having finished, but it was such a lovely evening that I decided it mustn't be wasted. Not that I ever waste my evenings – there's always too much to do. But the sun was still shining brightly and it was very warm so I decided to go for a bike ride. I went over the new bridge to the High Road, taking the left fork at Bancroft's, passed the path to Connaught Water and straight on up to High Beech. It was simply gorgeous up by the church on the hill, with the sun filtering down through the trees making shadows on the road.

When I reached the summit I intended to bear to the right and make my way back through Loughton, but ahead of me stretched a winding lane, obviously going downhill, so I just couldn't resist it and was soon flying along, tearing round bends, my hair flying in the wind, with my skirt somewhere round my waist and all the little insects going ping against my cheeks! It was grand! About four or five miles all downhill – I went on and on with no idea where I was going.

At the bottom I came to a major road and a huge field of corn. The men were gathering it and putting it into a machine which chopped the ears off and then passed the bundles out to be piled on to a stack. It was most interesting and I stayed a little while watching, till the men got too friendly! And then I cycled on. I rode on for quite a way and presently saw that I was coming into the village or town. I was riding beside iron railings enclosing some large buildings which looked like a factory and next I arrived at the gates, where two policemen stood on guard with revolvers in their belts! So I got off and asked where I was and they said 'Waltham Abbey'! It was the armament factory, of course.

Well, I knew my way into the town, so I went along and looked at the Abbey and then, as the time was getting on, decided I'd better be making for home. I enquired the way to Loughton and was soon speeding along through the forest [Epping Forest] and at length I seemed to recognise the road and I was on the road to the Wake Arms. I went straight on to Loughton, Buckhurst Hill and so along to Roding Valley and Woodford station, and I reached home just about two minutes after lighting up time! ...

As well as writing to Lily and his parents, Martyn regularly corresponded with Fellowship friends and his aero modelling club schoolfriends, including Bob Jacobs and Peter Matthews who he'd worked with as a teenager to build the Flying Flea. In one letter to Martyn, Peter wrote, 'Lily asked if I would take her photograph, as you had been agitating for some snaps of her. ... We therefore went round to Lily's last Saturday afternoon and had to take her photo in about three different frocks, her tennis rigout, and with – and <u>on</u> – her bicycle. She insisted on being photographed riding the bike and steering with only one hand! This was designed to improve your confidence in her riding ability, but it is just as well that you will not see the sequences before and after the photographs were taken. For goodness' sake do not tell her that I have said this because she really is making progress.'

Lily with her bike, close to home, on the corner of Grenville Gardens and Wansford Road

Thursday 4th September

My dearest girl,

… We've just had a letter from a fellow who was at Cerney with us and he mentioned that his wife, who had to register some while ago, has now been called up. So even if wives were allowed up here, once you left Shadrack's you would be liable to be called up and the only way that you could reach Iceland's shores would be as a member of the WAAFs!

And believe me, ducky, I'd much rather you were at home in Shadrack's than up here in the WAAFs.

Not, of course, that you would be given the choice of coming up here anyway, even if they did decide to introduce WAAFs for the entertainment of the troops!

So in this respect, I'm afraid, the outlook is pretty grim, though there's always the consoling thought that it's most unlikely that I shall be out here for more than a year, and a quarter of that time will have passed when you receive this letter …

Thursday 4th September

… Mr Chapman gave me a long sermon yesterday on the foolishness of getting married:

a. during a war
b. being under 25
c. if the husband had to leave his wife at home!

He'd just got back from the Wanstead office and Mrs Ashwood had told him about her daughter who married an RAF fellow a little while ago but while he was away had met someone she liked better and decided to ignore her marriage! They've agreed to part – her husband being rather annoyed.

I felt awful! As if my intentions of wanting to ask for two weeks' holiday for my wedding was written all over me in black-and-white!

I still haven't said anything about it to Mr Chapman, so he can't know. But I'd love to know how much he's guessed! I bet he'll have a lot to say when I do tell him.

You know you don't have to be afraid of me doing that, don't you. Margaret Ashwood has a lot of her father's bad blood in her and apparently she's always been flighty and undisciplined.

I know I'm going to love you ever so much more when you're my husband and I'm quite positive, certain, that I'll never love anyone else but you! So, don't be afraid of me being unfaithful to you ...

Saturday 6th September

My darling Martyn,

... I'm getting very disappointed and depressed because I still haven't had any letters from you – isn't it odd? I've had no letters from Iceland since 15th August – three weeks ago! I am beginning to wonder if you've met an Icelandic *stúlka* whose kisses are nicer than mine! I heard about *stúlkas* on the wireless. They had a recording of a troop entertainment in Iceland ...

Tuesday 9th September

My darling Martyn,

This morning the seemingly unending silence, in the way of letters from you, was broken at last! I tore to the door at the postman's knock and he handed me two letters in your dear familiar writing. I glanced at the envelopes first. One was quite normal but on the other was an ominous little note 'Damaged by seawater'!

I opened that one first and found to my consternation that inside, between pages on which the ink had run till the writing was almost unreadable, a solid white mass – the promised photographs!

At first I thought the photos were useless, but I got busy with a kettle of water over the gas and tried to steam them apart. The first one was stuck to the paper and all the others stuck fast to each other. I held them in the steam till they were soft and damp and then very, very carefully, with my heart in my mouth, I attempted to peel the top one off. First the inevitable gumboots appeared – then legs – and before it could stick on again I'd peeled it right off. The one of you sitting on the petrol can! It's lovely, darling! I do like it ever so much. It took me about half an hour to get the others unstuck but one by one I managed to peel them off …

The salvaged photo

I'm horribly afraid that lots of your other letters have been lost altogether. Assuming that you wrote every day, your letters from the 20th to the 26th and the 27th to the 31st have all gone missing – and the parcel of cheese! It makes me feel very sad to think that some of your letters, so very precious to me, may be at the bottom of the sea. Could you try and remember what you said, Martyn, and write them again? …

I was stricken with a sort of despair when I read the news about leave. Thank you for putting it in. It's about time that my soaring hopes were brought down to earth! It was a shattering blow, though. Since that letter when you talked about October as being fairly definite, I've hoped and prayed and pretended! In my most pessimistic moments I've never gone further than the end of November. But now, another four months at least! I don't think I can bear it, Martyn.

That's silly. Forgive me. I know I've got to somehow, though I'm still going to hope.

Three months, nearly four have gone already and I'm remembering how quickly the days go by. It will be lovely if you come at Christmas time and if you don't perhaps I shall be able to go back with you in the New Year? Is there any more hope of wives being allowed? That would be a marvellous compensation for waiting a long time. Do you think there is a hope?

My lovely costume, Martyn! (Bleak despair again!) I shan't be able to wear that at Christmas. All my lovely things will be moth-eaten or out of date by the time you come! Why is it? Has the leave been slowed down? What makes you think it will be so long in coming? Do tell me all you can?

You say some precious things that make my eyes go dreamy with longing. Yes, we have had ample time to discover whether our love is deep and real and sincere.

I will shore up my love till you come, Martyn – all the kisses, all the caresses, all the little things I want to say to you – and the longer it is, the more there'll be!

I'll think about that when I'm sad – it's the happiest thought I've had today.

Keep safe dearest,

Lily

My dearest girl,

I've just been deliberately making myself homesick, or should I say lovesick, for the two are very much akin in this case! To put it briefly, I've just been playing over my records of ballet music and trying to imagine myself back at Sadlers Wells or Covent Garden. And if I shut my eyes and let myself dream sentimentally it's not at all difficult to find myself back in the slips at Covent Garden or at the back of the gallery on the first night that we went there together.

I shall never forget how brave I felt to be taking a girl out for the first time and how terribly thrilled and romantic I felt whilst I was sitting beside you! I felt that we were just on the threshold of some most exciting and delicious years – and I was right, wasn't I?!

And then, when we came home from the performance in the train, I remember how I deliberated whether to sit beside you or opposite you – finally deciding to do the latter for I felt that to sit beside you would be going a 'bit too far'!

And then again, in the spring of 1940, there were those trips to Sadlers Wells when you came home from Torquay and I came home from Hastings.

By that time I was a sergeant and very much braver when I escorted you home after the show. I rather believe that I sat beside you in the carriage then. In fact I seem to remember kissing you quite a lot between Liverpool Street and George Lane and holding you in my arms for the whole of the journey!

What delightful memories. My blood tingles as I relive the glorious experience of falling in love and I am just longing for the day when I can fall in love with you again!

That seems a silly thing to say, for I'm loving you madly all the time, but how we shall enjoy the old ecstasy when we can see each other and talk to each other and kiss each other again.

I want to be to be with you so much, sweetheart,

Martyn

Monday 15th September

My precious Martyn,

... I love telling people about our wedding, don't you? It gives me an immense thrill to talk about something that seems too wonderful to ever really happen! And other people seem to accept it so calmly. It helps to persuade me that it will come about, though I shan't really be able to believe it until you are with me again, until we can talk about it together. We are missing a lot, aren't we, Martyn – not being able to discuss our own wedding! But we'll make up for it when you come home, won't we? ...

Wednesday 17th September

...When I cycled to Ilford, Martyn, I left my bike at the Stockdales so when I returned from the shops I stayed and chatted to Muriel's people for some time. I did so wish that someone would come running in and say, "Hello Auntie Liddy!" I miss Janet very much – it seems so different without her.

Won't it be fun when we have a little girl like Janet, Martyn? A little girl with black – sorry – 'dark' curly hair and blue eyes! I do want children so dreadfully, Martyn. But I want a little boy first. I want a little boy who's very, very like you! ...

Wednesday 17th September

My sweetheart Lily,

Now, ducky, I have some news that will no doubt interest you, though whether it will please or disappoint you I cannot say. It is, needless to say, about leave!

I have now ascertained that they are not sending us home in crews but are arranging it in the order of who has been up here the longest. By the end of November, according to my careful calculations, it should be my turn to come home, unless some new scheme is devised that fiddles me out of the privilege!

So now you have some more information that is at least a little more definite though not particularly helpful. To put it briefly – I shall definitely not get leave before the end of November, whilst there is quite a fair possibility that I shall be at home with you about Christmas time. So it will be a winter wedding, I'm afraid, and our honeymoon will not be quite as we had planned it to be. I fear that it will be too cold to lie for hours on end on the Devon cliffs or enjoy summer sunshine by the edge of the Devon seas! …

Saturday 20th September

My precious Martyn,

… Les has received a summons to appear at Stratford police court, for returning his call-up papers. He has to appear on 1st October and the usual procedure is six months' imprisonment starting from that day. So it looks as though we shan't see him for quite a time. Florence intends to keep the house and get a job. She wants to anyway.

I hope you won't feel too badly about having a future brother-in-law in prison? It's rather a blow to Mum and Dad, but, though I don't agree with him, I still admire his pluck. He's giving up a great deal.

I had my hair set last night. It took all evening! But it does look nice now. By the way, do you ever wash your hair these days? I think you should, ducky! And do you ever get your folding bath out now? – I bet you don't! ...

Sunday 21st September

My dearest Lily,

All day yesterday it was rumoured that mail was coming in the evening and in gleeful anticipation I hopped around all day like a cat on hot bricks – too excited to settle down to read or write! After dinner I went into the anteroom expecting to see masses of mail lying around but to my overwhelming distress the room was bare!

I waited and waited and at ten o'clock decided that I was waiting in vain and so went off to bed. The mail did come in, however – at midnight! – and so at breakfast time this morning I had the delight of opening eleven letters ...Lily, darling Lily, I do need you so terribly just now. Memories of months ago make me so impatient and I long for the delight of holding you in my arms. But maybe it's not so far away after all – yes, darling, I have some more news of leave!

Yet another leave list has come out and although it is not quite as I had anticipated, my name does appear thereon. And, if it is adhered to, which in this case is very probable, I shall be home, or rather on my way home, during the first week in November! Does that cheer you up again, darling? By the time you receive this letter it will be little over a month before I board the leave boat and less than six weeks before we are actually married!

Today I feel very, very happy! The appearance of the mail and the latest gen on the leave question have sent my spirits soaring! ...

29th September

... I should get home, Lily, either on the fifth or sixth of November. ... I reckon that it would be too much of a rush to arrange the wedding for Saturday 8th November and if we cannot have it on a Saturday we could fix it for any day during the following week. I expect that my last day at home would be either the 24th or 25th.

The only snag is that it's quite possible that the whole leave will be shifted to a fortnight later, so please don't attempt to make any kind of definite or even preliminary arrangements yet.

When I am about to board the boat, I shall send you a telegram worded simply 'NICE WORK – MARTYN' and then if everything is suddenly cancelled you will receive a further telegram saying 'TOUGH LUCK – MARTYN'. If 'nice work' is not followed by 'tough luck' you can then expect to receive a wire from a town in the British Isles during the next two or three days. In this way I should be able to tell you the approximate time of my arrival in London.

You could book Bodgers the caterers as soon as you receive my 'nice work' telegram and then cancel the booking if the fateful 'tough luck' follows! ...

… As I write this letter, Lily, I am practically sitting on the stove for it has got much colder these last few days and tonight it is very chilly. It is a lovely night though – bright moonlight (yes, we do have a moon up here!) and the northern lights are up in full force too. Yes, the northern lights are visible almost every night now, appearing as huge searchlights that stretch across the sky from north to south, east to west, or maybe forming a cone or painting in all directions. Usually the streaks of light are white, just like searchlights, but sometimes they appear to be vaguely tinted pink or green. They were quite an awe-inspiring spectacle at first but now we hardly notice them! …

Monday 6th October

My dearest girl,

Last night I received more letters and one was from Ken. He says he will be pleased to officiate at the wedding as best man, so that's a load off my mind. I don't know how he proposes to get leave for the occasion but he knows that the great event is taking place in November, so I imagine that there is at least a pretty good chance of him getting away from his unit for a day. As soon as you receive my 'nice work' telegram, please wire him and tell him the date decided for the wedding.

I'm naturally counting on you to send out all the invitations as soon as the 'nice work' telegram confirms the date …

Tuesday 7th October

My precious darling Martyn,

Imagine me more excited than you've ever known me before – imagine my love and longing for you simply bubbling over – imagine me absolutely crazy with excitement at the thought of seeing you again! And you will realise my state of mind at the moment!

I received your letter containing the wonderful news yesterday lunchtime and I've been in a fever of excitement ever since.

The postman was late this morning so I didn't know until I got home for lunch. There were two letters, one dated 21st and the other dated 24th. As I had already had one for the 25th I didn't anticipate any fresh news but as I reached the end of the first letter, well, I could hardly believe my eyes! I couldn't really take it in at first but the second letter confirmed it, and then I too felt as if I was to be 'plunged into paradise' without any warning! For what's a month? It will go in no time. The days seem to fly by now – I suppose it's being so busy. And I certainly try my utmost to speed them up. But now only four little weeks. Oh, darling, I'm so excited!

How like you to hold out all those pessimistic warnings about January and February and then to spring this glorious news almost casually at the end of the letter! Of course, I'm glad now. It's such a lovely surprise!

I think I'd better go up to town this week and buy my wedding dress. And my coat, too. I shall have to get busy or I shan't have my clothes in time.

I shall rely on you giving me instructions as to when to set the preparations going. But I know you'll deal with that ...

… I was most sorry, Lily, to read in your letter that your Les had received his summons to appear at Stratford Court. Though, like yourself, I think he's going rather too far, I also much admire his pluck and I could not feel otherwise than proud of someone who is prepared to suffer imprisonment for the sake of his convictions. …

Saturday 11th October

Lily dearest,

I think it would be as well if I devoted this letter to a discussion of the wedding arrangements for there are a number of things that I should like you to fix up as soon as I announce my departure from this isle. Even now you could make some further preparations – maybe you have already done them – but let me deal with the various points in some sort of order.

I believe that Dad should already have the licence in hand and preliminary arrangements regarding the church and fellowship room but I should find out whether he's done anything yet and keep him up to scratch.

When you have decided on the timetable it would be as well to approach Mr Lemon [the minister], and book him and also the organist.

Are you thinking of advising Bodgers of the possible date? It might be as well, even though you won't be able to notify them definitely until about a week before the event. What about a wedding cake? Are they unobtainable or will Bodgers be able to fix one up?

It will certainly be wisest to leave the date blank when you have the invitations printed. As far as I remember your people should send them out ...

Monday 13th October

Dearest Martyn,

... There was a very good attendance at badminton on Saturday night. We had some jolly good games and sat around the Fellowship room fire drinking coffee in between.

Our news has spread like wildfire! And I was the object of considerable publicity! I wish you'd been there to share it. The people I haven't told, your father has! It's all very exciting! George and Maisie insist on us having it on Saturday and I'm afraid unless we do there'll be lots of Fellowship people who won't be able to come, and I should very much like them to, after all. But we can't decide definitely until you arrive, can we? I'm telling them it's either the Saturday or Monday just to prepare them. ...

Wednesday 15th October

My darling Martyn,

... I've just come back from the registrar. I did the necessary formalities. I had to give full particulars about both of us and swear that we haven't been married before (have you?!) and pay the two shillings fee for the certificate. I thought it would cost a lot more than that, didn't you?

It was a lot easier than I thought but I'm very relieved to know it's all settled. I haven't yet received a letter from you asking me to do all this! It's rather a big responsibility getting a marriage certificate without one's future husband's request!

But I'm assuming that a letter telling me about these things is on its way from you. It would be awkward if you decided you didn't want to marry me after all!

I also called in at Bodgers and made a provisional booking for the reception on Saturday November 8th. I warned them it's only provisional – but I'm hoping that date will be alright. Saturday will be so much easier for everyone. I do hope you agree.

I've ordered a two tier cake but they can't ice it as there is no icing sugar.

Could you bring some with you? ...

Lily

Friday 17th October

My dearest Lily,

... Love is such a crazy, overwhelming, delightful thing, isn't it – it must be awfully unexciting for people who aren't madly in love, don't you agree?! All the folk up here – including the Wing Commander! – think that I'm quite mad because I try to write you a letter every day, but as I always tell them, this madness is extremely pleasant and I wouldn't be cured for anything.

Of course, you mustn't expect a letter a day when we are married! – But you'll get it all the same, for I just have to keep on writing to you.

I just have to keep on telling you that I love you with all my heart and shall always remain,

your most devoted lover,

Martyn

Saturday 18th October

... I was interested, Lily, to hear that you had listened to that wireless programme about the work of Coastal Command and was a little amused to read your remark that you wondered whether I didn't 'feel a little afraid sometimes'!

Heavens, ducky! I'm by no means an intrepid aviator and more often than not I am absolutely shaken to the core! But one gets used to it ...

Monday 20th October

My darling girl,

... You suggest leaving the actual date of the wedding till I get home but I really think it should be decided on as soon as possible. Saturday the eighth is very risky in view of the fact that I may not be home until the end of the week.

We must let people know the exact date at least a week beforehand for we want to get replies to the invitations and my best man will want a week's notice if he is to get off from his unit. So I suggest that you decide definitely on the date as soon as you receive this letter and send out the invitations as soon as you receive my telegram saying – 'NICE WORK' ...

Tuesday 21st October

Lily dearest,

... In just about a fortnight's time I should be at home with you but I'm sure that this coming fortnight is going to be quite as long as any previous month! It still seems too good to be true that after all these months I shall be with you again. I'm longing to see you so very, very much and I'm just bursting with impatience to get on that leave boat!

So, goodbye, sweetheart, until I see you,

Martyn

On 27th October Lily sent a telegram confirming arrangements.

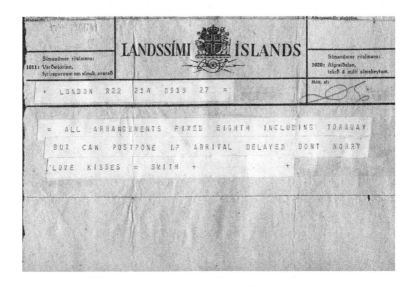

POST OFFICE

TELEGRAM

Charges to pay
s. d.
RECEIVED

Prefix. Time handed id. Office of Origin and Service Instructions. Words.
79

From

79 CA REYKJAVIK 1 1342 PBC 8

To

SMITH 89 GRENVILLE GDNS WOODFORD GREEN ESSEX =

NICE WORK = MARTYN + +

89 GRENVILLE GDNS +

No.

OFFICE STAMP

ELEGRAMS ENQUIRY " or call, with this form
anied by this form, and, if possible, the envelope.

B or C

Saturday 8th November 1941

Postscript

Fortunately, there was no need for Martyn to send Lily a telegram saying 'tough luck' and they were finally married on Saturday 8ᵗʰ November 1941 at the South Woodford Congregational Church with a reception that followed in the Fellowship Room.

Lily wore a pale blue dress with accessories of dark blue and burgundy and Martyn donned his RAF uniform. As they had agreed so long ago, their honeymoon was spent in Torquay and there was still time for them to stay for a few days at Martyn's parents' house before his leave ended and he returned to Iceland.

During the COVID-19 lockdown in Spring 2020, when I retrieved the battered cardboard box, I was not sure what I would do with the letters, written between my parents, that I knew it contained. On the side of the box was written 'Belles Lettres' – beautiful letters – but was it right for me, their daughter, to read this intimate correspondence? I took the plunge and read one or two of the loose letters that were stuffed into the top of the box and was immediately captivated and became convinced that the letters were so fascinating and so expressively written that they deserved to be read by others.

In creating this compilation, initially it felt counter-intuitive for me to be correcting my parents' punctuation and spelling errors but I have done so occasionally for ease of reading. Similarly, where I felt a word needed to be added, removed or changed to clarify the sense that I believe the letter writer intended to convey, then I took that liberty too.

More of their story for family and friends ...

In September 1942 Martyn was posted back to Silloth to become a Hudson flying instructor and, at last, he and Lily were able to set up home together in a cottage in the nearby village of Skinburness. Nine months later Martyn was moved to RAF Thornaby-on-Tees in Yorkshire and they shared a house then in Malton with Guy, Martyn's Iceland hut-mate, and his wife Rita.

Martyn was on the move again in the summer of 1943: this time to Nassau in the Bahamas to train to fly Liberators. Following this, with his new expertise he joined 547 Squadron at RAF Thorney Island and moved with them to RAF St Eval in Cornwall. Here the squadron's role was to keep U-boats out of the English Channel during the invasion period and patrol the Bay of Biscay. While in Cornwall Lily and Martyn lived in Newquay and their first son Christopher was born.

From Cornwall the family headed northwards to Scotland where Martyn was posted to RAF St Leuchars, near St Andrews, and they lived in the village of Balmullo in a cottage which lacked both electricity and gas. Luckily, Lily had always said that she would be content to live anywhere in order to accompany Martyn.

In March 1945 his crew took part in a Baltic sweep, code named Operation Chilli, and made a successful attack on a surfaced U-boat, for which Martyn was awarded the Distinguished Flying Cross.

Two months later he was posted to RAF Defford in Worcestershire where, following promotion to Squadron Leader, he became the Commanding Officer of the Coastal Flight of the Telecommunications Flying Unit. New radar devices were being developed at the nearby Research Establishment in Malvern and they were trialled at RAF Defford. In particular, at this time they were trying to perfect an automatic blind landing system, which Martyn recalled led to some alarming moments for the pilot.

While Martyn was at Defford the family lived in the village of Bredon in the ground floor flat of a crumbling Victorian mansion called Wellington Lodge and it was here that their daughter Cheryl was born.

After leaving the Air Force in 1946 Martyn went to university and rather than completing his original Aeronautical Engineering degree, he chose to study Geography and Geology at Bristol University with a view to school teaching. Once his studies were complete, and he'd experienced secondary school teaching, he decided instead to re-enter the RAF on a four year commission as an Education Officer. After a brief time spent at RAF Shenfield Park, Reading, and just as he and Lily were in the throes of buying their first family home on the edge of Reading in Caversham, he was posted to Singapore. This was during the period of the 'Malayan Emergency' when the Commonwealth Armed Forces had to deal with the pro-independence guerrilla fighters of the Malayan National Liberation Army.

Once more Lily was left behind, while Martyn flew out to start work at RAF Tengah. Three months later she bravely set out with Christopher and Cheryl to join him, sailing from Southampton on a three week passage aboard the troopship Dunera.Living in Singapore, initially across the causeway on mainland Malaya, was an amazing experience for all the family. Martyn was determined to make the most of the various cultural opportunities and took *the family to many unusual destinations in order to experience the jungle, see open tin mining, look at paddy fields and tea plantations, discover how rubber was tapped and processed, and appreciate the shops, markets and festivities of the three Singaporean races – Malay, Indian and Chinese.*

Martyn and Lily also indulged their love of theatre while in Singapore. Martyn produced a series of plays performed by the Tengah Drama Group in the camp cinema and needless to say, Lily invariably had a lead role.

Robin, later to be known as Bob, was born at the Changi RAF Hospital in 1953, making the family complete. The following year they were booked to travel back to England aboard HMS Windrush but at the last moment, to their immense disappointment at the time, their tickets were cancelled to give priority to another family. This proved to be the last journey of the Windrush as, while she was sailing through the Mediterranean, there was an explosion resulting in a fire on board and all the passengers had to be rapidly evacuated by lifeboats. This must have been a terrifying experience and so sad for those returning home to have lost all their possessions, including their treasured souvenirs from the Far East.

Since Martyn's next postings were relatively close to Reading, namely RAF Abingdon and RAF Uxbridge, the family were able to stay in their house in Caversham. In 1960, however, his posting was to France. Fontainebleau had become the command centre for NATO military forces and Martyn's responsibilities were with the British Air Force personnel there and the English section of the International School. Martyn and Lily embraced the opportunity of living in France and settled the family, minus Christopher who was boarding at Reading School, into a green-shuttered, typically French house – Les Volets Verts – in the village of Bourron-Marlotte. They bought their daily baguettes from the village baker, sampled the wondrous variety of charcuterie from the butcher's shop and employed a femme de ménage to do a bit of house cleaning, not for the benefit of a clean house but more for Lily to perfect her French and pick up the village news.

After a year of rural life, they moved into the historic town of Fontainebleau itself. Here they experienced the contrasting pleasures of living on the second floor of a modern block of flats constructed in the style of Le Corbusier, one of a row of four which served this international community. They revelled in exploring Fontainebleau, its chateau and forest, and interesting villages and towns nearby. They made frequent trips to Paris and each school holiday became an opportunity for a camping expedition to discover a different region of France.

With the benefit of Martyn's creative flair and ability to organise, and Lily's gregarious nature and love of cooking, they fruitfully socialised with other Forces personnel and the English teachers employed at the school. Martyn, as ever, went beyond the remit of his job description and organised various events and activities to support his fellow servicemen, teachers, wives and families. It was in recognition of this that in 1964 he was awarded an MBE.

Martyn's final RAF posting was in 1972, when as Group Captain he was assigned to the Joint Forces headquarters in Rheindahlen where he was Command Education Officer for the Royal Air Force in Germany. Lily played her role as a senior officer's wife and hosted dinners and parties but she also supported the wives of Air Force personnel of other ranks. As in the pastoral visiting she'd taken on previously for the Caversham church, she had an ability to reach out and empathise with those in need of support, giving practical help.

While in Rheindahlen, Martyn and Lily once again involved themselves in amateur dramatics and Martyn became aware that there was a desire amongst the theatre clubs throughout the RAF for an umbrella association which could bring them together for one-act play competitions and an annual drama festival. Martyn put his organisational skills to work and in 1974 the Royal Air Force Theatrical Association was established, which is flourishing to this day.

When Martyn retired from the Air Force in 1975, at the statutory age of 55, he then worked for the Southern Regional Council for Further Education. He became a governor at a local primary school and, keen to be hands on – as was his way – he would go into the school weekly to listen to children read.

One of Lily and Martyn's ideas which they were able to bring to fruition at this time was the setting up of a lecture society. To start with, they posted information cards round all the houses in Caversham to test interest; and finding the response to be positive, they held the first meeting of the Caversham Heights Society in 1975. It soon became so popular that to comply with fire regulations they had to have a waiting list for membership. Martyn then started to arrange coach trips to the theatre and the Proms for the society members and the success of these encouraged him next to try out a four day 'mini holiday'. For the three night stay he arranged affordable accommodation, often in university halls of residence, which he and Lily sampled in advance, and the holidays consisted of action-packed days with visits to various buildings of note, places of interest and invariably, some river, canal or steam-train travel. Both the society and the mini holidays continued from year to year – and possibly still do.

When Martyn finally took complete retirement, he and Lily were able to spend more time pursuing their common interests. With their love of music, theatre, ballet, film and the visual arts they became regular supporters of Reading's many arts events and rarely missed a concert at the Town Hall or Hexagon Theatre.

Lily's enthusiasm for keeping fit never waned. She always loved walking and especially in the countryside. During the 1950s she regularly attended the exercise classes run by the League of Health and Beauty; and once yoga became recognised in this country as being a valuable form of exercise for both mind and body, she became a devotee. With a desire to share this enthusiasm for yoga with others, she went on to arrange regular sessions in the Caversham church hall, even though at the time this was not approved of by many churches.

As a pro-European and staunch internationalist, Martyn took a keen interest in current affairs and political issues and both he and Lily were members of the Liberal Party – later the Liberal Democrats. On a number of occasions in the 1980s Martyn stood for election as a Liberal councillor, but with the political bias as it was at the time, there was little chance of him being elected. He was indefatigable, though, in promoting the Liberals' views and at election time would go out canvassing from door to door.

The church always remained central to Lily and Martyn's lives and when resident in Caversham they were active members of the Caversham Heights Methodist Church, taking on responsibilities when needed. In fact, they became involved in, and supported, so many activities, such as Christmas bazaars, summer fêtes, socials, concerts, and youth activities as well as the Sunday services, that it was said that there was a 'rut in the pavement between their home and the church!'

They championed the ecumenical movement whereby churches of different denominations and traditions would work closely together. Out of this development, and with Martyn's involvement, was born the charity Reading Churches Together, which still runs a valuable Drop-in Centre for the homeless and disadvantaged, and Caversham Churches Together.

Martyn had the idea of setting up a link between the Caversham Heights church and a church in a developing third world country and from that inspiration, in 1998, a link with the Racecourse

School in Kitwe, Zambia was established and money from church fundraising events was used to help support the school. A continuing annual church event for this cause is the Pancake Evening on Shrove Tuesday.

Lily became concerned with the problem of isolation for elderly people and suggested that the church should run a weekly luncheon club in the church hall. With Martyn's help they set this in motion, calling it Stay-Awhile. Lily, with gradually more volunteer helpers, produced a two-course home-cooked meal at a very reasonable price and those attending were encouraged to stay on well into the afternoon to enjoy each other's company. A further development from this was Out-Awhile. With the help of a number of voluntary car drivers, the regulars at Stay-Awhile were offered outings. Sometimes these would be to a place of interest like a National Trust House, or – the most popular treat – a trip on the river, followed by tea and cakes. There was also an annual outing to a musical show at Reading's Hexagon Theatre. The success of Stay-Awhile and Out-Awhile was largely due to Lily and Martyn's skill at encouraging people to offer voluntary help and inspiring others to participate.

Both Lily and Martyn were enthusiastic members of the Reading-Düsseldorf Association. Back in 1946, Reading's visionary mayor, Phoebe Cusden, had been concerned by the plight of those living in the many devastated German cities and was determined that Reading, which had hardly suffered any war damage, should offer humanitarian aid and friendship. In 1947 she visited Düsseldorf where forty percent of the buildings had been destroyed and where there was a severe shortage of food owing to the destruction of the town's two bridges over the Rhine limiting transportation. Following her meeting with the Düsseldorf Town Clerk, it was agreed that a group of disadvantaged children would be given the opportunity to travel to England and be looked after in the homes of Reading residents. So began the twinning of the two towns just *two years after the cessations of hostilities – the first such twinning of an English town with its former German enemy.*

Two years later, in April 1949, thirty German children made a trip to Reading and seventy-five children from Reading travelled to Düsseldorf and stayed at the International Youth Hostel. Then in July of that same year the whole of the Reading Youth Orchestra went to Düsseldorf to give a concert and thirty children travelled back with them to take part in Reading's 'International Fortnight'.

This movement was close to Martyn's heart and in 1977 he became the chairman of the association and masterminded its 30th Anniversary celebrations. He worked tirelessly in this capacity for twenty-two years and succeeded in broadening the society's activities to include many other interest groups such as churches, sports organisations and choirs. Together, Lily and Martyn welcomed many exchange visitors to their home and made many trips to Düsseldorf themselves, establishing close friendships. In recognition of his contribution to the Reading-Düsseldorf twinning, Martyn was made an honorary freeman of the borough of Reading in 1991 and the following year he and Lily made a special trip to Germany when he was presented with the Order of Merit of North Rhine-Westphalia, an honour never before awarded to an Englishman.

In addition to the trips to Germany, Martyn and Lily travelled widely. When friends moved abroad or returned to their homelands, Martyn and Lily would, if at all possible, take a holiday trip that incorporated a visit to see them. This took them to see friends in Canada, USA, Cyprus, Hungary, Portugal, Italy, Haiti and Japan. Wherever they travelled, they appreciated being able to see the everyday life of the local people as well as tourist attractions and places of interest.

The wide perspective that Lily and Martyn gained from their travels confirmed their conviction that there was a need worldwide to address social injustices and poverty. Through the charity Plan International, they began fostering a boy called Mohamed in Cairo, and their contributions helped not only him but also his family and his local community. They corresponded with him for a number of years and while on a holiday to Egypt made a detour to meet him where he lived. Convinced of the value of this charity, Martyn set up the Berkshire branch of PLAN, as it is now known.

Once a year Martyn assisted with the organisation of a number of events marking One World Week, which has as its aim 'to share understanding about some of the global issues that affect us all and to recognise we can all make a difference'. Each year a different topic of world importance was tackled, such as refugees, child labour, indebted poor countries and global warming. Martyn would produce an exhibition for Caversham Library and book a speaker and on the Saturday morning, in some thoroughfare in Reading's town centre, Lily and Martyn could be found with a large outline map of the world on the ground beside them which they would then coerce passers-by to cover with coins, whilst discussing the relevant world issue.

Leading up to the millennium year, the cause that occupied Lily and Martyn was Jubilee 2000, an international movement that was calling for the cancellation of debt for third world countries by the year 2000. In 1998 Martyn led a group from Caversham to take part in forming a human chain with fifty thousand or more protestors around Birmingham City Centre where the G8 Summit was being held. The demonstration made world news and increased awareness of the issue. Two years later Jubilee 2000 did achieve promises of debt relief from different countries but in the subsequent months very little was accomplished, so a new campaign – Drop the Debt – was launched with the aim of ensuring that Debt Relief was on the agenda at the forthcoming G8 meeting in Genoa. Lily and Martyn, now both 81, were *determined to go to Genoa and to join other protestors in a mass demonstration. They set off for Italy and stayed their first night with friends in Turin. The headline news that evening was of riots, overturned cars, one death and brutal police intervention. Lily and Martyn's Italian friends pleaded with them not to go, but to no effect. They still made their way to Genoa and added their voices to the thousands who were there.*

Martyn saw Fair Trade as being a practical way to support poorer nations as well as being beneficial to the environment and he coordinated Reading's efforts to reach the necessary goals to gain the status of a Fairtrade Town. In 2008, as a result of Martyn's encouragement, Caversham Heights Methodist Church achieved the status of having an Eco Congregation, the first in Reading.

Both Lily and Martyn loved meeting new people and making new friends, and friendships once established were nurtured and never allowed to fade. Right through their lives they kept in touch with many of those early friends from their schooldays and from the Fellowship who are mentioned in the letters and though their Christmas card list was particularly lengthy, they delighted in being in touch with past acquaintances.

Lily's warm, open personality enabled her to strike up a conversation with complete strangers. And some became lasting friends. On a holiday in Venice in her eighties she became lost, having got separated from the family; and the person who took pity on her and came to her rescue was a young architecture student from Portugal who somehow managed to reunite her with the rest of her party. Afterwards, addresses were exchanged; and a wonderful friendship developed between an elderly English woman and a young Portuguese girl. They corresponded by letter and visited each other's houses in Caversham and Lisbon.

Above all, Lily and Martyn cherished their family – and it was an extended family. They kept abreast of what everyone was up to, celebrated their successes and were supportive when times were hard. Janet, their niece – that little girl who Lily loved so much – went on to be an actor. In fact, the family's theatrical gene also emerged in Janet's brother Andrew, Cheryl's daughter Lucy, and Bob's son Patrick, all of whom were performers in very different ways, encompassing children's theatre, indie rock and 16th century polyphony. Often Lily and Martyn would figure out where they were performing and travel some distance to surprise them by turning up to a performance unannounced.

Over the years, a week's holiday in August for the family became a regular event, organised, unsurprisingly, by Martyn and Lily. In the 1970s when the canal network was being restored and becoming navigable again, the holidays would be on a narrow boat; but as the family grew in number and there were too many to fit on board, this event became land-based in self-catering accommodation. Martyn and Lily would check out the venue first and one of their main requirements was that it should have a dining room large enough to seat everyone, even when the number was edging over twenty. A feature of these family holidays was that whatever people did in the daytime they would always be back together for the evening meal. In the early years these meals were cooked by Lily but later on other members of the family took their turns. This gave everyone the opportunity to catch up with each other's news, discuss their latest interests, compare books read, films seen and theatre performances enjoyed. Traditionally, the meal always ended with cheese and biscuits and some good red wine which doubtless helped the conversation to flow. These holidays enabled the family, who were scattered all over the country, to meet together, as well as – importantly – giving Lily and Martyn a chance to enjoy their grandchildren's and great-grandchildren's company.

Lily and Martyn certainly lived life to the full and their love for each other never faded. In those wartime letters Martyn often referred to Lily's 'infernal optimism' which she herself called her 'elasticity of optimism' and there is no doubt that this characteristic of hers, in combination with Martyn's ambition to make the world a better place, helped them to accomplish great things.

Lily and Martyn were able to celebrate 60 years of a loving and eventful marriage and had a further nine years together before Martyn died in 2010. Lily died three years later. In one of her letters, Lily had written that she was "never more certain of anything in my life than that we were made for each other ... Our love will last, Martyn – I'm sure of it."

Lily and Martyn enjoying life in their eighties

A photo taken by Martyn whilst on holiday in Paris in 1955,
with Lily and their three children Christopher, Cheryl and Robin

Maps

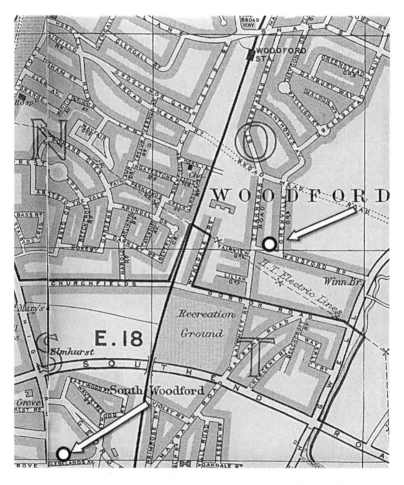

A section of a Bartholomew map showing Grenville Gardens and Glebelands Avenue

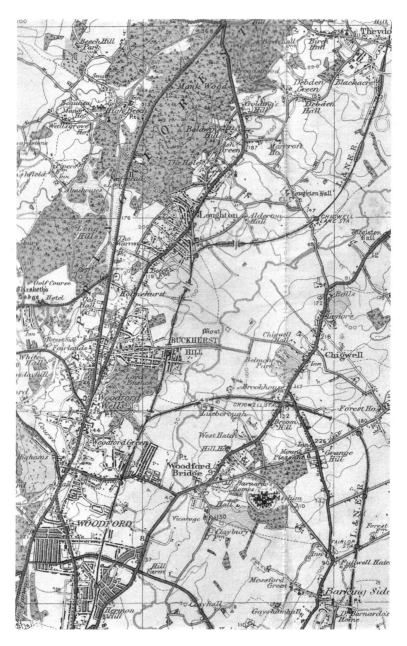

Reproduced from Lily's own 1930 Ordnance Survey map

The Flying Flea

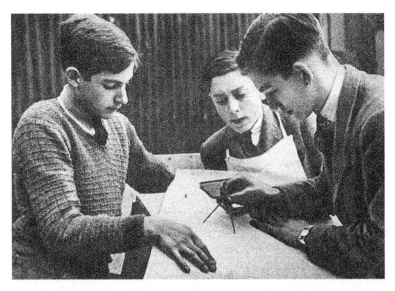

*Peter Matthews, Martyn and Bob Jacobs building their Flying Flea.
All three of them became RAF pilots during the war*

The three boys at work

A photo taken by Martyn of Southampton's Flying Flea

The Young People's Fellowship

A Sunday afternoon Fellowship meeting in Tony's garden

Stopping off on a Saturday ramble

Martyn and Maisie clamber over the old tree trunk on an Epping Forest ramble

The Garden Party – July 1939

Lily watches on with her friend Prissie on her left-hand side

The Young People's Fellowship entertain with country dancing

E.J. plays the fiddle

The appreciative audience

Lily with her close friends Maisie, on her left, and Nora on her right

Acknowledgements

I could thank my parents for many, many things, but in this instance, I'm thanking them for keeping the battered, jam-packed cardboard box that had written on the side of it 'BELLES LETTRES' – beautiful letters – and for the insight into their lives that the letters have given me.

I am indebted to Penny Dunscombe, not only for her skills in editing, but also for holding my hand from the first conception of this project.

Thanks go to my lovely writing group friends: Jean, Pat, Anne, Wendy, and her husband Brian, who read through the initial portions as I produced them.

I am grateful to my brothers Chris and Bob, my daughter Lucy and my cousins Janet and Andrew, who have all assisted with comments and encouragement; especially Chris, who designed the cover.

I have leant heavily on Maybelle, herself a writer, who has offered much appreciated advice.

Mike Asbury has kindly been my expert in all Air Force and aeroplane matters; and Tim Baker gave his blessing to my use of his poignant poem 'Hudson Bay'.

I am grateful for the time that kind friends Maurice, Annette, Barbara, Wendy, Kay, Sylvie and Eileen have spent in reading the completed manuscript.

And lastly, thanks are due to my husband Peter, who has shared the lockdowns of 2020 and 2021 with me and my unceasing delving into the Allies and Smith family history.

Should you be interested in sharing with Cheryl
any information concerning people and places
mentioned in the book,
she would be pleased to hear from you at
- chrylunderhill@gmail.com

Printed in Great Britain
by Amazon

79384213R00210